W9-ACR-760

SOURCE BOOKS ON EDUCATION

1. Bilingual Education: *A Source Book for Educators*
   by   Alba N. Ambert and Sarah Melendez

2. Reading and Study Skills in the Secondary Schools: *A Source Book*
   by   Joyce N. French

3. Creating Connections: *Books, Kits, and Games for Children*
   by   Betty P. Cleaver, Barbara Chatton, and Shirley Vittum Morrison

4. Gifted, Talented, and Creative Young People: *A Guide to Theory, Teaching, and Research*
   by   Morris I. Stein

5. Teaching Science to Young Children: *A Resource Book*
   by   Mary D. Iatridis

6. Microcomputers and Social Studies: *A Resource Guide for the Middle and Secondary Grades*
   by   Joseph A. Braun, Jr.

7. Special Education: *A Source Book*
   by   Manny Sternlicht

8. Computers in the Classroom . . . What Shall I Do?: *A Guide*
   by   Walter Burke

9. Learning to Read and Write: The Role of Language Acquisition and Aesthetic Development, *A Resource Guide*
   by   Ellen J. Brooks

10. School Play: *A Source Book*
    by   James H. Block and Nancy R. King

11. Computer Simulations: *A Source Book to Learning in an Electronic Environment*
    by   Jerry Willis, Larry Hovey, and Kathleen Hovey

12. Day Care: *A Source Book*
    by   Kathleen Pullan Watkins and Lucius Durant, Jr.

13. Project Head Start: Past, Present, and Future Trends in the Context of Family Needs
    by   Valora Washington and Ura Jean Oyemade

14. Adult Literacy: *A Source Book and Guide*
    by   Joyce French

15. Mathematics Education in Secondary Schools and Two-Year Colleges: *A Source Book*
    by   Louise S. Grinstein and Paul J. Campbell

16. Black Children and American Institutions: *An Ecological Review and Resource Guide*
    by   Valora Washington and Velma LaPoint

17. Resources for Educational Equity: *A Source Book for Grades Pre-Kindergarten–12*
    by   Merle Froschl and Barbara Sprung

18. Multicultural Education: *A Source Book*
    by   Patricia G. Ramsey, Edwina Battle Vold, and Leslie R. Williams

19. Sexuality Education: *A Resource Book*
    by   Carol Cassell and Pamela M. Wilson

20. Reforming Teacher Education *Issues and New Directions*
    edited by
    Joseph A. Braun, Jr.

REFORMING TEACHER EDUCATION
Issues and New Directions

Joseph A. Braun, Jr., editor

GARLAND PUBLISHING, INC. • NEW YORK & LONDON
1989

Library of Congress Cataloging-in-Publication Data

Braun, Joseph A., 1947–
    Reforming teacher education : issues and new directions / Joseph
A. Braun, Jr.
        p. cm. — (Garland reference library of social science ; vol.
370) (Source books on education ; vol. 20)
    Includes index.
    ISBN 0–8240–3712–X (alk. paper)
    1. Teachers—Training of—United States. I. Title. II. Series:
Garland reference library of social science ; v. 370. III. Series:
Source books on education ; vol. 20.
LB1715.B7   1989
370'.7'30973—dc20
                                                                            89–7876
                                                                              CIP

Printed on acid-free, 250-year-life paper
Manufactured in the United States of America

To my father, Joseph A. Braun, Sr., you remain one of my greatest teachers. From you I learned a vital lesson in life: face the future enthusiastically and filled with optimism.

Contents

Acknowledgments..xi

Preface...xiii
    Bob Schuck

Introduction...xv

PART I.
REFORMING TEACHER EDUCATION: ISSUES

Chapter 1. Conditions and Forces Influencing
            Educational Reform
            Wesley J. Little...5

Chapter 2. The Three Ghosts of Teacher Induction:
            Past, Present, and Future
            John M. Johnston..23

Chapter 3. Master Teachers: A Way to Restructure the
            Profession
            Judith C. Christensen.......................................49

Chapter 4. Change in Teacher Education: Focus on
            Field Experiences
            Marvin A. Henry...69

Chapter 5. Technology and Teaching: Trends for the
            Future
            Rhonda Robinson & Peter West....................97

Chapter 6. A Futurist View: Forces Framing the Future
            of Teacher Education Programs
            Robert Alley...117

Chapter 7. Where Have All The Futurists Gone?
            Linda S. Tafel...143

PART II.
REFORMING TEACHER EDUCATION: NEW DIRECTIONS

Chapter 8.   New Directions in Teacher Education:
             Which Direction?
             Walter Parker...161

Chapter 9.   Building a Better Mousetrap for Teacher
             Education
             Michael Wolfe & L. Giandomenico.............187

Chapter 10. Moral Education in Reforming Teacher
             Education: Issues and New Directions
             Richard L. Hayes.......................................209

Chapter 11. Research in Humanistic Education:
             Implications for the Future of Teacher
             Education
             Gary F. Render...233

Chapter 12. Measurement and Research in the
             Classroom: Directions for Preservice
             Education of Teachers
             Kathy E. Green...253

Chapter 13. The Many Voices of Multicultural
             Education
             Phyllis F. Maxey..279

Chapter 14. Global Education: The Future Is Now
             Frederick J. Baker.....................................295

Chapter 15. Challenge Education: A Model for
             Individualizing Teacher Education Courses
             Devon J. Metzger......................................321

Chapter 16. Developing Preservice Teachers' Self-
             Awareness: An Examination of the
             Professional Dynametric Program
             Bonnie Johnson..335

Index 351

The Authors

Wesley J. Little is Vice President for Academic Affairs, Northeastern Oklahoma State University in Tahlequah, Oklahoma.

John M. Johnston is Associate Professor in the Department of Curriculum and Instruction at Memphis State University in Memphis, Tennessee.

Judith C. Christensen is Associate Professor and Director of the Master of Arts in Teaching Program at National College of Education in Evanston, Illinois.

Marvin Henry is Chair of the Department of Secondary Education at Indiana State University in Terre Haute, Indiana.

Rhonda S. Robinson is Associate Professor in the Department of Instructional Technology and **Peter C. West** is Associate Director of the Learning Center at Northern Illinois University in DeKalb, Illinois.

Robert Alley is Associate Dean and Professor of Secondary Education at Wichita State University in Wichita, Kansas.

Linda S. Tafel is Assistant Professor in the Department of Interdisciplinary Studies at the College of Education in Evanston, Illinois.

Walter C. Parker is Associate Professor of Education at the University of Washington in Seattle, Washington.

Michael P. Wolfe is Director for Center of Teacher Education and **Lawrence Giandomenico** is Associate Professor of Education at State University of New York at Plattsburgh in Plattsburgh, New York.

Richard L. Hayes is Associate Professor, the Department of Counseling and Human Development at the University of Georgia in Athens, Georgia.

Gary F. Render is Professor of Educational Psychology in the Department of Educational Foundations and Instructional Technology at the University of Wyoming in Laramie, Wyoming.

Kathy E. Green is Associate Professor in the School of Education at the University of Denver in Denver, Colorado.

Frederick J. Baker is Professor and Coordinator of Basic Credentials Program at California State Polytechnic University in Pomona, California.

Phyllis F. Maxey is Associate Professor in the Department of Teacher Education at California State University at San Bernardino in San Bernardino, California.

Devon J. Metzger is Associate Professor in the Department of Education at California State University at Chico in Chico, California.

Bonnie J. Johnson is Assistant Professor in the Department of Education at California State University in Chico, California.

Acknowledgments

Several people played key roles in the development of this book of readings on teacher education. Marie Ellen Larcada, my editor at Garland Publishing, was of great help and encouragement in the process of developing the idea for the book. She showed great patience and insight when answering the countless questions I posed as I proceeded with the editing process. Similarly, she was very understanding of the brief delays that developed as I coordinated the work of sixteen authors.

I would also like to acknowledge Barbara Ryan and Marlene Baer for their word processing skills and emendations to bibliographic entries to make them uniform. I would also like to thank Doris Brodeur, John Godbold, and Larry Kennedy for their review and comments on parts of the manuscript. Their assistance made the final production stages of the book a much simpler process.

I would like to thank my wife, Anne Elizabeth Gosch, for her patience and understanding about the fact that I was occasionally preoccupied with completing this project. She was always most supportive and encouraged me at those moments when I had second thoughts about this undertaking.

Finally, I would like to acknowledge my daughter, Sage Elizabeth, and beg her forgiveness for those times when I had to postpone reading a story at bedtime because I had a chapter that needed editing. Like my father, in her own way she is one of my greatest teachers. If this book has any impact on making her school experiences enjoyable and rewarding, then I will consider it an ultimate success.

Preface

There is a sign on my desk that constantly reminds me to "Keep It Simple Stupid." The problem is I constantly find difficulty applying this Law of Parsimony as it operates in my chosen profession, teacher education. This is partially related to the fact that the role of schools, and the individuals that comprise the profession who are engaged in them, is so complex. Being social institutions schools are subject to several varied and often contradictory expectations. For example, we expect academic excellence and athletic prowess, the passage of traditional value systems and the nurture of cultural diversity, and the inclusion of elite criteria of academic performance and the exclusion of none: the beat goes on.

It would seem, however, that there is some hope. Certainly we appear to have some clarification of the professional knowledge base related to teacher roles beyond that of the early 20th century rules that were devoted exclusively to the psychology of learning. The wheels of teacher competence continue to grind but even the often revered protocols, exemplified by the paper and pencil dominated National Teachers Examination are being revised within the broader perspective of performance based evaluation. Political leaders are starting to recognize that social issues, such as desegregation, malnutrition, teenage pregnancy, and yes even AIDS cannot be solved by the schools *alone*. Education is slowly being viewed as important but not the panacea it has too often been considered.

Reform in teacher education presents both challenge and a caution. We are challenged to review, analyze, synthesize, and act upon the issues that confront us: the professionalization of teaching, the role of technology in teacher education, and the preparation of our students adequately for the inevitable change of the future. There is no single source of wisdom. The diversity of perspectives presented to us in this book pays testimony to this fact. Those of us engaged in processes so crucial to the professional and temptation of Alexander to cut the Gordian Knot. Rather, we must accept the burden of seeking to understand the human condition and education's role in improving it. The new directions that are described in this book provide us with opportunities for successfully assuming this burden.

A light illuminates the end of the tunnel of teacher education reform. These readings, together with a sense of commitment, perseverance, and tenacity, will go a long way toward insuring that this light is the light of the sun and not the beam from an on-rushing locomotive of despair and confusion.

Robert F. Schuck, Dean
School of Education and Human Development
Rhode Island College

Introduction

Joseph A. Braun, Jr.

Amidst much national media attention, the U.S.
Department of Education released a jeremiad on education
about five years ago. It was titled *A nation at risk* and the
resulting furor over the perceived poor performance of our
schools resulted in a number of follow-up reports and recommendations that focused on teacher education as one key
ingredient to improving the nation's schools.

Politicians, teachers, and academics all have voiced
strong, but sometimes conflicting opinions, about how teacher
education should change to achieve the type of reform that is
needed. These have ranged from simply raising admission
standards into teacher education programs, all the way to
eliminating teacher education as an undergraduate major.
The variety of the reform proposals, and reactions by
constituents that could possibly be affected, is almost staggering.

In taking on the task of editing a book of readings about
the issues raised by the reform proposals and new directions
that teacher education might take, it became clear that the book
could not possibly be all things to all those who have a vested
interest in reshaping teacher education. Thus, there are some
elements that are not addressed by the authors. For example,
the issue of minority recruitment is not directly addressed, nor
are other points of contention such as alternative certification,
the reactions of teacher unions, or better partnerships between
teacher education and other academic departments in arts and
sciences who also have a role in the preparation of teachers.

A second point that the reader should be aware of is the
fact that the various authors were given considerable latitude
in the way they approached the writing of their chapter. Thus,
differences in individual writing styles will be apparent, but
there are commonalities that tie together the chapters in the
first section. For example, it can be argued that many of the
issues raised by the recent reforms are nothing new and have

been raised in previous reform efforts dating back to the end of the last century. With this in mind, each author in the first section, which deals with the reform movement and issues it raises, begins by providing a historical look at the topic. When appropriate, those chapters in the second section, which describe new directions for reforming teacher education, also provide a historical perspective. Obviously, some of the directions in this section are so new that a historical frame of reference does not yet exist. A feature common to all chapters, however, is the annotation of selected references.

The authors who were solicited represent some of the leading scholars and researchers on their subject. A review of the list of authors will reveal geographic diversity, with almost every region of the country being represented.

The first part of the book looks at issues that relate to some of the themes of the national reports recommending changes in teacher education. The first chapter provides a historical overview of some of the reform proposals, and addresses some of the conditions and forces that are influencing educational reform. It summarizes and analyzes the recommendations from a number of the reforms that have focused on teacher education. How beginning teachers are introduced to the profession is commonly referred to as teacher induction. This issue is the focus of the second chapter. In this case, the author elects to provide in-depth annotations to this body of literature. As with other issues in the first section, the author begins by tracing the historical antecedents of the induction movement. The development of career ladders through differentiated staffing is examined in the third chapter. It includes a review of previous efforts in this regard as well as a summary of the author's research into teacher and administrative perceptions of plans to distinguish novice from intermediate and master teachers. The role of field experiences in previous attempts to reform teacher education is considered in the fourth chapter. Additionally, the author argues that field experiences will continue to play a key role in achieving the various goals of reform. The effective use of technology in teacher education is another issue relevant to the reform movement as we enter what futurists have dubbed the "Information Age." In the fifth chapter the authors describe some of the promises and limitations for educating teachers about the use of technology. Examples of applications of technology in education and an evaluation of technology and teacher education are also provided. The first section of the book concludes with an eye to the future in Chapters Six and Seven. Chapter Six discusses eight major social trends that futures research indicates will have a major impact on our world and teacher education. Chapter Seven is a critical appraisal of the underlying assumptions of the reform movement. A reconstructionist perspective on how teacher education might be changed is also described.

The second part of the book takes a much different focus and addresses new directions that teacher educators are exploring. The reader will find a cross section of ideas and thrusts that could help revitalize schools of education to achieve the kind of results that we, as a nation, expect of our schools. This look at new directions for teacher education begins with a provocative discussion of three ethics that appear to compete for control of the direction of teacher education. It is argued that all three ethics have a place in the direction that teacher education should go. Research related to the areas of teacher education as they address classroom practice are highlighted in Chapter Nine. Specifically, the role of the teacher, the school, the curriculum, and the learner are analyzed relative to developing more effective teacher education programs. Chapter Ten examines the moral development of teachers and its role for enhancing teacher education curriculum. Readers are also introduced to basic issues surrounding the controversy over moral education in the schools and to the major curricular responses addressing these issues. A historical overview of research in humanistic education and the education of teachers is provided in Chapter Eleven. Contemporary humanistic education research results, based on twenty years of data collection and their implications for teacher education, conclude this chapter. Chapter Twelve describes the current status of preservice teacher education in research methods and measurement. The extent of use of research by inservice teachers is considered and the discrepancies between university recommendations and teachers' practices are presented. The next two chapters look at global and multicultural education from a teacher education perspective. Chapter Thirteen describes the history of global/international studies as they relate to teacher education. Additionally, this chapter examines conflict resolution, critical thinking skills, and foreign language learning as elements of teacher education. The challenging task of preparing teachers to teach students of many different subcultures–based on race, sex, religion, ethnicity–is the focus of Chapter Fourteen. Strategies for providing cross-cultural experiences for preservice teacher education are also highlighted. The final two chapters describe specific innovative approaches that are being used in a secondary teacher education program. A model known as Challenge Education is an attempt to redress the "preach but not practice" oversight that characterizes much of teacher education. Its rationale, components, and recommendations for future use in teacher education are described in Chapter Fifteen. An assessment instrument designed to help teacher education students develop self-awareness is presented in Chapter Sixteen. Specifically, the instrument measures a preservice teacher's orientation to dominance, extroversion, patience, and conformity, and the impact of these dimensions on teaching style, classroom management, and leadership roles.

While there is almost unanimity among educators in their belief that teacher education is in dire need of reform and new direction, there are many notions of how this might be accomplished. Nonetheless, I remain sanguine about the changes that must come. Part of this optimism is based on a faith in the American spirit. In his trilogy, *The Americans,* Daniel Boorstin describes this virtue as "stick-to-it-ive-ness," and he asserts that this is a historical and pervasive cultural trait. Perhaps this is best exemplified by the renewed efforts to explore beyond our world. It was only two and a half years ago that our space program lay in shambles and disgrace after the tragic loss of the Challenger. With renewed commitment and a sense of "we can do it," the shuttle flies again. While not accompanied by such a dramatic and tragic calamity as the Challenger disaster, in a sense the schools and teacher education can be compared to the space program after January 1986: a shambles and a disgrace. But I, like the authors whose chapters you are about to read, remain committed and conscious of our important responsibility which was most aptly described by Christa McAuliffe before her doomed flight, "We touch the future, we teach."

REFORMING TEACHER EDUCATION

PART I.

REFORMING TEACHER
EDUCATION: ISSUES

Conditions and Forces Influencing Educational Reform

Wesley J. Little

Following the 1983 release of the National Commission on Excellence in Education report, *A nation at risk;* teacher education programs in American colleges and universities began to experience unprecedented national scrutiny and criticism. While the report focused on the failure of American high schools to produce literate and functional graduates, it clearly established a link between some of the nation's public education problems and teacher education. The report, under the direction of Secretary of Education Terrel Bell, set the tone for numerous additional reports calling for educational reform in many areas of public K-12 and teacher education (National Commission on Excellence in Education 1983).

This landmark report on public secondary education initiated a media blitz highlighting the negative findings and conclusions of this and each successive report on public education and teacher training. President Reagan used this report to create a national political debate on public education following his earlier statements of intent to dismantle the United States Department of Education (Bell 1986). Ironically, the report appeared to have the opposite effect on public opinion. When United States citizens began to comprehend the potential seriousness of the problem, President Reagan's plan to dismantle the Department of Education was tabled. The Commission's well-publicized report generated national interest and concern related to the status of public schools and teacher education and subsequently provided many state and national legislators with a new and timely political issue.

Within a few months of the release of the Commission's report, little doubt remained that teacher training was to become a major target of educational reform. Teacher educators were challenged as never before in every aspect of teacher training. Criticism came from parents, public school educators, state departments of education, university colleagues and administrators, national critics of teacher education, and state and national legislators. Since the problems associated with public and teacher education developed over several decades, the first part of this chapter will review the historical antecedents and educational changes that had a significant impact on the events leading up to the report. The second part of this chapter will review some of the major reports that followed *A nation at risk*. The chapter will conclude with an analysis of the potential impact of the reform movement on the future of teacher education.

The National Economy Threatened

Reform in public education and teacher training might not have received national attention in the early 1980's had not a series of significant international events occurred. From a historical perspective, the Arab oil embargo of 1973 will likely be identified as a critical point in American history. Without question, the embargo set in motion a chain reaction of economic and political events that would change the American economy and the American standard of living for decades (Halberstam 1986). It is the author's opinion that this single event played a key role in later focusing attention on the need for national reform in education.

Beginning in 1973, primarily as a result of the embargo, our national economy began experiencing longer and more severe cycles of inflation, unemployment, and recession. The American automobile industry, caught napping during the oil embargo, allowed inexpensive and more fuel efficient Japanese imports to gain an unprecedented market share of sales, which soon led to increasing unemployment for many American workers. Between 1973 and 1983, a significant number of American industries began to collapse, producing an economic ripple effect. This decline was rapid, unexpected, and traumatic. Thousands of auto, steel, and mine workers, accustomed to earning $25,000 to $30,000 yearly, found themselves unemployed and with little hope of ever regaining a comparable paying job or their previous standard of living (Yates 1983). Further, this sudden economic decline caused both state and federal deficits to escalate. This problem was made worse by the resulting unemployment, inflation, growing pressure on entitlement programs, and increased defense spending. Within an extremely short period, our nation's historical and traditional industrial-based economy began shifting toward the service sector and high-tech labor needs. This rapid shift in the need for and expectations of the nation's work force occurred more rapidly than our educational system could adapt. As our nation's industrial base eroded, corporate America, and to a degree, state and federal officials, were quick to place blame for our nation's economic decline on the public educational system.

Changing K-12 Educational Goals

Since the civil rights movement began, public educators have struggled to respond to the special needs, rights, and governmental mandates with regard to racial minorities, women, the handicapped, the gifted, and economically disadvantaged children. Significant time and resources were directed toward creating educational access and opportunity in these areas. "Equality of opportunity" was emphasized for specific groups who previously had not had "appropriate" access to educational opportunities. Criticism of education coming from the federal government, prior to *A nation at risk*, was directed almost entirely to the issue of the system's "failure" to provide access for these specific groups of individuals. Therefore, the student population in 1980 differed significantly from the population of 1960, as did the curriculum, standards, and expectations. Public school educators had been engaged in a major effort to educate more children than ever before. Prior to this time, for the most part, it was the educationally "advantaged" or highly motivated student who stayed in school. By 1980 the student population contained significantly more educationally "at risk" and often academically unmotivated students. While the national effort to educate all children was and is both a necessary and noble goal, it nevertheless changed the nature of the public education system in America.

The period following the Johnson Administration's "War on Poverty" saw limited attention paid to the crisis that had developed in public K-12 schools and teacher education. Our poorly defined state and national education policies, loosely founded on the Cardinal Principles of Secondary Education from an earlier era, needed attention, redefinition, and a new national commitment. During this time period, teacher education programs were unable to adjust rapidly enough to produce teachers who were prepared for this changing public education environment. With the publication and subsequent publicity associated with the *Nation at risk* report, the emphasis and criticism shifted to a different type of "failure." Each published report presented more evidence attempting to verify the failure of public education, and by the mid 1980's, national confidence in our public schools and teacher education had reached an all-time low.

Teacher Education Within the University Setting

Teacher education played a significant role in the development of the nation's state university systems. Between 1900 and 1970, more than one hundred state normal schools, originally intended to be two-year teacher training programs, evolved first into state teachers' colleges, and later, into state universities, as requirements for becoming a teacher began to include the possession of a college degree.

Beginning with the emergence of education as a specialized discipline, teacher education programs primarily attracted women; however, following World War II thousands of male veterans enrolled in colleges and universities in order to be certified to teach (Gosman 1985). A teaching degree became a common vehicle for many students, including veterans, to move into a respected middle-class occupation. Likely, many thousands of first generation college students who became teachers, would not have attended college if there had not been a national market for teachers.

When the post-war "baby boom" generation entered the public schools, the demand for certified teachers outpaced production. Between 1950 and 1970, state teachers' colleges and teacher education enrollments grew at a significantly faster pace than did traditional college and university student enrollments (Rudolph 1962). In most state teachers' colleges, as well as most major state universities, teacher education enrollments generated significant revenue that supported other programs. During this period teacher education programs expanded in order to train the growing number of undergraduate and graduate education students.

Colleges, schools, and departments of education often dominated credit hour production. During this period, higher education administrators and faculty were willing to "tolerate" teacher education programs as long as this new discipline kept producing enrollments and credit hours for the arts and sciences and other areas. This unofficial, unspoken arrangement existed in many institutions because most teacher education programs required students to complete a major portion of their degree program in courses outside the field of education. While many critics of teacher education programs have argued that prospective teachers are required to take excessive hours in pedagogy, education students have consistently been required to take over 70 percent of their total degree program in courses outside of the field of education (Holmstrom 1985). The ratio of hours taken in teacher preparation course work to "context" or liberal arts and sciences courses does not differ significantly from the ratio required by other human services undergraduate degree programs such as nursing, social work, or psychology.

Even though teacher training standards were maintained at a respectable level during this period, the decline in student enrollments during the 1970's eventually impacted program quality through retrenchment of faculty and programs. Between 1973 and 1983, as a result of the declining K-12 school population and the decreased demand for K-12 teachers, the number of teacher education graduates decreased by as much as 50 per cent in some institutions (Feistritzer 1985). The eventual impact of this enrollment decline left many teacher education programs in disarray. As collegiate-level enrollments declined nationally during the seventies, administrators in many institutions elected to redirect resources into growth or research areas. Consequently, as colleges, schools, and departments of education lost enrollment, comparable percentages of faculty and staff positions were eliminated. Faculty positions lost to resignations or retirements were not replaced, and many of the faculty losses occurred without adequate planning for program transition or, in some instances, program continuation. As a consequence of the declining enrollment and the resulting faculty retrenchment, an overall reduction of program quality was experienced in many institutions. By 1980, large numbers of teacher education programs had been seriously impaired by a somewhat random reduction of faculty and staff. Throughout the nation, many teacher education programs were operating without sufficient faculty necessary to deliver quality basic programs or to meet even minimum accreditation standards. Unfortunately, the general reaction from many university administrations to this situation was neither sympathetic nor supportive in regard to long-term implications for teacher training.

Ironically, the decline in teacher education program quality paralleled the emergence of the Civil Rights and Women's Movement in America. Traditionally, many talented women considered a teaching career as their only viable career option in a male-dominated work world. As the Women's Movement began to open new career choices for talented women, the education profession lost what had been a near monopoly on female talent. This same shift in career options occurred within the minority population among both females and males.

Decades of resentment from university colleagues in other academic areas toward teacher education as a discipline began to emerge. Based on a European model, most colleges and universities were organized around the traditional academic disciplines of the arts, sciences, and humanities. Educational pedagogy was a relative newcomer to the university curriculum and at best, there existed an uneasy truce between teacher educators and traditional university faculty and administrators. Integration of teacher education pedagogy into the university curriculum was never completely accomplished. During most of the twentieth century, teacher educators struggled to shape an applied field of study into a traditional university discipline. New and substantive research on teaching and learning was beginning to emerge during the late 1970's and early 1980's, just as the resources necessary to field quality programs were being cutback (Graham 1984).

The Call for Reform in Teacher Education

Long before the first report calling for reform in education was published, professional educators were in general agreement that teacher education needed immediate attention. For many years leaders in teacher education had been pleading for assistance to implement needed educational reform, but had been unable to generate sufficient support from higher education administrators, state and federal officials, or the public (Bok 1987).

Unfortunately, when national attention finally focused on teacher education, the views of most educational leaders were virtually ignored. Based on an analysis of the membership of the major education reform reports, national leadership in teacher education often had only token representation on these commissions.   Consequently, many outstanding professional educators were in effect silenced on teacher education issues.   As a result of this silence, the changes already underway in American education and teacher training were not articulated to the public. In the final analysis, following the publication of numerous reform reports, public education and teacher training took a devastating blow without significant protest, explanation, or defense from those in the profession.

For a number of years critics have advocated the elimination of traditional teacher training programs, arguing that there is no relationship between the completion of teacher training programs and a teacher's ability to affect student achievement (Bok 1987).   However, numerous studies have demonstrated that teachers who have had teacher training are better prepared to teach (Ashton & Crocker 1987).   Those who would eliminate teacher training demonstrate a vast underestimation of the complexity of what is involved in "effective teaching."   Those who work successfully with students with varying needs and backgrounds know that "teaching" is much more than merely presenting well-planned lectures and sorting students according to their ability to pass tests.   In an interview published in *Phi Delta Kappan*, Linda Darling-Hammond has pointed out the significance of well-trained teachers in the lives of children.

> To individual students, education is much more than the acquisition of facts.It is an act of self-affirmation, a moral act, an act of empowerment for the student. Or it can be an act of disempowerment. (Strother 1988)

A Look at Major Reform Proposals And Recommendations

This section will analyze some of the major reports that followed *A nation at risk*. Specifically, the reports of the Holmes Group, the Carnegie Corporation's Task Force, and the educational task forces comprised of the nation's governors will be reviewed. Additionally, the redesign of accrediting standards by the National Council for Accreditation of Teacher Education will be addressed.

Tomorrow's teachers: A report of the Holmes Group created shock waves with some of its controversial recommendations. This committee, made up of deans of education schools and chief academic officers from noted research universities, proposed the elimination of the undergraduate education major. Acknowledging their own past lack of commitment to teacher education, especially at the undergraduate level, this group suggested that the route to the teaching profession be confined to a liberal arts degree followed by a graduate professional program in education at a research university. The discussion launched by this recommendation has initiated serious reevaluation of the many and varied four and five year designs for teacher training. The resulting reevaluation of what content is essential and the amount of time needed for appropriate preparation for teaching, has been beneficial to teacher education.

Another recommendation from the Holmes Group involves a three-level career ladder concept for teachers. Under the plan, an "instructor" would teach under the supervision of and with assistance from a "career professional." The career professional teacher would assume responsibilities in many areas currently associated with principals who ideally function as "instructional leaders." In addition, the career professional would have responsibilities with regard to teaching and research within the school district and cooperating university. The "professional" teacher would function autonomously within the classroom setting with responsibility for the learning of the students assigned.

Partnerships between university faculty and practicing teachers and administrators is a recommendation from the Holmes Group that addresses a real need for ongoing interaction between university and K-12 educators. Other recommendations refer to entry and exit standards for teacher training programs that would ensure that teachers demonstrate basic mastery of writing and speaking and demonstrate competence in the subject(s) they will teach (The Holmes Group 1986).

The recommendations coming out of this report have generated serious debate throughout the educational community and among educational reform activists. Any one of the recommendations within the model has far-reaching logistical and educational implications. Even prior to implementation of pilot programs, the proposed model has served the function of stimulating reevaluation and redefinition of "essentials" for effective teacher training. However, serious reservations must be expressed regarding the viability of these recommendations, both economically and functionally.

From an economic perspective, the potential cost of the implementation of the Holmes Group proposal could be staggering. For example, the increased salary structure for the "professional teachers" and "career professionals" could necessitate a major restructuring of local and state school finance. Even if this component of the proposal could be proven effective in the education of children, the current economic situation in school districts and states across the country would not indicate support for a costly educational reform plan. A common-sense understanding of our current national and international economic situation would suggest that future educational reform having an exceptionally high cost will have little chance of being widely implemented.

From a functional perspective, the Holmes Group initiative bases much of its premise on "elite" professional teachers being trained by "elite" state research institutions. Given the magnitude of both teacher education and public education, this exclusive reliance on research universities for teacher training would appear to be neither functional nor realistic. Currently, state and other research universities are not producing the majority of our nation's certified teachers. Again, from a common-sense perspective, if future certified teachers came primarily from these universities or through alternative certification programs, a crisis in the production of certified and qualified teachers would be inevitable. Closely related to this problem is the extended time and expense that would be necessary for teachers to be certified through the Holmes Group plan. Further, these concerns must be considered with regard to our current difficulties in attracting and training minorities and in meeting the needs of a growing minority population.

Released soon after the Holmes report was the report *A nation prepared: Teachers for the 21st century* This report was prepared by the Carnegie Corporation's Task Force on Teaching as a Profession, a committee formed by the Carnegie Forum on Education and the Economy. With powerful business and political leaders involved, with representation of teachers by the heads of both major teachers' unions, and with a strong influence from the chairperson of the Holmes Group, many of the recommendations from the Carnegie group were similar to those proposed in the Holmes report. Requiring a bachelor's degree in the arts and sciences as a prerequisite for studying education and completing a professional curriculum in graduate school leading to a Master of Teaching degree are reflective of the Holmes influence on this plan.

One of the Carnegie Task Force recommendations is the creation of a National Board for Professional Teaching Standards. Funded with a Carnegie grant, an advisory group has been formed to work on creating a national board that will specify what teachers need to know and be able to do. The development of specific tests for these knowledge and skill areas is currently underway.

Restructuring the schools to allow teachers more autonomy in deciding how to meet goals for children and the restructuring of the teaching force to allow more teacher involvement in evaluation, school, and curricular design, are reflective of a theme of teacher "empowerment" which is sounded in many of the major reports, including the Carnegie Report. However, teachers and administrators are to have leeway only as long as they "demonstrate results" that are deemed acceptable, generally based on such measures as standardized tests, drop-out rates, and attendance rates.

Tying teacher incentives to student performance has created much debate and concern among educators. Not only is there concern regarding the criteria to be utilized in determining what is to be tested, what constitutes acceptable "student performance," and what determines the validity of the measurement instruments to be used, there is a great deal of concern regarding the basic underlying assumptions about teaching and learning that this "marketing approach" to education implies.

While most reports recommend increasing teachers' salaries, the Carnegie Group's proposal to raise top teachers' salaries to a level as high as $72,000 has attracted a great deal of attention. Moreover, this report mentions the need to attract more minority teachers to the field of education only briefly, while providing little in the way of a substantive plan to accomplish that objective (Carnegie Forum on Education and the Economy 1986).

The recommendations coming out of the Holmes and Carnegie Groups, if adopted in their entirety, could have the effect of dismantling traditional teacher education. These groups have been effective in promoting images of "failure," and thus preparing the public to be supportive of drastic--as opposed to well-thought-out--change. Instead of sorting out what is sound versus what needs improvement in teacher education, the emphasis has been on the elimination of undergraduate teacher training and the restructuring of training at the graduate level, based on what various interest groups "believe" will provide better teachers. These plans have little research data upon which their recommendations for improvement were based. Their assault on traditional teacher education has been fueled by an appeal to emotions encouraging haste instead of reason. To abandon a proven and improving structure for teacher education, without substituting a functional, viable replacement could very well mean educational and economic disaster.

Time for results: The governors' 1991 report on education represents a compilation of the recommendations of seven governors' task forces set up by Governor Lamar Alexander of Tennessee, chairman of the National Governors' Association. The recommendations center around providing incentives, support, and encouragement for programs to improve training, standards, and the learning environment for educators and students at all levels of the educational system, as well as on encouraging the involvement and cooperation of parents in their children's education. The seven education issues studied by the task forces were: Teaching, Leadership and Management, Parent Involvement and Choice, Readiness, Technology, School Facilities, and College Quality. Each task force report reflects the views of the specific governors who served on the particular task force, and are not necessarily the views of the governors as a whole. The significance of this report lies in the interest and commitment to improving education demonstrated by the nation's governors (National Governors' Association Center for Policy Research and Analysis 1986).

NCATE's new Standards for the National Council for Accreditation of Teacher Education is a major example of the reform that has been taking place within the teacher education profession. Most institutions with teacher education programs had been working to maintain and upgrade standards prior to the redesign at NCATE, and in most cases welcomed the national efforts that would help to establish assurances regarding the quality and type of training being provided. In response to needs expressed from within their member organizations, NCATE has made substantive and far-reaching changes in procedures and standards for national accreditation of teacher education programs. The redesign effort has received strong backing from such professional educational organizations as the American Association of Colleges for Teacher Education (AACTE) and the National Education Association (NEA) (Gollnick & Kunkel 1986). Many teacher educators see this as an important step toward insuring quality in teacher education.

Past criticism of NCATE centered around ambiguous standards that could not be applied uniformly, the fact that standards were not applied consistently, redundancy in reviews for national accreditation and state approval, and a structure that allowed program category approval without the total education unit being accredited. This often resulted in confusion regarding the actual accreditation status of the overall unit (Wheeler 1980).

NCATE responded by adopting principles for its redesign process that would address the major areas of concern and by soliciting input from teacher educators across the nation through cooperative efforts with its member institutions. The major principles that guided the specific changes in standards and procedures include:

1. Accreditation decisions would be made for the teacher education unit as a whole.

2. Continuing accreditation would replace the concept of reaccreditation.

3. Articulation would be provided between the program review for state approval and the program review for national accreditation.

4. Visiting team members would be selected from a board of examiners, the members of which would be highly skilled in evaluation techniques and well trained in NCATE processes and standards.

5. Five sets of standards, focused on the teacher education unit as a whole, would replace the six sets of standards then in use to evaluate basic and advanced programs.

6. The NCATE annual list would be expanded to include a description of each teacher education unit and data that describe the support level for professional education programs within that unit. (Gollnick and Kunkel 1986)

The new NCATE standards fall into five categories: (1) knowledge base for professional education, (2) relationship to the world of practice, (3) students, (4) faculty, and (5) governance and resources. Within each category specific standards are supported by criteria of compliance.

Within the "knowledge base for professional education" category, institutions must describe the knowledge base that supports the curriculum, demonstrate that the curriculum is based on educational research and accepted practice, and clearly state the philosophy and objectives of the curriculum. The curriculum must reflect global and multicultural objectives, and demonstrate that the faculty within the unit utilize effective teaching practices as they work with students. Institutions are to provide students with a well-rounded background in general studies and a strong academic background in areas in which they plan to teach or work. Students must be provided with the opportunity for acquiring sufficient knowledge in academic subjects, knowledge of professional practices and methods of research, and knowledge relating to professional ethics and values.

Within the "relationship to the world of practice" category, institutions must provide opportunities for students to apply and evaluate what they are being taught through the coordination of clinical and field-based experiences. Education majors are required to fulfill a minimum of ten weeks of full-time student teaching. In addition, institutions must provide follow-up assistance during the first year of teaching to graduates within the unit's service area, and meet criteria for selection of cooperating teachers and supervisors.

The "students" category details criteria for determining entry and exit requirements for the teacher training program. Admission procedures must encourage recruitment of a culturally diverse student population, and have in place procedures for providing adequate advisory services and for monitoring students' progress.

The "faculty" category details standards for qualifications of teacher education faculty members. Limitations are placed on the use of graduate assistants as faculty, and criteria regarding number and qualifications of faculty required within areas of specialization are spelled out. Limitations with regard to faculty load are detailed and institutional resource support requirements are included as well. Evaluation must be balanced among teaching ability, scholarly performance, and use of research.

The "governance and resources" category requires that the governance system be spelled out, have a clear mission, and function as described. The unit must demonstrate that it has adequate space, facilities, materials, equipment, support staff, and sufficient financial resources to meet program needs.

As the national representative of professional teacher educators, NCATE reflects the efforts of its member institutions in providing the public with assurance of high standards in the preparation of its nation's teachers. Through the redesign and upgrading of its standards, procedures, and governance structure, NCATE has taken a major step in providing a measure against which alternative programs for teacher education can be judged.

Summary

The 1980's has seen a proliferation of reports, plans, and designs from numerous foundations, committees, and organizations purporting to offer the answer to America's educational needs for the twenty-first century. The reports have served to keep the sense of urgency and importance of education alive in the consciousness of legislators and the general public. Recommendations from many of the reports emphasize the importance of program design, inviting thoughtful reexamination of not only the essential components of teacher training programs, but the sequencing and time required for initial teacher preparation. Most reports emphasize the importance of high standards for entry into and exit from teacher training programs, as well as the importance for standardization of certification and licensing requirements. All of the major reports acknowledge the importance of improving the professional status and working conditions of teachers.

Recommendations from the reports need to be evaluated and considered on the basis of the potential for the recommendations to accomplish the intended objectives and in light of the background and understanding of teaching and learning, as well as the motivation of those making the various proposals. Proposed solutions and recommendations must be evaluated with concern given to the long-term implications of their implementation. The tendency to react emotionally instead of thoughtfully must be overcome.

Our educational system is reflective of our nation as a whole, and just as we need reasoned change and improvement in many aspects of our governmental system, we need reasoned, carefully-thought-out change and improvement in our educational system.   We must avoid finger-pointing and turf protecting and the temptation to reach for trendy or "quick-fix" solutions."   Our nation's consciousness has been raised concerning the very real need for attention to our educational system.

It is time for professional educators to speak out on the critical education issues facing our nation. It's time to give the proposals that show promise the opportunity to be piloted in environments where they have the greatest chance to prove their worth, keeping in mind that there will be no easy answers or "one best way" to train teachers. We must reevaluate and reaffirm our national education mission, and be realistic about allocation of both our people and financial resources. The decisions made in the next few years regarding educational reform will have far-reaching implications for our nation's future. Educators who are deeply involved in and committed to education must be active in determining the direction of educational reform. In the United States, we have a tradition of standing firm for both excellence and equity.   With rational and forward-looking leadership, educational reform can be a long-term positive force ensuring a successful future for our nation's children and society as a whole.

References

American Association of Colleges for Teacher Education. *Report to the profession.* Washington, D.C.: AACTE, 1984.

Ashton, Patricia, and Linda Crocker. 1987. Systematic study of planned variations: The essential focus of teacher education reform. *Journal of Teacher Education* 38, No. 3 (May-June).

   This article provides an overview of the various educational reform recommendations with an analysis of their implications.

Bell, Terrel H. 1986. Education policy development in the Reagan administration. *Phi Delta Kappan* 67, No. 7 (March).

Bok, Derek. 1987. The challenge to schools of education. *Harvard Magazine* (May-June).

   Bok challenges faculty of schools and colleges of education to assume the role of educational leaders by utilizing the knowledge available concerning teaching and learning, and to serve as models exemplifying the highest standards of effective teaching.

Carnegie Forum on Education and the Economy. 1986. *A nation prepared: Teachers for the 21st century.* New York: Carnegie Forum Task Force on Teaching as a Profession.

Feistritzer, Emily. 1985. *Teacher education reports.* Washington, D.C.: Feistritzer Publications.

   As a major reporter on teacher education and educational reform, Feistritzer documents the training, certification, and employment of the American teacher with valuable data and interpretation.

Feistritzer, Emily. 1984. *The making of a teacher: A report on teacher education and certification.* Washington, D.C.: National Center for Educational Information.

Gollnick, Donna M., and Richard C. Kunkel 1986. The reform of national accreditation. *Phi Delta Kappan* 68 (December): 310-314.

Gosman, Erica. 1985. *Quality in teacher education: A crisis revisited.* Boulder, Colorado: The Western Interstate Commission for Higher Education.

Graham, Patricia A. 1984. Schools: Cacophony about practice, silence about purpose. *Daedalus* 113, No. 4 (Fall).

Graham traces the major educational issues and concerns from the turn of the century to the present, highlighting the fact that in the current climate of educational criticism there is a noticeable lack of meaningful discussion concerning what the purpose of schooling "should" be.

Green Joslyn. 1987. *The next wave: A synopsis of recent education reform reports.* Denver, Colorado: Education Commission of the States.

Halberstam, David. 1986. *The reckoning.* New York: William Morrow and Company, Inc.

Halberstam provides a comparison of the development of American industry with that of Japan's, while relating economic development to education.

The Holmes Group. 1986. *Tomorrow's teachers: A report of the Holmes group.* East Lansing, Michigan: College of Education, Michigan State University.

Holmstrom, E. and I. Engin. 1985. Recent changes in teacher education programs. Washington, D.C.: American Council on Higher Education. Panel Report Number 67.

National Commission on Excellence in Education. 1983. *A nation at risk: The imperative for educational reform.* Washington, D.C.: U.S. Department of Education.

National Governors' Association. 1986. *Time for results: The governors' 1991 report on education.* Washington, D.C.:

National Governors' Association Center for Policy Research and Analysis.

Roth, Robert.   1986.   *Teaching   and   teacher   education: Implementing   reform* (Fastback No. 240).   Bloomington, Ind.: Phi Delta Kappa Educational Foundation.

Rudolf, Frederick.   1962.   *The American college and university, A history.* New York: Vintage Books.

Strother, Deborah Burnett.   1988.   A wide-ranging look at current issues in education: An interview with Linda Darling-Hammond.   *Phi Delta Kappan* 69, No. 6 (February): 447-450).

Wheeler, C. W.   1980.   *NCATE: Does it matter?*   East Lansing, Michigan: Research on Teaching, Michigan State University.

   This in-depth study of NCATE in 1980 summarizes many of the problems associated with teacher education accreditation under the "old" standards.   This timely and critical review of the overall accreditation process helped provide focus for later NCATE reform.

Yates, Brock.   1983.   *The decline and fall of the American automobile industry.* New York: Empire Books.

The Three Ghosts of Teacher Induction: Past, Present, and Future

John M. Johnston

Men's courses will foreshadow certain ends, to which,if persevered in, they must lead.

Ebenezer Scrooge

This chapter provides an annotated bibliography which includes differing perspectives on the induction of new teachers into the profession. The bibliography is set in a context which provides first, an overview of how first year teachers and teacher induction have been viewed in the past; second, a discussion of current teacher induction programs and practices; and finally, a consideration of selected issues for the future of teacher induction.

Induction is a concept in teacher career development that is applied to beginning teachers. Generally, teacher induction refers to the first one to three years of teacher career development and is viewed as a bridge between the preservice and inservice career phases. Fessler broadly describes induction as ". . . a period when a new teacher strives for acceptance by students, peers, and supervisors and attempts to achieve a comfort and security level in dealing with everyday problems and issues" (1985, 186). More specifically, induction refers to the first years of teaching following the completion of pre-service preparation. Johnston (1985) notes that the induction period often coincides with the probationary years in a teacher's career. Induction can also be identified in relation to specific practices often extended to beginning teachers (e.g., reduced class size, assignment of a support teacher, additional orientation, and extra released time for planning and observation). Such practices are generally not made available to experienced teachers.

The future of teacher induction is considered by examining the ebb and flow of past and present induction practices and attitudes. How have the process of beginning teachers and the process of beginning to teach been perceived by the profession? What attitudes and perceptions affect our thinking about the needs of beginning teachers? Current induction efforts are discussed with particular emphasis on current issues and trends which will likely affect future efforts. The future of reform in teacher induction is assessed. What teacher induction policy should be developed and implemented? What research should be undertaken to strengthen the knowledge base for teacher induction? What changes need to occur? Who is responsible for the various teacher induction components? Will the fledgling teacher induction reform movement continue to prosper in coming years, or like Scrooge's dark glimpse of his own fate, will we discover Teacher Induction graven on a fresh headstone?

A View from the Past

Are the chances for significant reform of beginning teacher induction any better than were the prospects for reform of Ebenezer Scrooge prior to his nocturnal visits from the Ghosts of Christmas's Past, Present and Future? Scrooge's now famous "Bah! Humbug!" view of Christmas was shaped by his experiences: a lonely boarding school childhood, benign neglect from his parents, a young clerk and unsuccessful suitor, and as an avaricious partner in the firm of Scrooge and Marley. In much the same fashion, contemporary American society's attitudes toward the induction of beginning teachers into the teaching profession are also considerably influenced by past experiences and perceptions. The introduction of beginning teachers to the work of teaching is inextricably linked to a history of schools and teaching that predates the republic. Significant reform of teacher induction is shackled by dated traditions and societal attitudes about schools, teachers, and teaching.

Past professional attitudes about teacher induction are clearly displayed in the many articles, papers, monographs, and books which comprise the published induction knowledge base. The professional literature about beginning teaching is a narrowly focused, but helpful, reflection of how educators have thought about and valued the induction of new teachers into the profession. Between 1930 and 1977 there were published just a handful of books and only about 300 articles, papers, and research reports related to beginning teachers (Johnston 1978). These written documents represent one obvious means by which messages about the first year of teaching are introduced and circulated within the education community. As such, professional publications about beginning teachers or the first year of teaching represent a rich, unobtrusive view of the profession's past perspective on teacher induction.

In the first recent comprehensive analysis of the first year teacher literature, Applegate, Lasley, Flora, Mager, Johnston, Newman and Ryan (1977) proposed five useful topic categories. First, advice on the first year of teaching included not only advice to beginning teachers, but also advice about understanding and helping newcomers. Second, are (usually) first-hand reports of first year teachers' experiences, unadorned by interpretation or commentary. Similarly, the third category includes first-hand accounts of beginning teachers, but these include scholarly, discipline-based interpretation. Fourth, are carefully reasoned explanations of more global experiences of first year teachers, and thoughtful commentaries on the first year of teaching. Fifth, are empirical studies of the first year of teaching, including teacher induction program evaluations.

Beginning teacher and induction literature prior to 1975 is characterized by an overwhelming emphasis on problems and concerns of first year teachers. Research of this period is primarily descriptive, with little emphasis on contextual variables. Comprehensive descriptions of induction programs coupled with reliable and valid program evaluation studies are scarce. Positive efforts to understand and explain induction problems and process were initiated from anthropological, sociological, and psychological perspectives. Literature from this period provides little attention to comprehensive program or policy issues such as funding, relationship to system evaluation needs, certification, or career long development.

The Present View

Professional literature since the late 1970's provides a very different view of thinking about induction of beginning teachers. Concomitant with the current public concern with educational reform and legislative activity in teacher induction, there has been a significant increase in scholarly attention to teacher induction (e.g., Brooks 1987; Griffin & Millies 1987; Huling-Austin in press; Johnston 1985; Ryan et al. 1980; Zeichner 1983). A marked increase in the quality and utility of professional publications about beginning teaching is but one result of teacher induction becoming a significant feature of the educational reform movement.

The focus of current induction literature has expanded beyond description of the difficulties of teachers in the induction phase of their career development. The present literature is characterized by attention to larger issues of policy, resource allotment, and program design, with the general goal of improving the induction experience (cf. Brooks, 1987; Griffin & Millies 1987). Matters being addressed include induction program financing; new teacher assignment (Rosenholtz 1987); identification of program components (Carter & Koehler 1987); identification, training, and assignment of support or mentor teachers; and the most appropriate roles and activities for the community, school, school system (Johnston 1985; Kester & Marockie 1987), state departments of education (Burke & Notar 1986; Ward, 1987)), teacher unions and professional organization (Ishler & Kester 1987), and institutions of higher education (Hegler & Dudley 1987; Howey & Zimpher 1987; Johnston & Kay 1987).

The current teacher induction literature is also marked by broad based interest in development of theoretical perspectives from which to understand the experiences of beginning teachers and upon which to base design of teacher induction programs. Veenman (1984), for example, suggests that the development of beginning teachers can be understood from three different perspectives. One theoretical framework focuses on teacher socialization, on how teachers adapt to their new role in the context of their own beliefs and those of others in the workplace. A second framework is a cognitive development perspective which is supported by the view of the beginning teacher as an adult learner. Finally, Veenman suggests a developmental framework based on stages of concern.

Current writing about teacher induction is characterized by much more detailed attention to a broad range of specific components relevant to understanding the experience of beginning teachers and to designing functional induction programs. In contrast to earlier more simplistic prescriptions such as "Assign a buddy teacher to assist the neophyte," current literature is characterized by many thoughtful considerations of appropriate roles for mentor teachers, necessary mentoring skills, training of mentor teachers, and policy matters related to funding and workload of support teachers.

Similarly, current literature reflects thoughtful concern about concrete matters of roles and responsibility for teacher induction efforts. For example, the role of institutions of higher education has come under particular scrutiny. Johnston and Kay (1987) surveyed institutions about existing and planned programs and common induction activities. They also investigated arrangements between teacher education programs and school districts; faculty workload and assignment procedures. This state-of-practice perspective is nicely complimented by Howey and Zimpher's (1987) comprehensive proposal for appropriate roles of institutions of higher education.

Another outstanding feature of the current teacher induction literature is its attention to public policy and the general relationship between public education and induction as one phase of career long teacher development. In part this policy literature was the outgrowth of statewide induction or entry year programs mandated by state legislatures (Hawk & Robards 1987). Griffin's (1987) chapter is an excellent example of thoughtful, knowledge based policy recommendations for a statewide induction program; and is also a good example of a level of discourse not present in earlier teacher induction literature.

In summary, the present view of teacher induction appears rosier now than it ever has in the past, much like the view provided Scrooge by the jovial Ghost of Christmas Present. National commissions, critical reports, and professional debate all trumpet the importance of teacher induction. Executive and legislative actions have mandated induction programs at the state and local levels. Public school teachers, administrators, and higher education faculty are now involved in designing, implementing, and evaluating induction efforts. Increased funding for teacher preparation provides better financial support than ever previously afforded teacher induction efforts. Research on teacher induction has received commensurate attention and the knowledge base is expanding. Increased induction efforts are providing exciting opportunities for evaluating induction programs. Induction research issues and directions are being debated and are emerging more clearly drawn.

A Glimpse into the Future

Much of the future for teacher induction programs will be dictated by the extent to which thoughtful, comprehensive induction programs are institutionalized by school systems, institutions of higher education, and state departments of education. Such institutionalization depends, in part, on the demand for new teachers, and the perceived value of induction efforts. Establishing clear expected outcomes shared by all participating constituencies is essential for the success of future programs.

Future programs also must clearly define the relation of induction to initial teacher certification. This is a particularly difficult though fundamental issue for the future of teacher induction efforts. How will necessary support mechanisms be related to the equally necessary evaluation and quality control measures? Failure to attend to this critical component could result in the institutionalization of ineffective and counter-productive programs which may well drive beginning teachers toward rather than away from Lortie's (1965) Robinson Crusoe syndrome.

Cooperative participation by involved constituencies is another critical factor affecting future induction programs. As states such as Illinois and Tennessee, for example, develop initial year of teaching programs, consideration must be given to the unique perspectives and contributions to be provided by schools, colleges and universities, teachers organizations, local communities, and state departments of education. These groups must be involved with induction program planning from its initial stages. A variety of perspectives and resources can be accommodated through development and testing of different models of teacher induction, with each model attending to differing content.

Evaluation of teacher induction programs is essential in order for continued growth in our understanding of this critical period in teacher development. Availability of a variety of induction program models will create opportunities for future research. Little is known about the effects of specific induction interventions, or their cumulative effects. The development of future induction programs will provide increased opportunities for researchers to study what induction practices work best under what conditions.

The Ghost of Christmas Yet to Come provided Scrooge only a shadowy and ambiguous view of the future. Our view of the future of teacher induction is equally cloudy and uncertain. On one hand the education profession may know what is good and proper for the induction of new teachers into the profession. On the other hand it is entirely another matter to make the changes in society's collective attitudes and actions necessary to effect substantial and lasting change in teacher induction practices. What is the likelihood that teacher organizations and school administrators will agree on positive practices for assigning new teachers' initial workplace and workload? Will institutions of higher education restructure teaching load and productivity expectations for faculty working in field based induction programs? Can institutions of higher education faculty embrace new conceptions of their role in induction efforts? Teacher induction programs are expensive; will voters continue to support appropriate funding for induction efforts? How can the need for teacher evaluation be met without destroying the often fragile induction process? Though positive opportunities exist for the future of teacher induction, difficult problems and serious challenges must be overcome if the current expansion of the teacher induction knowledge base is to continue.

References

Applegate, J.H., T. Lasley, R. Flora, G. Mager, J.M. Johnston, K. Newman, and K. Ryan. 1977. *The first year teacher study.* Columbus, Ohio: ERIC Document Reproduction Service No. ED 135 766.

Ashburn, Elizabeth A.   1987.   Current developments in teacher induction programs.   *Action in Teacher Education*, 8 (Winter):   41-44.

> Provides an overview of the induction scene from the need for induction programs, to sources for existing induction programs, to the need for comparative analysis of different types of programs. Written by the Director of the ERIC Clearinghouse of Teacher Education, this article provides a quick overview and useful starting point for further inquiry about teacher induction.

Barnes, Susan.   1987.   Assessment issues in initial year of teaching programs.   In *The first year of teaching: Background papers and a proposal*, ed. Gary A. Griffin and Suzanne Millies, 115-127.   Chicago: University of Illinois-Chicago.

> Addresses the thorny problem of combining support for and evaluation of beginning teachers. Barnes' purpose is to address selected issues related to the assessment of beginning teachers as a component of an induction program. Her perspective is one of an assessment system operating within the induction program within the political, educational, and social systems in a school system, not in isolation. From this perspective, Barnes discusses policy, technical, and implementation issues encountered in developing an assessment system. The paper includes a brief discussion of the relationship of the assessment system to preservice and inservice training.

Brooks, Douglas M., ed.   1987.   *Teacher induction: A new beginning.*   Reston, Va.: Association of Teacher Educators.

> Reports the results of two years of inquiry by members of the Association of Teacher Educators National Commission on the Induction Process.   This monograph provides the most up-to-date report available on induction programs

and activities currently in progress in local school systems across the country; state induction programs which have been implemented or which are now being piloted; the involvement status of institutions of higher education in beginning teacher induction; and positions on teacher induction of a variety of professional education organizations. It is a timely, highly readable resource that provides an invaluable starting point for surveying the state of current teacher induction practice in the United States.

Burke, Peter, and Ellen Elms Notar. 1986. The school and the university: Bridging the gap in teacher induction. *Action in Teacher Education* 7 (Winter): 11-16.

Outlines the role of the university in an induction program, along with factions in the University and the school culture which both support and thwart program development. Burke and Notar explore issues in the development of a collaborative teacher induction program and consider rewards for assisting beginning teachers.

Carter, Kathy, and Virginia Richardson Koehler. 1987. The process and content of initial year of teaching programs. In *The first year of teaching: Background papers and a proposal*, ed. Gary A. Griffin and Suzanne Millies, 91-104. Chicago: University of Illinois-Chicago.

Proposes content and processes for initial year of teaching programs. Carter and Richardson develop the general goals of a beginning teacher program by describing the ways in which beginning teachers differ from both preservice and experienced teachers in terms of knowledge, skill, attitudes, cognitive processes, and their needs in these areas. They lay out a foundation for such a program based on a conception of teaching, of knowledge needs of beginning teachers, and of the learning-to-teach process. The authors suggest that the development and use of a case literature holds particular promise for meeting specific objectives proposed for initial year of teaching programs.

Eddy, Elizabeth M. 1969. *Becoming a teacher: The passage to professional status*. New York: Teachers College Press.

Examines the professional development of twenty-two first year teachers in inner city elementary and junior high schools. Using weekly tape recorded sessions as a data base, Eddy was able to study classroom events, the experiences of these new teachers, their satisfactions, problems, and changing perceptions. The purpose of this classic and still informative study is "to provide a greater understanding of the social relationships within the school which deeply affect new teachers and their teaching performance and which must be taken into account if teacher education and recruitment is to become more meaningful for those who teach in slum areas" (7).

Eddy uses the anthropological concept of social transition to explore how beginning teachers learn the responsibilities and activities appropriate to their new role. She also uses the concept of rites of passage to examine the experience of beginning teachers as they separate from their secure home and college existence, their transition from student to teacher, and their eventual incorporation as a teacher in a particular school setting. She carefully considers the roles played by administrators, other teachers, students and their parents in shaping the new teachers' professional self-expectations.

Becoming a teacher is one of the few publications to date that not only chronicles the experiences of the beginning teacher, but also offers discipline-based explanations for why and how those experiences occurred. Those responsible for planning induction of new teachers--particularly for those beginning to teach in urban settings--will find much of value in this book.

Fessler, R. 1985. A model for teacher professional growth and development. In *Career-long teacher education* , ed. P.J. Burke & R.J. Heidemann, 181-193. Springfield, Ill.: Charles Thomas, Inc.

Gehrke, Nathalie J. 1987. On helping the beginning teacher. *In The first year of teaching: Background papers and a proposal,* ed. Gary A. Griffin and Suzanne Millies, 105-113. Chicago: University of Illinois Chicago.

Examines the kinds of help for beginning teachers in light of what is known about beginnings. She discusses creation of a new helping community for teachers, a community that benefits both beginning teachers and experienced teachers as well. Gehrke's model is based upon the notion that conditions must be created within schools which will assure sustained care for beginning teachers beyond those times when the public is concerned about teacher retention. She illustrates her helping community by using perspectives from sociology, anthropology, psychology, linguistics and education. Gehrke cautions that the building of helping communities within each school should receive attention equal to, if not greater than, the development of large-scale technical assistance programs and training packages.

Griffin, Gary A. 1987. A state program for the initial year of teaching. In *The first year of teaching: Background papers and a proposal*, ed. Gary A. Griffin and Suzanne Millies, 129-137. Chicago: University of Illinois-Chicago.

Sets forth a number of recommendations about how the state might act in relation to developing an Illinois Initial Year of Teaching Program. His recommendations attend to planning that must be engaged in as well as specific features of an initial year of teaching program that are believed to be essential. Griffin's capstone proposals are preceded by a brief presentation of the background against which any consideration of new teacher programs must be understood.

Griffin, Gary A. 1985. Teacher induction: Research issues. *Journal of Teacher Education* 36(1): (January-February) 42-46.

Asserts that although available research on beginning teachers and on induction programs has serious limitations, progress can be made by changing the research questions asked, and by improving the balance of qualitative and quantitative research methods employed to answer those questions. As have others, Griffin claims that there is little useful research available for use in induction programs. Great Britain and Australia, he notes, have studied induction more extensively, and can provide useful perspectives for researchers in the United States.

Griffin discusses the important distinction between "research that describes the experience of new teachers and research that gives attention to the influence of intentional interventions in the lives and work of new teachers" (42). He notes that most research on new teachers has concentrated on describing problems in adjusting to their new role, but that few ameliorative programs are available. Griffin cautions against an over-reliance on research on teaching as a basis for designing induction programs, particularly those tied to certification of new teachers. He discusses several dilemmas associated with using research on teaching as the primary basis for induction programs. Griffin concludes this useful article by posing a series of questions for future research on teacher induction, and by presenting five pressing issues for teacher induction research.

Griffin, Gary A., and Suzanne Millies. eds. 1987. *The first years of teaching: Background papers and a proposal.* Chicago: University of Illinois at Chicago.

Commissioned by the Illinois State Board of Education, this most useful collection of papers was one component of an exploration of the desirability of moving ahead with an Illinois Initial Year of Teaching Program. Written by recognized national experts in their respective fields, the topics of the papers are ones that have been shown in other states and regions to be of importance in planning, implementing, and assessing the impact of beginning teacher induction programs. This collection of papers, in combination with the reports of current teacher induction practices provided in the ATE National Commission (see Brooks 1987 above), provide an excellent starting point for understanding the current teacher induction knowledge base, issues, and practices.

Hall, Gene. 1982. Induction: The missing link. *Journal of Teacher Education* 33(3) (May-June): 53-55.

Notes the gap between higher education and the local school district responsibility for teacher induction and calls for a career long view of teacher development which would include the transition from preservice to inservice. Hall observes that relatively little research has been done on the induction phase and that "almost no research has focused on strategies to assist teachers during this time" (52). Like Griffin, Hall recognizes that educators in Great Britain and Australia have induction programs in place, and have conducted systematic studies of induction. He goes on to suggest that socialization research from industrial and organizational theory can provide useful starting points for educators' study of teacher socialization. He concludes by offering an extensive list of research questions generated by participants in an invited AERA Division C forum on induction. Hall suggests five topics as starting points for induction research: (a) the phenomena of induction, (b) induction teacher education programs, (c) selection, (d) retention, and (e) linkage.

Hawk, Parmalee. 1984. *Making a difference: Reflections and thoughts of first year teachers.* Greenville, N.C.: School of Education, East Carolina University.

Based on over one hundred hours of tape recorded interviews with twenty-eight first year teachers employed in public school systems in rural northeastern North Carolina, this publication captures the thoughts and experiences of these teachers in an enlightening and interesting manner. Hawk writes that *Making a difference* "was not written to report hard empirical data from which highly reliable inferences or generalizations can be made. Rather it was written to capture some of the impressions of . . . beginning teachers" (11). Drawing heavily on quotes from the first year teachers, the book is organized in seven chapters around such themes as reasons for choosing to teach; facing the realities of paperwork and continuous responsibility; planning; instruction; evaluation; discipline; and relations with parents and principals.

Hawk, Parmalee, and Shirley Robards. 1987. Statewide teacher induction programs. In *Teacher induction: A new beginning,* ed. Douglas M. Brooks, 33-44. Reston, Va.: Association of Teacher Educators.

Reports results of a survey of the status of statewide teacher induction programs. Reporting responses from 50 states, they discuss components of implemented statewide teacher induction programs, as well as components of statewide programs in the pilot stage of implementation. A useful name/address list of contacts for each state is included. An excellent and current overview of induction activity at the state level.

Hegler, Kay, and Richard Dudley. 1987. Beginning teacher induction: A progress report. *Journal of Teacher Education* 38 (January-February): 53-56.

Documents implementation of an induction program as one component in teacher education reform. Hegler and Dudley identify the general purposes of induction programs and describe how this specific induction program addresses these purposes. The role of the college supervisor and the support teacher are explained. The program's unique features and its strengths and weaknesses are described. The authors recommend the implementation of college-based induction programs and present suggestions for program development and additional research.

Hitz, Randy, and Susan Roper. 1986. The teacher's first year: Implications for teacher educators. *Action in Teacher Education* 8 (Fall): 65-71.

Assigns the general needs of beginning teachers into four categories based on a conceptual analysis of related professional literature. The authors maintain that beginning teachers need to (a) learn to work with other adults: parents, administrators and aides; (b) to learn to work effectively with other teachers; (c) to acquire a more realistic view of the work of teaching; and (d) to be provided a more useful and comprehensive theoretical framework on which to base initial professional development.

Howey, Kenneth, and Richard Bents, ed. 1979. *Toward meeting the needs of the beginning teacher: Initial training/induction/inservice.* Minneapolis: Midwest Teacher Corps Network and University of Minnesota/St. Paul Schools Teacher Corps Project.

Addresses the needs and issues concerning beginning teachers; reviews lessons learned from past induction efforts; offers conceptual, theoretical and operational models for teacher induction; and presents challenges, issues and research questions for the future. This unified collection of nine papers provides an historical overview of some of the more common efforts which have been employed to help beginning teachers; discusses problems facing beginning teachers; outlines the need for a comprehensive set of guidelines for policy makers; reviews issues associated with internship programs; reinforces the need for cooperation among public school personnel, higher education, state legislatures, boards of education and certification officers; explores needed research and research issues related to the beginning years of teaching; outlines an operational model for support of beginning teachers from the perspective of a school administrator; expresses concern about the amount of time and type of initial preparation, the over-emphasis on "hands on" activity and, the tendency of teacher selection and socialization to foster a conservative outlook and resistance to change in teachers; provides a model for the induction of beginning teachers based on developmental theory; and concludes with a general framework for induction and continuing teacher education which provides a means of considering each of the various decisions faced in planning a comprehensive and unified induction program.

Howey, Kenneth R., and Nancy Zimpher. 1987. The role of higher education in the initial year of teaching programs. In *The first year of teaching: Background papers and a proposal*, ed. Gary A. Griffin and Suzanne Millies, 35-64. Chicago: University of Illinois-Chicago.

Examines appropriate roles for those in institutions of higher education (IHE) in terms of enabling beginning teachers in their initial years of teaching. Howey and Zimpher begin by emphasizing that major changes in funding arrangements and cooperative working relationships are necessary. Their comprehensive paper is based on the assumptions that (a) new teachers first learn much essential knowledge about teaching on-the-job rather than in preservice preparation programs, (b) induction support and opportunities for learning are necessities rather than niceties for many beginning teachers, (c) initial education of teachers is a joint responsibility of IHEs and K-12 schools, and extends well into the beginning years of teaching, and (d) intensive intervention to correct induction problems is long overdue. They discuss in detail eight specific activities in which IHEs should engage collaboratively with those in K-12 schools in order to contribute to improved assistance to beginning teachers.

Huling-Austin, Leslie. In Press. Teacher induction and internships. In *Handbook of research on teacher education*, ed. W. Robert Houston. New York: Macmillan Publishing & the Association of Teacher Educators.

Defines and establishes teacher induction in relation to career-long teacher education. In her comprehensive examination of current developments in the field of teacher induction and internships, Huling-Austin reviews state and national induction policy; describes and discusses various sponsors/sources of induction programs; discusses various common components of induction programs and internships, and explores potential conceptual paradigms useful for structuring teacher induction programs. Her consideration of research on teacher induction includes studies of needs and concerns of beginning teachers; research on induction programs, practices and internships; and closely examines research on the influence of context on beginning teachers. Huling-Austin summarizes areas of consensus about teacher induction and then reviews unresolved issues. This well-organized chapter concludes with discussion of needed next steps in the areas of policy, practice, and research. This chapter is timely and will be of assistance to those developing induction programs and conducting research in this important area.

Huling-Austin, Leslie. 1987. Teacher induction. In *Teacher induction: A new beginning,* ed., Douglas M. Brooks, 3-24. Reston, Va.: Association of Teacher Educators.

Summarizes progress on teacher induction that has been made in the United States during the past decade and provides a knowledge-based context for understanding teacher induction programs and activities. She considers several critical professional issues that must be addressed if teacher induction programs are to be successful in accomplishing their goals and concludes with a discussion of needed next steps and recommendations for future directions in teacher induction research and practice.

Huling-Austin, Leslie, ed. 1986. *Induction directory.* Washington, D.C.: Association of Teacher Educators.

Contains brief descriptions of over one hundred teacher induction programs on-going in schools systems and higher education institutions across the United States. Initially a project of the Model Teacher Induction Program (MTIP) established by the Research and Development Center for Teacher Education at the University of Texas at Austin, the Association of Teacher Educators National Commission on the Induction Process has updated the Induction Directory based on information obtained from school systems, professional organizations, and institutions of higher education. Each directory entry contains a contact name, address and a brief description of the program.

Ishler, Peggy, and Ralph Kester. 1987. Professional organizations and teacher induction: Initiatives and positions. In *Teacher induction: A new beginning,* ed. Douglas M. Brooks, 61-68. Reston, Va.: Association of Teacher Educators.

Discusses teacher induction initiatives and positions of professional organizations. Within a meaningful historical context, Ishler and Kester summarize professional organizations recommendations on nine critical issues in teacher induction. A useful overview of the professional perspective on beginning teacher induction.

Johnston, John M. 1985. Teacher induction: Problems, roles and guidelines. In *Career-long teacher education,* ed. Peter J. Burke and Robert G. Heideman, 194-222. Springfield, Ill.: Charles Thomas.

Proposes goals to be accomplished by a comprehensive induction program and then reviews problems of beginning teachers as a context for planning induction programs. Johnston's review of the professional needs and problems of beginning teachers includes topics of: (a) pupil instruction and classroom management; (b) relations with other teachers, administrators, parents and community; (c) reality/culture shock; and, (d) isolation, anxiety and self-doubt. He also considers the personal needs and problems of beginning teachers. He discusses problems related to clarity of purpose for induction programs, problems of tradition, and problems of financing. Johnston presents guidelines for designing teacher induction programs, and discusses the need for cooperation among the three groups sharing major responsibility for teacher induction. Roles and contributions from the local school level, university and teacher education programs, and state or intermediate state agencies are presented and discussed. This essay concludes with a call for individualized and personalized teacher induction programs.

Johnston, John M. 1979. Conceptions of the first year of teaching: An analysis of periodical professional literature. Dissertation Abstracts International 39, 4882A.

Johnston, John M., and Richard Kay. 1987. The role of institutions of higher education in professional teacher induction. In *Teacher induction: A new beginning,* ed. Douglas M. Brooks, 45-60. Reston, Va.: Association of Teacher Educators.

> Reports survey results from 300 responding teacher education institutions who were members of the American Association of Colleges of Teacher Education. Johnston and Kay consider roles to be played by institutions of higher education (IHE) in the professional induction of beginning teachers. Five goals of teacher induction programs are presented as a context for IHE participation in teacher induction. Selected factors affecting optimal IHE involvement are discussed. The survey results are reported and discussed and suggestions for IHE involvement in beginning teacher induction are presented.

Jordell, Karl. 1987. Structural and personal influences in the socialization of beginning teachers. *Teaching and Teacher Education* 3 No. 3: 165-177.

> Discusses the relative importance of different forms of influence on the beginning teacher and teachers at large. The personal and structural influences of the classroom, the institution, the society and the teacher's own recollections of experiences as pupils in schools and students in teacher education are explored. Jordell's useful conceptual analysis suggests that the structural influences at the classroom level are of primary importance, while experiences as a pupil and as a teacher education student probably have more limited impact.

Kester, Ralph, and Mary Marockie. 1987. Local induction programs. In *Teacher induction: A new beginning,* ed. Douglas M. Brooks, 25-32. Reston, Va.: Association of Teacher Educators.

> Kester and Marockie report the results of the Association of Teacher Educators National Commission on the Induction Process survey of beginning teacher programs in 1,100

local school systems in seventeen states. Information is provided regarding teacher induction strategies employed, amount of time spent for induction, the intent or purpose of induction programs, evaluation of induction programs, issues of compensation for time spent in induction, voluntary or mandatory participation in induction activities, and concludes with a report of what factors facilitate successful induction programs.

Lasley, Thomas, ed. 1986. Teacher induction programs and research. *Journal of Teacher Education* 37 No. 1 (January-February)

Contains a powerful and useful thematic collection of articles on programs and research in teacher induction. Leslie Huling-Autsin presents four goals for teacher induction programs, as well as reasonable and unreasonable expectations for such programs. This article represents an excellent starting point for those who are designing induction programs for beginning teachers. Cleta Galvez-Hjornevik presents a review of some of the most important, recent research on mentoring among teachers. She identifies the salient characteristics of successful mentor-protege relationships. She also argues that knowledge of induction from other disciplines and fields be incorporated into planning teacher induction programs. Sandra Fox and Ted Singletary propose a set of goals for teacher induction programs and discuss components for induction programs. James Hoffman and his colleagues from the University of Texas Research and Development Center for Teacher Education report findings from a large scale investigation of two state mandated beginning teacher programs. The research was designed to document how beginning teacher programs affect the transition from student of teaching to regular classroom teacher. Gail Huffman and Sarah Leak report their study of 108 new teachers' reactions to a mentoring support program. Of particular value are their research-based recommendations for design and conduct of beginning teacher mentor programs. Sandra Odell reports a study of the needs of both first year teachers and "new to the system" teachers participating in a teacher induction program. Of particular interest is her finding that experienced teachers who are new to a school system do not have remarkably different needs from those of first year teachers. Leonard Varah and his colleagues describe the University of

Wisconsin-Whitewater Teacher Induction Program, and present results of a program evaluation study. Dorothy Stewart presents a useful annotation of selected articles and documents indexed in the ERIC system. Of particular interest, Stewart notes that "teacher orientation" is the ERIC descriptor used for the concept of teacher induction, a term so new that it is not yet included in the current ERIC Thesaurus. She further notes that "beginning teacher induction" is being developed as a descriptor, and is currently in use as an identifier. The collection of teacher induction articles in this issue of JTE concludes with reaction to the articles from Marilyn Rauth, Executive Director of the Educational Issues Department, American Federation of Teachers; and G. Robert Bowers, Assistant Superintendent of Public Instruction, State of Ohio.

Lortie, D.C. 1965. Teacher socialization: The Robinson Crusoe Model. In *The real world of the beginning teachers: Report of the nineteenth national TEPS Conference*. New York: National Commission on Teacher Education and Professional Standards, National Education Association.

McDonald, Frederick J., and Pat Elias. 1982. *The transition into teaching: The problems of beginning teachers and programs to solve them. Summary report.* Berkeley, Calif.: Educational Testing Service.

Reports a study "undertaken to determine with greater precision what is known about the problems of beginning teachers, and to describe as accurately and completely as possible the means which have been used to anticipate, prevent, resolve or ameliorate these problems" (3). McDonald and Elias go on to present a diversified survey of two kinds of programs: (1) internship programs, and (2) induction programs (". . .programs in which the beginning teacher participates when they are first employed full time with full teaching responsibility assigned to them" [3]). As McDonald and Elias offer an analysis of characteristics of existing programs, they chronicle the problems of beginning teachers, discuss existing internship and induction programs, and conclude with recommended studies of the beginning teacher. In the introduction, however, they point out that after completing the study "We are left with a conundrum. We do not know whether to improve the quality of teacher preparation or whether some special form of assistance is required during the transition into teaching, or whether radically new forms of teacher preparation should be tried" (1982, 2).

Odell, Sandra. 1987. Teacher induction: Rationale and issues. In *Teacher induction: A new beginning*, ed. Douglas M. Brooks, 69-80. Reston, Va.: Association of Teacher Educators.

   Considers rationale and issues for teacher induction. She explores beginning teacher concerns, stages of teacher development, administrative structural consideration, personnel considerations, and concludes with an excellent discussion of pedagogical considerations and issues.

Peterson, Ken. In Press. Assistance and assessment of beginning teachers. In *Handbook for the evaluation of elementary and secondary school teachers*, ed. Jason Millman and Linda Darling-Hammond. Beverly Hills, Calif.: Sage Publishing.

   Explores the characteristics and the needs of beginning teachers, then discusses teacher induction assistance systems and presents components of comprehensive induction programs. Peterson includes consideration of evaluation for tenure and beyond. Throughout this chapter he is careful to consider issues related to formative and summative evaluation of beginning teachers, as well as the relationship between beginning teaching and career-long development. He argues that beginning teachers are in an unusual position with respect to evaluation: they expect it; they have not been socialized against it; they have not had bad experiences with it; and they need the feedback it provides. Peterson believes that educational systems should provide enhanced evaluation opportunities and procedures for beginning teachers.

Rosenholtz, Susan J. 1987. Workplace conditions of teacher quality and commitment: Implications for the design of teacher induction programs. *In The first year of teaching: Background papers and a proposal*, ed. Gary A. Griffin and Suzanne Millies, 15-34. Chicago: University of Illinois-Chicago.

Explores the alarming trend for teachers with the potential for making the greatest academic contributions to schools to be the most likely to leave teaching early in their careers. In this important paper Rosenholtz considers several school conditions required for teachers' productive commitment to schools. She also explores the discouraging picture of the consequences where these workplace conditions fail to be met. In considerable detail she outlines how schools can be structured to enhance teachers' learning opportunities and their sense of teaching efficacy, with particular emphasis on beginning teachers. Finally, she details ten specific policy implications for the design of teacher induction programs.

Rossetto, Celeste R., and Judith K. Grosenick. 1987. Effects of collaborative teacher education: Follow-up of graduates of a teacher induction program. *Journal of Teacher Education* 38 (March-April): 50-52.

Investigates perceptions of graduates in a program which combines on-the-job training with induction activities. Program graduates from the past 13 years were surveyed regarding the training they received. Results indicate that most graduates remained in teaching, and rated program objectives as having been attained.

Ryan, Kevin. 1986. *The induction of new teachers.* (Fastback #237.) Bloomington, Ind.: Phi Delta Kappa Educational Foundation.

Details six of the most common problems that face first year teachers: the shock of the familiar, students, parents, administrators, fellow teachers, and instruction itself. In this well-written booklet, Ryan eloquently describes how assistance with these problems can come from beginning teachers themselves, school districts, and teacher training institutions.

Ryan, Kevin, Katherine K. Newman, Gerald Mager, Jane Applegate, Thomas Lasley, V. Randall Flora, and John M. Johnston. 1980. *Biting the apple: Accounts of first year teachers.* New York: Longman.

Provides a detailed exploration of the mismatch between beginning teacher expectations and on-the-job realities based on an intensive ethnographic study of eighteen first year teachers. Most of the book consists of accounts of the first year teaching experiences of twelve of the study's eighteen participants. Using an inside voices/outside eyes perspective, these accounts combine the experiences of the first year teachers with the perspective of the researchers who intensively studied them during their first year. Based on hundreds of hours of interviews, observations, informal conversation, questionnaires, and contacts with other inhabitants of the first year teachers' world, the researchers' field notes have been woven into accounts which document the successes and failures of first year teachers in a variety of settings. The twelve accounts in *Biting the apple* are fertile sources of information about beginning teachers' lives both inside and outside the classroom, and as such provide a valuable perspective for those seeking to understand the needs of new teachers in the induction phase of teacher career development.

Schlecty, Phillip. 1985. A framework for evaluating induction into teaching. *Journal of Teacher Education* 36 No. 1 (September): 37-41.

Identifies the indicators and characteristics of effective induction systems. In this very useful article, Schlecty writes "an effective induction system is a system that creates conditions in which new members to the occupation so internalize the norms peculiar to the group that they conform to these norms even when informal authority is not overtly present to uphold the norms" (37). Schlecty discusses norms in relation to the induction of professionals, and then identifies three indicators of effective induction systems: (a) the way in which the norms are distributed throughout the group; (b) the patterns of conformity that develop around the norms; and (c) the patterns of deviation from the norms. The bulk of the article is devoted to discussion of eight characteristics of effective induction systems. He then describes efforts within the Charlotte-Mecklenberg Schools' Career Development Program to incorporate these characteristics. Schlechty concludes with an analysis of the fundamental changes needed in the way teacher education is conceptualized by school personnel.

Smith, David C., and Garfield W. Wilson. 1986. The Florida beginning teacher program. In *The dynamics of change in teacher education. Volume I: Background papers for the National Commission for Excellence in Teacher Education,* ed. Thomas J. Lasley, 127-141. Washington, D.C.: American Association of Colleges for Teacher Education.

  Describes how a comprehensive and integrated system of support, training, and evaluation is designed to accomplish two central purposes: the improvement of beginning teachers and the documentation of their successful performance. The legislative background, development of the model, and implementation of the program is described. The outcomes yielded by the Florida Beginning Teacher Program are described.

Veenman, S. 1984. Perceived problems of beginning teachers. *Review of Educational Research* 54(2): 143-178.

  Reviews and analyzes research on the perceived problems of beginning teachers in the most recent and most comprehensive treatment of this much publicized topic. Veenman's abstract of this paper is presented below. Perceived problems of beginning teachers in their first year of teaching are reviewed. Studies from different countries are included. Issues such as the reality shock and changes in behaviors and attitudes are considered also. The eight problems perceived most often are classroom discipline, motivating students, dealing with individual differences, assessing students' work, relationships with parents, organization of class work, insufficient and/or inadequate teaching materials and supplies, and dealing with problems of individual students. There is a great correspondence between the problems of elementary and secondary beginning teachers. Issues such a person-specific and situation-specific differences, views of the principals, problems of experienced teachers, and job satisfactions of beginning teachers are discussed also. Three frameworks of teacher development are presented which provide conceptualizations of individual differences among beginning teachers. Finally, forms of planned support for beginning teachers are noted. Research using an interactionist model for the explanation of behavior is needed (143).

Ward, Beatrice. 1987. State and district structures to support initial year of teaching programs. In *The first year of teaching: Background papers and a proposal,* ed. Gary A. Griffin and Suzanne Millies, 1-14. Chicago: University of Illinois-Chicago.

Explores state and district structures to support initial year of teacher programs. Ward considers several structures which have promise for supporting development and installation of initial year of teaching programs. Her perspective is shaped by research on effective teaching, effective teacher training, school-based staff development, and knowledge production and utilization in education. She recommends specific action in three areas (a) provision of training and services for novice teachers, (b) inter-institutional arrangements which foster collaborative design and implementation of training and support services, and (c) standards to guide design and implementation of initial year of teaching programs. Six structures are proposed and discussed that support action in these three areas: (a) mentor teachers, (b) teacher development schools, (c) school district-university collaboratives, (d) a center for quality teaching, (e) initial years of teaching program standards, and (f) teacher advancement standards.

Yinger, Robert, J. 1987. Learning the language of practice: Implications for beginning year of teaching programs. In *The first year of teaching: Background papers and a proposal*, ed. Gary A. Griffin and Suzanne Millies, 65-89. Chicago: University of Illinois-Chicago.

Argues persuasively that a major task confronting the beginning teacher is a learning to think and behave in ways appropriate to the demands of teaching, or what he refers to as "learning the language of practice" (65). Yinger further argues that beginning teachers cannot learn this language of practice until they actually engage in teaching. Yinger presents a comprehensive argument by examining two sets of questions: (a) How might the knowledge and skill of the experienced practitioner best be described? and (b) How do teachers learn to teach? Using a study of beginning teachers learning to teach in order to illustrate some of the issues involved in acquiring a language of practice, he proposes ideas for describing the language of practice of teachers.

Zaharias, Jane Ann, and Thomas W. Frew. 1987. Teacher induction: An analysis of one successful program. *Action in Teacher Education* 9 (Spring): 49-55.

Describes an induction program designed by one university to provide a non-threatening forum wherein beginning teachers could discuss common concerns and seek the advice and assistance of master teachers. Program goals are stated, program implementation details related to staffing, recruitment, location and scheduling are described. Program structure and content, and program outcomes are reported.

Zeichner, Kenneth. 1983. Individual and institutional factors related to the socialization of teachers. In *First years of teaching: What are the pertinent issues?*, ed. Gary Griffin and H. Hukill. (ERIC Document Reproduction Service No. 240 109.) Austin, Tex.: Research and Development Center for Teacher Education.

Argues that the induction process is more complex, contradictory and context specific than has been commonly thought. In this comprehensive essay, one of four papers published in the proceedings from a national working conference on teacher induction, Zeichner first considers who and what appear to influence the socialization of beginning teachers. Next he examines how beginning teachers impact the system. Third, he addresses the thorny issue of generalization in relation to studies of beginning teacher socialization. Finally, discusses the need for an administrative response to the presence of beginning teachers. Ken Zeichner is a teacher educator who has studied and published widely about the socialization of beginning teachers. This thoughtful essay is an excellent introduction to his scholarship, and includes a rich reference list on teacher socialization and induction.

Master Teachers: A Way to Restructure the Profession

Judith C. Christensen

Introduction

The Federal government's involvement in education has taken many forms over the past three decades. The launching of Sputnik I triggered a fervor for curricular reform especially in the areas of science, math, preservice teacher education and inservice education. Federally funded research and development centers as well as individuals created curricular programs and materials. Publishing companies scrambled to package programs that would help America's students catch up to the Russians. The claim that these materials were "teacher proof" indicates the trust placed in the profession in the 1960's and 1970's.

In the 1980's, the mood of the country shifted. Federal intervention subsided as states and local districts were encouraged to assume a greater leadership role in education. Businesses were encouraged to get involved. At the Federal level the Department of Education was in jeopardy. In 1983 the National Commission on Excellence in Education published its findings based on 18 months of study. The report painted a bleak picture of education in America from the quality of teaching to the motivation of children.

The Commission report did not specify ways to solve the problems in education. Instead, the education profession, states, businesses, parents, and citizens in general were given the task of finding solutions to the dilemmas outlined in the report. Secretary of Education Terrel Bell suggested making the teaching profession more attractive to the "best and brightest." He stated, "We desperately need to establish the teaching profession as a prestigious and esteemed calling where promising young people can readily realize an opportunity to move up through a series of recognitions and promotions to command the salary and esteem that more gifted and talented individuals would pursue" (Bell 1983, 3). He promoted the idea of a master teacher. "That new position should be a much esteemed and sought-after distinction among teachers. It should provide a step beyond the ranks of beginning teacher and regular teacher and it should command a salary that is commensurate with other salaries that recognize accomplishment of great worth to American society" (Bell 1983, 4).

Secretary Bell supported his stance with grants made available for pilot projects for teacher incentives including career ladder and master teacher plans. Prior to the publication of the Commission Report, *A nation at risk*, Governors Hunt in North Carolina and Alexander in Tennessee promoted plans to upgrade the quality of education. Within two years 38 states in the nation would have, or would be considering, some type of merit pay or career ladder plan. The latest review of the states with some type of incentive program (either state or local level) indicates that 40 of the 50 states report some type of teacher incentive program (Cornett 1987).

While reform was being stimulated at the national level, state politicians and business leaders were taking the major leadership roles. Educators responded with cautious interest. The National Education Association (NEA) and American Federation of Teachers (AFT) both extended support for plans which would retain and reward excellent teachers. In the process, the questions that would be most difficult to answer were what type of program would provide the rewards for excellence and how would excellence be determined?

Toward a Common Definition

Merit pay, mentor teacher, master teacher, career ladder, and differentiated staffing are all terms used in discussions of incentive plans. They are likely to draw heated discussions from proponents and opponents alike. This debate can be helpful as the ensuing dialogue may enable planners to take the best from each model and custom-design a program to meet specific needs. On the other hand, educators can be "turned off" to new ideas because of connotations which terms carry. Good ideas may be disregarded because of "bad press." To help clarify the concepts discussed in this chapter, the following definitions will be used.

- Incentive plans. Any plan which rewards teachers for excellent performance or for providing extra service.

- <u>Merit pay</u>. A plan which recognizes outstanding levels of performance. It is additional pay for <u>better</u> work.

- <u>Mentor teacher</u>. A plan in which qualified teachers work with beginning or experienced teachers in a staff development role. It could be part of a career ladder model.

- <u>Career ladder plan</u>. Any plan which uses differentiated staffing and performance as incentives.

- <u>Differentiated staffing</u>. A plan which incorporates a variety of levels and roles for teachers and involves a pay differential.

- <u>Master Teacher plans</u>.

  a) A plan which recognizes teachers for exceptional performance.

  b) Part of a differentiated staffing plan which recognizes teachers for exceptional performance and extra duties. This definition will be used in this chapter.

A further exploration of the master teacher concept will help determine its value in the restructuring of professional roles within education.

The idea of a master teacher is certainly not new. Rather, as with many "new ideas," its time has come again. People who were in the profession in the 1960's will recognize the idea as part of the differentiated staffing plans of that decade. The Temple City, California, model was one of the most publicized plans and is the blueprint for many current career ladder initiatives, specifically, the Tennessee Career Ladder Plan (Furtwengler 1985). The Temple City model provided four career levels: the associate teacher, the staff teacher, the senior teacher and the master teacher. Each stage had specific levels of expertise, role differentiation and compensation differences. In this plan the master teacher could earn more money than the district superintendent (Freiberg 1984/1985). Fenwick English, who was personally involved with the Temple City Model, feels that too much may have been expected from its implementation. He states,

"Differentiated staffing was not as successful as its leaders imagined because it failed to produce the dramatic and revolutionary changes within the teaching ranks that were promised. People expected large change. Instead they got subtle role shifts or no discernible alterations at all" (English 1984/1985, 23).

The role definition for master teachers (as well as other levels of a career ladder) has been subjected to many debates. Allen (1987) conducted a study of effective teaching literature, career ladder program descriptions, and master teacher literature and developed a description of behaviors for master teachers. The behaviors indicate that the master teacher:

1. displays evidence of superior preparation for classroom instruction

2. displays exceptional teaching strategies to meet individual needs

3. motivates students to achieve beyond previous performance levels

4. is extremely skillful in using a variety of verbal and nonverbal communications

5. provides specific evaluative feedback with reinforcement and encouragement

6. demonstrates superior knowledge of the curriculum and subject matter

7. selects learning content congruent with the prescribed curriculum which goes beyond the requirement of instructional objectives

8. provides maximum instructional opportunities for individual learning styles by designing learning activities that meet the mastery levels of students

9. is extremely skillful in maintaining students on the learning task

10. sets high expectations for students and is able to demonstrate a history of high student achievement as a result

11. assesses and adjusts the setting to provide a variety of learning styles

12. plans and implements strategies to encourage student self-discipline

13. promotes a good working relationship with others by providing active leadership

14. is self-motivated and assumes employee responsibilities willingly

15. provides leadership in curriculum and instruction development

16. provides leadership in the development and improvement of school and district regulations and policies

17. is self-motivated and assumes extra responsibilities willingly

18. initiates professional growth activities and encourages other staff members to participate. (Allen 1987, 44-46)

This comprehensive list of behaviors for master teachers leaves one feeling reinforced and inadequate at the same time. Reinforced, because many of us have worked very hard to live up to these behaviors and inadequate because the standards are so high. The standards, however, must be high if the rewards are to be meaningful. If everyone can achieve the status of a master teacher, the expectations are not high enough.

There are many excellent teachers who would fit the behaviors outlined above, but the questions of who decides and how, are ever present. Evaluation plans are being developed and refined in almost every district in the country. However, until effective evaluation procedures have been developed, it would be easier to assess progress toward a master teacher level by viewing the role from a "more than" perspective rather than a "better than" perspective as described by Griffin (1985).

The master teacher concept has been praised, damned, ignored, and implemented. Research indicates increases in job satisfaction and positive school climates occur where career ladder/master teacher plans are in place. Shared leadership, new reward systems, and increased teacher involvement are all benefits in the Utah plan (Cornett 1987).

Perceptions about the master teacher concept will vary greatly depending on whom you ask. The potential for restructuring the profession is great, but education is a complex enterprise and no change takes place without influencing many people.

The next section will examine the view of the major players in this enterprise of change: teachers, administrators, and teacher educators. What do they think of master teachers? What other forces or agencies might be affected by master teachers?

Perspectives on Master Teachers

One is usually not tempted to give advice to one's dentist or doctor (or plumber or electrician), but most people will not hesitate to give specific suggestions on what teachers should be doing. Everyone has been through some level of schooling; therefore, "experts" on education include just about everyone.

Recently politicians have added their voices to the debate with opinions on restructuring the profession and/or improving the quality of education. The state and national government have a variety of bureaucratic structures intended to help the profession. But educational decision making should belong to the students, teachers, administrators, and teacher educators–those people directly influenced by and influencing schools. Too often, these principal actors in education decision making become secondary.

This section will explore the impact of the master teacher concept on teachers, administrators, and teacher educators. The goal of any such plan is to improve the quality of education for students by upgrading the competency of the professionals involved.

Teachers

The master teacher concept has been promoted as a way to recognize and reward excellence in teaching, thus making the profession more attractive to "the best and the brightest." It is also a way to provide leadership roles for teachers without forcing them to leave the classroom. The need for career patterns which could include master teachers is evident in the literature on differentiated staffing (Freiberg 1984/1985; English

1984/1985; Christensen 1987). Lortie (1975) states, "Compared with most other kinds of middle-class work, teaching is relatively 'career-less.' There is less opportunity for the movement upward which is the essence of career" (84).

Teachers need alternative roles within the profession to stimulate professional growth, new challenges and new responsibilities. Professions with little change or opportunity for advancement and/or recognition can produce frustration or stagnation which, in turn, lowers morale and productivity. In teaching, as with any career, people could pass through a number of stages. The work of Fessler (1985) outlines a number of career stages a teacher could experience.

Figure 1. A model of the stages of the Teacher Career Cycle and the environmental factors that affect it.

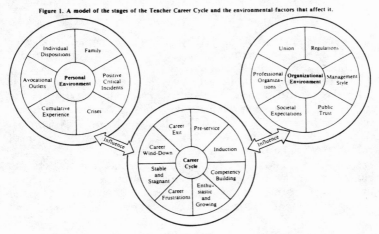

This model incorporates the complex nature of a career cycle by including the influences of the personal and organizational environments. The use of a career-ladder, master-teacher model provides for teachers' needs at a number of stages in their careers.

Inherent problems with most master teacher plans include availability of only upward movement, and a quota on how many positions are available. More lateral movement would increase the number of leadership positions available and allow teachers to move in and out of leadership roles as their personal needs or the organizational needs change. An image of a career lattice would accommodate the vertical and horizontal movement needed at various times in a teacher's career.

A study conducted in Wisconsin (Collegial Research Consortium, March 1985) asked teachers, principals, and

- helping teacher training institutions design preparation programs

- organizing staff development programs.

Teachers expressed disagreement with some duties which could be assumed by master teachers. These included:

- evaluating teachers for the purpose of retention

- evaluating teachers as a member of an assessment team for the purpose of granting performance awards.

Teachers also disagreed with the statement that master teachers should remain in the classroom full time without additional duties or responsibilities.

These responses indicate teachers' willingness to try out roles that would provide alternative responsibilities as long as they were not asked to evaluate their peers. This is a common response in a number of studies (Collegial Research Consortium 1986/1987; Harris 1986) and reflects the sense of collegiality in the profession (Rosenholtz 1984).

When asked about the competencies, skills and personal characteristics which master teachers should exhibit, teachers in the Wisconsin study had high expectations and expressed strong agreement that master teachers should exhibit:

- superior subject matter knowledge

- exemplary teaching and management skills

- good interpersonal skills

- comprehensive curriculum planning and implementation skills

- competence in producing demonstrable student learning

- active participation in personal growth and development activities

- leadership in and out of the classroom.

This list of competencies and qualities teachers would expect of a master teacher does not point toward a teacher who is a technocrat or who has a simple formula for teaching. The tendency to use the research on teaching results to determine who is a master teacher is not appropriate. Much of the accountability-in-teaching movement runs counter to the expectations we should have for master teachers. Zumwalt (1985, 51) sums up this dilemma when she says, "In an era when direct instruction, time on task, and teacher and school effectiveness defined by achievement scores are popular, teachers find themselves thrust more and more into a techno-logical rather than a deliberative orientation to teaching. . . ."

Administrators

If master teachers take on leadership roles, what will be the role of the principal, assistant principal, curriculum specialist, and others? This is a question heard many times in any district which contemplates a move to restructuring the profession. It is not a question asked in idle conversation but a question with far-reaching implications for many people. There is no doubt that roles will change if master teacher plans are implemented. Money will be spent in different ways. Authority will have to be shared along with responsibility.

What types of responsibilities do administrators see as appropriate for master teachers? In the study of Wisconsin teachers, principals and superintendents (Collegial Research Consortium 1985), administrators strongly agreed with all the duties favored by teachers listed earlier. In addition, they tend to more strongly agree on the following:

- conducting staff development workshops

- working on an extended contract

- advising teachers concerning instructional problems.

Principals and superintendents agreed more favorably than teachers on the following duties:

- evaluating teachers for the purpose of professional development

- evaluating teachers as a member of an assessment team for the purpose of granting performance awards

- advising teachers concerning instructional problems

- being involved in the budgeting process for program development.

These results seem to show an accepting attitude by administrators for teachers to become involved in a variety of roles often seen as their sole responsibility. It is frequently pointed out that administrators cannot possibly perform all the duties expected of them. Sergiovanni (1985) stresses the need for a better mix of roles among teachers, principals, supervisors, coordinators, etc. He discusses the idea of leadership density which. . . . "refers to the total amount of leadership which exists in the school. . . . The more dense leadership is, the more effective is an organization likely to be" (Sergiovanni 1985, 8). Administrators in this study seem to agree with Sergiovanni's proposition.

Teachers cannot and should not move into new roles without additional preparation. For example, if they are to take on a role as a curriculum developer, they need to develop special skills in curriculum theory, instructional strategies, evaluation techniques and leadership skills to work with other teachers. What then is the role of teacher education in the restructuring of the profession?

Teacher Education

If teachers need new skills to assume new roles, part of the responsibility for preparation rests with the schools of education in our colleges and universities. The preservice programs must change to stress the need for a variety of expertise within the teaching profession. They must, according to Zumwalt (1985) ". . . instill within preservice students the self-analytic and reflective skills necessary for continued professional growth" (8).

The Carnegie (1986) and Holmes Group (1986) reports call for graduate level teacher education programs after completion of a degree in liberal studies. They stress the need for a rigorous program in pedagogical studies with collaboration and cooperation with the personnel in pre-kindergarten through secondary schools. Both reports call for some type of differentiated staffing patterns to provide career steps for teachers.

Inservice teacher education is another important component in restructuring the profession. The local districts and teacher education graduate schools are the two primary providers of inservice programs. Packaged programs with "the answer" for excellence in teaching and learning are not what is needed by reflective intelligent teachers. They need well designed programs that will provide opportunities to combine theory with practice. They need to experiment with new ideas in their classrooms and discuss results with their colleagues. They need to ask questions on their own and learn how to find answers. They must practice leadership skills and practice developing, implementing, and evaluating new curriculum. Programs with these emphases will produce the type of person who can assume the leadership roles expected of a master teacher.

The Government

Restructuring the profession to incorporate the master teacher concept will cost more money. If monetary incentives are used, the programs will cost more than some type of differentiated staffing plan which will distribute existing funds in a variety of ways.

A review of the current status of career ladder/incentive projects in the United States indicates that eight states have local programs only, eight states have pilots with state funding or assistance, fourteen states have state-funded programs and six have programs under development. (SREB 1987, 9) An example of costs can be seen in the California Mentor Teacher Program where,"State law authorizes districts to designate up to 5% of their certified teachers as mentors. Each mentor receives a $4,000 stipend and the local district receives an additional $2,000 per mentor for support costs, such as training and released time" (SREB 1987, 10). In 1984-85, $30.8 million supported 4,362 mentors in 742 districts which represented 2.84 percent of the teachers in the state. In 1987-88 $49.75 million is available to support 8,273 teachers or approximately 4 percent of the teachers in the state (SREB 1987,11).

Unfortunately the trend is not toward continued funding for incentive programs. States and local districts are withdrawing support and teachers are feeling let down. Terrel Bell (1988) recommends that career ladders should be standard in all states and that, "Those states that already have mandated career ladders must keep their commitments with regard to incremental increases in salary; those states that have not yet done so should enact the necessary legislation to get such programs underway" (406). Bell suggests that the additional funding for such projects should come from state and national budgets. He states that, "Funding American education adequately and guaranteeing taxpayers that the educational system will be more effective in the future than it has been in the past are both problems and obligations for the next President, the nation's governors and Congressional and legislative leaders" (Bell 1988, 407).

Future Directions for Master Teachers

The professionalization of the teaching force is at a crossroads. Changes in the composition of the teaching force, the student body, family structure, societal expectations, the bureaucratic structure of the schools, and government involvement have had an impact. It is time for a change and teachers have a chance to be involved in setting the goals and direction. The role of teacher as leader seems appropriate. Leadership at the local school level is seen as important and effective in increasing teacher accountability, staff morale, and a better learning environment for students. The benefits of teacher empowerment are recognized and promoted. Financial support is more tangential. In this context it is time to move ahead toward continued restructuring of the profession.

Change will not be easy. Tradition is strong within the educational establishment and the bureaucracy is firmly in place. Some teachers do not want change and if put to a vote–which teacher unions often do–change might not win a majority. That does not mean it should not take place, however. The process should move slowly but deliberately to provide alternative roles for teachers in the school setting.

Change in the structure of the teaching profession will be important to a wide variety of people and their alternative roles as discussed earlier in this chapter. In order to help create the changes needed, it is important that:

1. teachers are involved in the development of new roles and leadership decisions;

2. teachers are willing to accept new responsibility and to take risks in exercising authority when it is offered to them;

3. teacher unions work collaboratively with their membership and school officials to "try out" new roles for teachers;

4. funding is provided to train teachers for new leadership roles;

5. time is provided for teachers to take on new tasks and responsibilities;

6. teachers see their peers as having expertise which will be useful to them. They must be willing to accept their colleagues in roles other than classroom teachers;

7. teachers have a variety of roles to choose from and have an option of assuming a leadership role. They should be able to move into and out of roles as their personal needs change or as organizational needs change;

8. roles and incentives are viewed in a horizontal as well as hierarchical organizational structure to provide incentives for teachers at a number of stages within their careers;

9. teacher organizations accept a variety of pay options for teachers and flexibility in the use of their time;

10. principals reorganize their job expectations to include teachers in decision making and leadership roles within the school;

11. central office staff examine some of their tasks and share leadership with teachers at the local school level and at the district level;

12. superintendents support principals by modeling shared decision making and by placing less emphasis on centralized decision making;

13. state governments continue to seek alternative funding structures for education and support pilot projects to find new ways to structure the profession. This funding must not be for one or two years but for a longer term (at least five years) to give an innovation a chance to work;

14. higher education institutions change their preparation programs for new teachers to include prepara-

tion for a variety of roles within teaching. The graduate programs must reflect the need for teachers as leaders rather than programs that will lead teachers out of the classroom; and

15. everyone involved in the change process understands the stress and role ambiguities caused by role shifts.

Change is not comfortable for all people and new roles will not be appealing to everyone. The day of turning out teachers at age 21 to assume a role that will be the same for 40 years is coming to an end. The profession must provide variety within its structure to offer its members alternatives for recognition and leadership without leaving the classroom. It does not matter what labels are applied to positions within the profession. Master teachers, lead teachers, teacher specialists, career teachers are equally useful if they represent a change in the way the role of teacher is viewed and rewarded by the profession and the public at large. Educational leaders at every level, especially teacher leaders, must be involved in the reform movement. Master teachers can lead the way to teacher empowerment. They must accept the challenge of change and lead the way for change in a new definition of the role of teacher.

References

Allen, Tom. 1987. Identifying behaviors of the master teacher. *ERS Spectrum* 5 (Spring): 42-46.

Reports on a research project on excellence in teaching. The profile created by the analysis provides a comprehensive list of behaviors expected from master teachers.

Bell, Terrel H. 1988. Parting words of the 13th man. *Phi Delta Kappan* (February): 400.

The former Secretary of the Department of Education discusses the events since the *Nation at risk* report marked the beginning of current educational reform. Twelve recommendations are given to upgrade and transform the teaching profession in America.

Bell, Terrel H. 1983. Building a better teaching profession. *American Education* (March): 2.

Burke, Peter J., Judith C. Christensen, and Ralph Fessler. 1984. Teacher Career Stages: Implications for Staff Development. *Phi Delta Kappan.*

Can the schools be saved? 1983. *Newsweek*, 3 (May): 50.

Carnegie Forum on Education and the Economy. 1986. *A nation prepared: Teachers for the 21st century.* Hyattsville, Md.: Carnegie Forum on Education and the Economy.

Christensen, Judith C. 1987. Roles of teachers and administrators. In *Establishing career ladders in teaching,* ed. Paul R. Burden, 88-110. Springfield, Ill.: Charles C. Thomas.

This book provides a comprehensive look at many aspects of career ladders including chapters on evaluation, costs, perspectives of teacher organizations, and the process of change. The chapter cited here presents an overview of differentiated staffing plans from the past and role change necessary in teaching and administration if differentiated staffing patterns are to be used in career ladder plans.

Collegial Research Consortium. 1986. *Incentives and teacher career stages: Influences and policy implications.* Carol A. Bartell, ed. Proceedings of a seminar on "Incentives that Enhance the Teaching Profession: A Discussion of the Policy Issues." Elmhurst, Ill.: North Central Regional Educational Laboratory.

   A report of the proceedings of an invitational seminar on incentives. This chapter contains a report of a research project in which a national sample of teachers were asked to identify their career stage as well as appropriate and available incentives. Results of the study reveal the need to provide a wide range of incentives to meet needs of teachers at different stages of their careers.

Collegial Research Consortium. 1985. Master teachers: Do educators agree? Paper presented as the annual meeting of the American Association of Colleges for Teacher Education. Denver, Colorado, March.

Cornett, Lynn. 1987. More pay for teachers and administrators who do more: Incentive pay programs. *Southern Regional Board Career Ladder Clearinghouse*, December.

English, Fenwick W. 1984/1985. We need the ghostbusters! A response to Jerome Freiberg. *Educational Leadership* 22 (December/January).

Fessler, Ralph. 1985. A model for teacher professional growth and development. In *Career-long teacher education*, ed. Peter J. Burke and Robert G. Heideman, 181-193. Springfield, Ill.: Charles C. Thomas.

   This chapter presents a model for looking at a teacher's career not in a linear fashion but rather as ever-changing cycles which are influenced by one's personal and organizational environment.

Freiberg, H. Jerome. 1984/1985. Master teacher programs: Lessons from the past. *Educational Leadership* 16 (December/January).

Furtwengler, Carol. 1985. Tennessee's career ladder plan: They said it couldn't be done. *Educational Leadership* 43 (November): 50-56.

Griffin, Gary A. 1985. The School as a workplace and the master teacher concept. *The Elementary School Journal* 86: 1-16.

Part of a theme issue on master teachers, this article presents a view of the pressures from the profession and the institution on teachers and how these pressures inhibit change. Griffin proposes four recommendations to implement a master teacher program.

Harris, Louis. 1986. *Metropolitan Life survey of the American teacher, 1986: Restructuring the teaching profession.* New York: Metropolitan Life and Affiliated Companies.

Holmes Group. 1986. *Tomorrow's teachers.* East Lansing, Michigan: Holmes Group, Inc.

Klein, M. Frances. 1985. The master teacher as curriculum leader. *The Elementary School Journal* 86: 35-43.

The master teacher who understands schools, children and curriculum is an ideal person to be a curriculum leader according to Klein. The importance of local school leadership in curriculum improvement is stressed in this article.

Kohut, Sylvester, and Jill D. Wright. 1984. Merit pay movement 1980's style. *Educational Horizons* 62: 52-54.

Lortie, Dan C. 1975. *Schoolteacher: A sociological study.* Chicago: University of Chicago Press.

Report of a comprehensive survey of 1,602 teachers and 702 leaders including principals, superintendents, state legislators, state education officials, deans of colleges of education, and teachers union officers. The survey analyzes their views about the structure of the teaching profession and ways to restructure that profession in the future.

Moore, Richard W. 1984. *Master teachers.* Bloomington, Indiana: Phi Delta Kappan Educational Foundation.

An overview of some of the issues involved with career ladders/master teachers. Includes sections on identification, characteristics, selection, rewards, and funding.

Rosenholtz, Susan J. 1984. *Myths: Political myths about reforming teaching*. Denver: Education Commission of the States No. TQ84-4.

 Presents ten myths often heard as truths in the reform movement and gives reasons why the statements are misleading. Concise, clear reasoning in small, attractive publication. Excellent for use with general public and teacher groups.

Sergiovanni, Thomas J. 1985. Teacher career ladders: Myths and realities in implementation. *Teacher Education and Practice* 2 (Spring): 5-13.

Southern Regional Education Board. 1987. *Career Ladder Clearinghouse* (December).

 This newsletter is published several times a year and includes current information on career ladder programs state by state. For additional information, contact Lynn Cornett, SREB, 592 Tenth St. N.W., Atlanta, GA 30318-5790, Phone: 404/875-9211.

The teacher career cycle: Model development and research report. 1987. Paper presented at the annual meeting of the American Educational Research Association, April.

Zumwalt, Karen K. 1985. The Master teacher concept: Implications for teacher education. *The Elementary School Journal* 86: 45-53.

 An excellent article for higher education faculty involved in teacher education. Zumwalt stresses the need to change both preservice and graduate programs by stressing alternative roles within teaching rather than forcing teachers to leave the schools and classrooms to assume leadership roles.

The author wishes to thank the following members of the Collegial Research Consortium, Ltd., for their parts in the research and writing projects cited in this chapter: Peter Burke,

Ralph Fessler, and Jay Price and to extend a special thank you to John H. McDonnell for editing assistance.

Change in Teacher Education: Focus on Field Experiences

Marvin A. Henry

The history of change in teacher education has been intertwined with field experiences. Persons and groups with reform agendas have invariably advocated more field participation for teaching candidates. In this chapter the author will argue that the new reforms with their emphasis on accountability, quantitative standards, increased subject-matter preparation, and a deemphasis on pedagogical training must still confront the fact that field experiences are inextricably involved in any successful program of teacher preparation. Field experiences will continue to be central to the success of changed standards and procedures for teacher preparation. This chapter will review the role of field experiences in reforms throughout the history of teacher education, share the reasons that field experiences have been successful, look at the changes that are occurring in teacher education, and conclude with desirable goals for teacher education and how these goals are involved with field experiences.

Field Experiences and Reform in Teacher Education

Field experiences have been in existence as long as teacher education has occurred. The history of teacher education suggests that the first field experience may have been a quasi-apprenticeship in France 300 years ago (Johnson 1968). The writings and teachings of Rosseau, Herbart, Pestalozzi, Froebel, and others in Europe suggested direct involvement as a part of teacher education. America may have seen the existence of a very early forerunner of student teaching in the 1600's when Franciscan friars apparently used supervised teaching experiences among the Indian pueblos of New Mexico (Williams 1942). In spite of this and a few activities from the

Europeans who came to America, early schools mostly saw teachers serving lengthy apprenticeships.

The practice teaching movement became established as the normal schools developed in the mid 1800's. Initially, practice teachers were assigned in pairs for a period of two weeks or so. Practice teaching continued to grow through the normal school and into the teachers college era. It continued to survive and expand with each reform movement (Johnson 1968).

The value of field experiences was emphasized by Dewey (1904) when he stated that some form of practice teaching in public school classrooms is essential. Indeed, many educators would say that field experiences are the most visible embodiment of Dewey's notion of experimental education.

As the discipline of teacher education began to take shape, a limited amount of student teaching was included. Teacher candidates who were completing their studies would go to the laboratory school between their university classes, teach a class or two and then return to campus to their academic studies.

A great boost to field experiences was given by the Flowers Report (1948). In the mid to late 40's, a committee of the American Association of Teachers Colleges (now AACTE) studied the question of what part professional laboratory experiences play in the education of teachers. After studying data, conducting conferences, and meeting with individuals across the country, members of the AATC and the Association for Student Teaching (now ATE), a series of recommendations was developed and reported by Flowers which still influence field experiences in teacher preparation. These far-reaching recommendations included:

1. A series of laboratory experiences extending over the period of college work and designed to help the student to participate in and study the major activities of today's teacher.

2. Laboratory experiences prior to student teaching which are integrated with other parts of the college program.

3. Full-time student teaching in settings other than laboratory schools.

4. Supervision by both college and public school supervisors.

5. An internship which would provide continuity between preservice and inservice education, gradual induction with part supervision by those who know the beginning teacher, and to afford the college opportunity to study its work and make needed curriculum modifications.

This monumental study, remarkable in its foresight, still serves as the Flexner Report (1910) of professional field experiences. The long-term result was full-time student teaching in school settings away from the campus and the beginning of more serious thinking about the initiation of systematic early field experiences. Full-time student teaching gained instant popularity and has been universally accepted. Exploratory field experiences are nearly as prevalent, and now internships are beginning to emerge as the necessary conclusion for an adequate program of teacher preparation.

The Conant Report (1963) analyzed the nature of teacher education, made a number of recommendations for change, and then concluded that full-time student teaching should remain and be expanded. Mr. Conant recommended a minimum period of eight weeks' practice [sic] teaching for the elementary teacher and nine semester hours of practice teaching for secondary school teacher candidates. The latter recommendation was to have practice teaching be the majority of effort which would be devoted to the study of teaching.

The social advocacy movement in the 60's ushered in further reforms in teacher education with field experiences being increased. Teaching internships became popular with the goals of improving the human condition through such agencies as the Teacher Corps and as a means of attracting teachers to the classroom when teachers were in short supply. The emphasis on relevance in education and in society created a fertile climate for downward extension of direct activity in the seventies and field experiences became part of a teacher preparation pattern early in a student's program of professional study.

In a few short years teacher education has moved from limited field activity to the threshold of a year-long supervised internship preceded by a number of field experiences at all levels of professional study. Each reform effort has reinforced the value of and expanded the focus on field experiences.

The New Reforms

We have now experienced the most intensive series of reform proposals ever for improving teaching. Teacher education programs have been questioned, even ridiculed, but once again the call for field experiences has come through unscathed. Although *A nation at risk* (1983) failed to mention field experiences specifically, the criticism was sufficient to cause an analysis of present practices and to spawn a plethora of reports and recommendations which did deal with field experiences. The latest criticism continues to reflect the desirability of student teaching while questioning the rest of teacher education. Lynne W. Cheney (1987), author of a report sponsored by the National Endowment for the Humanities which criticizes the way teachers are prepared to teach humanities, commented on the *Today Show*, September 3, 1987, that student teaching was worthwhile but methods of teaching courses should be replaced by more subject matter courses in a teacher candidate's area of study.

The Carnegie Report (1986) argued that the existence of a sufficiently solid . . . clinical knowledge was necessary to produce verifiable expectations that improve practices and outcomes in teaching. This would include internships and residencies in schools.

Three educational groups have stressed the importance of field and clinical experiences. NCATE Standard Two (1985) requires that clinical and field-based experiences be interwoven throughout the professional education curriculum in order to relate to classroom knowledge in a variety of settings for which education students are being prepared. The Holmes Group (1986) advocates the development of clinical experiences in schools as opposed to apprenticeships. It commits itself to strengthening clinical experience to relate more closely to systematic development of practice. Sikula(1986) in the ATE Blue Ribbon Task Force Report includes teacher induction in the recommended criteria for the training of personnel.

Murray (1986a) reviewed the recommendations for change and concluded that "the sole exception to a pronounced decrease in the traditional education courses was an increase in clinical experiences." He noted that today's gospel calls for better students, more time on basic academic subjects, *more clinical experience* (italics added) and more rigorous and standardized evaluation of students at all points in the program.

Sikula (1986) reported the findings of the ATE Blue Ribbon Task Force which was charged with preparing a response to the growing body of proposals for reforming teacher education. The group prepared a matrix of recommendations based on NCATE Redesign, the Holmes Group Report, and the Carnegie Forum. He observed that all three groups made ten similar recommendations. Of those ten, three related to field experiences: the development of clinical experiences, the promotion of internships and residences, and support for teacher induction.

Teacher educators joined with non-teacher educators in stating that part of the cause of the problems in teacher education today was poor structure and content in teacher education programs and placed more emphasis on field experiences.This is illustrated by a statement made by Saunders (1985) in reporting on a new program at Memphis State University, "while pedagogical training is reduced, the 'more intensified' internship will enable students to benefit more resulting in 'increased respect and credibility.'" Learning by doing is alive and well.

The Case for Field Experiences

Why have field experiences survived and grown? The research base shows conflicting results about their impact. Zeichner (1978) reviewed the research on student teaching and noted that the acceptance of student teaching and the trend to include more field experiences did not have a research base. Most criticisms center around the argument that student teaching is a conservative institution which serves merely to socialize prospective teachers into existing patterns. He further states that a review of the literature of student teaching indicates that it is not as beneficial as the testimonials for it. Instead, student teaching seems to entail a complicated set of both positive and negative consequences that are often subtle in nature.

Although there are many studies such as the one reported by Tamashiro (1982) which report that involving more time and greater responsibility early in the teacher education program were valuable, practicable, and beneficial, Bennie (1982) concluded that "in spite of the recent emphasis in preservice teacher education on more and earlier field experiences, studies are challenging the contributions of full-time student teaching to professional growth. Although pragmatic findings favor the inclusion of field experience in teacher preparation programs, the importance of field experience has not been empirically established."

The momentum continues, in spite of the lack of a firm research base supporting field experiences. It is necessary to look at the reasons for this popularity in order to develop a perspective on their role in educational change. The following factors seem to be central to the continuing popularity of field experiences in change in teacher education in spite of the lack of firm research data to support them.

1. Field experiences link teaching candidates to the actual teaching setting. In field experiences, teaching candidates are in what is often referred to as the "real world." Students are confronted with what is being taught, who is being taught, who is teaching it, and how it is being done. Learning is no longer in the abstract. There is a high motivating factor in applying knowledge and seeing the outcome. If the results are not what is desired, there is a receptiveness to change. If the results seem to work, practices are reinforced. Persons are learning by working with students in classrooms under the direction of teachers who face the challenge daily. Although some may observe (even complain) that this creates a "marry the natives" syndrome, the popularity of the development of teaching skills in the actual environment cannot be denied.

2. Field experiences exemplify the classical concept of learning by experience. Field experiences present problem-solving situations. The participants are confronted with problems, consider alternative solutions, test courses of action, and observe their results. In addition, there is a degree of independence in the ability of the teacher candidate to determine one's own needs and to develop appropriate solutions. This type of environment is in marked contrast with most university courses which may offer little or no opportunity for problem solving or independent decision-making.

3. Field experiences have a higher degree of emotional involvement; most of it satisfying. The design of field experience programs with their high levels of involvement present more opportunities to achieve satisfaction which results in more positive feelings. Teacher candidates are likely to be encouraged and praised from various sources during their experiences. School officials appreciate having them, supervising teachers are generous with their praise,

and college supervisors are generally supportive and empathetic. Even pupils often show very visible support.

4. Field experiences are growth-producing. Teachers admit that their field experiences were very influential in their learning about teaching. Recently, the author worked with an intern who was having considerable difficulty early in his first year of teaching with classroom management and instructional methodology. His classes were characterized by threats, frequent interruptions, rearrangement of students, and disorganized presentation of material. He and the students were in an adversarial stance. With the assistance of a mentor, he managed in a few months to become more student oriented and gained control of the class. When he did so, he began to have more creative classroom activities and provided more opportunities for logical and creative thinking among his students. He was aware of the improvement and continued to grow. There are numerous other similar examples in the experience of supervisors which visibly illustrate growth during field experience.

5. Field experiences offer the opportunity for one-to-one teaching encounters. In reality, field experiences are methods classes taught on a one-to-one basis. This provides opportunity to learn at the student's level and to focus on the learnings that seem to be the most necessary or imminent at the moment.

6. Goals are internally determined rather than externally imposed. The intrinsic motivation of direct activity overshadows the concern for a grade. The rewards are self-satisfaction and the ability to see immediate results. Field participants can determine their own goals and observe the results. With the support system that is associated with field experiences, the opportunities for success are enhanced and positive results are accompanied by student satisfaction. There is a poem by John Preston that begins, "I am the captain of my soul; I rule it with stern joy." Field experiences to a great extent permit an individual to be responsible for what he does and to have some latitude for the way that he does it. This

climate can produce a quicker response than one which is imposed through a set of formal requirements.

7. Prospective teachers are socialized into existing patterns. Zeichner (1978) referred to this condition as a possible negative consequence. However, the fact exists that student teachers do begin to become familiar with and accustomed to the realities of the teaching setting. Students tend to feel that they have some understanding of the school setting and how they fit into it.

8. Field experiences are popular. Field experiences enjoy the acclaim of critics, professional educators, public school personnel, and teacher education candidates. This popularity causes more receptiveness to change and presents a broader support base than exists in other areas of teacher education.

9. Public Schools and teacher education institutions have the greatest amount of trust and respect for each other in the area of field experiences. Change must involve respect and cooperation for and among the participants in teacher education. Field experiences extend from one institution into another. In so doing, working relationships develop which cause each to feel that problems are being solved and mutual respect develops. This climate is conducive in instituting different kinds of programs.

The rest of this chapter will be an attempt to place field experiences in the context of the present educational structure and to speculate as to the role they will assume in the new directions which teacher education may take. Finally, an agenda for improving teaching through involvement in field experiences will be presented.

The Present Changes

The current milieu presents an interesting set of internal and external factors which are influencing teacher education. When one addresses the future of teacher education, especially as it relates to field experiences, the following conditions will undoubtedly play an important role.

Emphasis on Accountability and Quantitative Standards

Abrell (1982) notes the demand for accountability as one of the present realities and current trends which will affect clinical experiences in the 21st century. The likes of Watergate, ABSCAM, and questionable management of financial resources in some large school systems have all coalesced to make every profession more accountable. The difficulty of finding quality teaching jobs has done much to make young and old alike question the value of certificates, diplomas, and degrees. Many media articles have spotlighted the alleged incompetence of professional educators and have affected the image of teachers and teacher educators adversely.

An example of what has happened is illustrated by a law passed by the 1987 Indiana Legislature in a comprehensive education bill which has been hailed as an "A+" measure for the improvement of education. It contained a thread of accountability throughout the law. Public school students are to be tested six times during the twelve years of schooling and results will be compared. Students who perform at unacceptable levels will be required to take remedial courses in summer school. Schools which show gains on the knowledge tests will be rewarded with visible symbols of accomplishment. The school year has been extended five days. New teachers must not only pass the National Teachers Examination for an initial teaching license but are to be evaluated after a year of teaching using criteria developed by the state. If they cannot meet these criteria within two years in the estimation of the principal, they will no longer have a license to teach in accredited schools in that state.

The Indiana experience is not unique. In 1985, 30 states required some type of minimum competency testing for teaching (Sandefur, 1985). The nation seems preoccupied with the need for some kind of measurable criteria to demonstrate that students are learning.

Increased Study of Subject Matter

The reform proposals, including those from professional educators such as the Holmes Group, come up front with the need to "make teacher education intellectually sound" (Murray 1986b). Proposals such as the previously mentioned Memphis State plan advocate the increase of subject knowledge as a method to improve teaching. The state of Indiana now requires that all teachers who secure a professional teaching license must have 18 hours of academic study in that degree, reducing the option for professional study. There seems to be general agreement to add more subject matter to teacher preparation without any analysis of the content being taught. On one hand, we have the "more is better" mentality provided to academic knowledge and "they must do better with less" applied to professional education study. This is contrary to the evidence that teachers have problems not so much with subject matter knowledge as with professional concerns, such as discipline, classroom management, and motivation (Henry 1986).

Dwindling Supply of Teachers

According to information from the National Center for Educational Information reported by Feistritzer (1987), the need for additional teachers by the year 2000 ranges from 13.4 percent additional for secondary to 36.3 percent for elementary. Harris (1986) in the Metropolitan Life survey of the American teacher states that "educational leaders think that the coming teacher shortage will be very serious" (9).

Given current conditions, we cannot be optimistic that numbers sufficient to meet present needs will be available. The Metropolitan Life survey further reports that such factors as low salaries, the status that society gives to the profession, the working conditions that teachers face, and a temporary imbalance between the growth of the school-age population and the number of people who are entering teaching will lead to an inadequate number of certified teachers (9).

Furthermore, the traditional pool of potential teachers is no longer available. The days are gone when teaching was virtually the only profession open to women. The healthy economy will provide job openings for persons who at one time would have looked at teaching for a secure future. It is the author's belief that teaching is not, and probably will not, be considered to be socially prestigious or economically rewarding in the near future.

If history is a guide, there will be attempts to alleviate the teaching shortage with field experience programs that provide students with direct teaching responsibility while they simultaneously earn a teaching license. Internships may be resurrected combining experiential learning with full- or part-time teaching. Twenty years ago, interns were used to place a needed teacher in the classroom. The door stands wide open for a similar phenomenon in the near future.

The general consensus is that a serious teacher shortage looms in the immediate future. One midwestern state issued 873 limited licenses in 1986 (limited licenses are issued when regularly certified teachers cannot be secured). Licensing regulations sometimes become more flexible to allow for lesser-trained teachers to secure valid licenses (Indiana recently returned to a secondary license for junior high and high school students instead of separate licenses because of the difficulty in securing licensed junior high teachers). If history is a precedent, the certification laws will be relaxed to ensure that persons are available for classroom teaching regardless of the quality of their training. In some cases, supervised field experiences are expected to help provide the essential training missed in a conventional program. New Jersey (Cooperman & Klagholz 1985) and Los Angeles Unified School District (conversation with Joel Colbert, Director of the Professional Development Center, May 20, 1987), already have such programs in place.

Bureaucratic Nature of Schools

Schools are larger and more bureaucratic. Procedures are established and individual initiative is often stifled. The bureaucratic character of the schools will continue to be a factor which discourages creative and talented people. Abrell (1982) notes that there is an increasing demand for more legal contracts, formal agreements, record keeping, and "forms for everything." Mandates and policies set at the state level are adding to what is already considered to be a cradle of red tape.

The problem is compounded by the fact that adversarial relationships often surface as bargaining becomes more prevalent in teacher contracts. Policies for field experiences may be formulated as a result of negotiations and administered in a bureaucratic fashion. Supervisors of student teachers and field participants may be selected on a rotating basis, for example, rather than from quality performance.

These two conditions are detrimental according to Frymier (1987) in an article in the *Phi Delta Kappan* entitled "Bureaucracy and the Neutering of Teachers." The conditions of work, according to Frymier, blunt teacher enthusiasm and stifle their creativity. The bureaucratic nature of schools is hindering enthusiasm and motivation for the work of teaching. Something is out of whack when the bureaucratic nature of the enterprise seems to have acquired a purpose all its own.

Future programs in teacher education must consider the above factors. Any scenario will have to reconcile the conflicts and develop procedures for solving the problems. This must be reconciled to the goals that seem to be the most appropriate for teacher education. The following section suggests such goals.

Desirable Goals

The future calls for changes. The goals depend upon who is espousing them. Given that caveat, the author suggests the following goals for the improvement of teacher education.

1.   Recognize that teachers must possess a repertoire of teaching skills as well as a body of subject matter knowledge. As indicated, reform efforts have tended to place a great amount of emphasis on the cognitive domain. While the knowledge of subject is indisputable, one must wonder how much knowledge is enough. How much advanced mathematics is necessary for the elementary or even the secondary teacher who is teaching basic math courses? Good teaching is recognized as much by the ability to communicate as by knowledge itself. There is no teaching unless there is learning and the process of instruction is the vital link to that objective.

Teachers must be able to be aware of and use a great variety of instructional techniques. They must know their own skills and use them. They should have an understanding of what kinds of procedures are most likely to produce desirable results in teaching. Such skills must include development of affective and technical skills of teaching as well as subject knowledge.

2.   The knowledge base in teacher education should be more visible in teacher preparation programs. One of the best kept secrets in teacher education may be the fact that there is a knowledge base in teaching. Unfortunately, it is not used as a basis for the development of teacher education programs as much as it should be. We frequently hear that teachers "ought to have a course in philosophy (or whatever)" but there is little or no evidence which indicates that performance is better from such a course. Research on effective teaching and effective schools exists. It should be systematically applied in a teacher education curriculum and constantly revised as new data

become available. This research should be illustrated and highlighted in educational textbooks on methods of teaching. Scientific knowledge has a role to play in educational practice, although there will always be room for artistic interpretation by the individual instructor.

3. <u>Teachers should develop models of procedures</u>. Teachers are confronted with hundreds (perhaps even thousands) of decisions each day. If there is no model to work from, it becomes more difficult to make correct or consistent decisions. There is standard procedure in some professions. The author recently had an experience with a physician who outlined three sequential courses of action to correct a health problem. The procedures had been established and were recognized by the medical community. Similarly, teacher education should see that teachers develop protocols of procedures which can be used whenever typical problems occur. An example might be the employment of a discipline technique. If one procedure fails, what is the next alternative? There are models for discipline and other areas available. Teachers would feel more in control if they were aware of them and practiced them regularly instead of relying on their impulse at the moment to solve problems.

4. <u>Teacher preparation should extend into the first year of teaching</u>. The expectations placed upon teachers from the reports and other sources cannot be totally achieved in a four-year preparation program (Griffin and Millies 1987). The present system has complications which should be addressed. The high dropout rate among new teachers points to the fact that something is wrong. Based on reports that a great number of teachers will leave the profession within the next few years (Grissmer & Kirby 1987), one can assume that present teacher educations may be inadequate.

Studies of first-year support programs seem to indicate that an internship was instrumental in the retention of teachers. Parker (1986) found that 75 percent of teachers who participated in an internship indicated a desire to remain in teaching compared to 25 percent of a control group. In a pilot intern program, Henry (1987) found that 100 percent of the interns who had a multiple support base planned to remain in teaching and are now in their second year of teaching. He also found that the teachers who participated in the first-year support program experienced less stress than a control group and showed significantly better teaching skills in 30 areas.

The first year of teaching is unique and calls for continued assistance. For the first time in one's career, the teacher has sole responsibility for a class in a room where he or she is isolated from other teachers. There is frequently no one to turn to, not even a peer who might also be in the first year of teaching. A new teacher will also likely experience what Carl Glickman (remarks made at ASCD Institute on Supervision, January 16, 1986) calls the Inverse Qualification Syndrome–the least qualified teacher gets the more difficult classes.

Teacher preparation must not conclude when a college student receives a license. It must continue into the initial teaching experience with supervision and intervention from more experienced professionals who can assure that competency has been developed and who is available as teachers learn the basic skills which can only be learned through direct experience.

5. Teacher-education institutions and public schools should link more closely in teacher preparation. Universities and public schools need each other. Universities are needed to provide research, ideas, theories, and perspective to the preparation of teachers. Public schools are the sites where the scenarios developed by the universities are played out. Universities must have a direct knowledge of public school classrooms in order to adequately prepare teachers for their roles. Academic knowledge and practical experience must be the responsibility of universities and public schools alike.

6. Academic content should be structured with teaching in mind. One of the unfortunate aspects of the reform agendas has been the fact that more content has been advocated without much concern for what is presently being taught. The pursuit of knowledge for its own sake may not be the appropriate content for a new teacher. Future teachers should know something about the structure of their particular discipline and understand what is taught at the basic level where they will work in the public schools.

Concepts and generalizations should be intertwined
with the academic principles in such a way that
persons may know how to introduce them to young
people.

The above goals are not complete, but they propose an
agenda that might place teachers in a more professional position because they will perform more as other professionals do
and be more thoroughly trained for the task of teaching. They
should have a more rounded preparation and be able to use
methods and techniques which are professionally justifiable.

An Agenda for Improving Teacher Education through Field Experiences

The final section of this chapter will be a series of
recommendations for change in teacher education through
field experiences. Recognizing that external forces have an
impact on teacher education and in recognition of the goals
stated previously, the following agenda is submitted for the
improvement of teacher education focusing on field experiences.

1. Field experiences should be early and continuing.
    There are necessary professional skills which should
    be learned at all levels. If any one area is neglected,
    damage can result. Early experiences provide the
    opportunity for decision making on the part of both
    students and professional educators before a lot of
    time has been spent on a particular career goal. Early
    experiences also allow for the beginning of the
    development of basic teaching skills and the applica-
    tion of subject knowledge in a real setting.

As students develop, they should have the benefit of
continued field experiences which are modified to build upon
what is known and to develop more complex skills. Continuing experiences also present the opportunity for learning in a
variety of settings. Schools are not all alike, and teacher education candidates should prepare to cope with different kinds of
students in different types of communities. Continuing field
experiences can provide such variety.

Finally, field experiences should continue until a teacher
has demonstrated the ability to perform competently in the
classroom without the intervention of another professional

person. It is fairly well established that such proficiency cannot be expected at the end of a typical preparation program.

2.   Specific learning tasks should be identified and developed at all levels. Field experiences should progress with a purpose, or perhaps more appropriately, a variety of purposes. Specific tasks should be identified for all developmental levels and related to the affective, cognitive, and technical domains of activity. The affective domain would move, for example, from mistrust to empathy. Teachers must learn to understand the behaviors of pupils and to respond at a sophisticated level. In the cognitive domain, candidates would develop higher orders of thinking and develop the ability to perform such tasks as asking questions which develop creative and divergent thinking on the part of pupils. The technical domain would see the development of more complex teaching procedures that are more appropriate to the learning task at hand.

3.   Select superior teachers as role models for field participants. The present scene is placing a lot of emphasis on career ladder approaches. These levels of accomplishment allow for the identification of teachers who are exceptionally competent, highly motivated, or who have had advanced training of some sort. The bottom line is that they are recognized as superior teachers. These persons should be able to serve as the best role models that teaching candidates and incoming teachers can have. It would present the opportunity for young persons to learn from the best teachers in the building instead of experimenting alone or turning to teachers whose qualifications and ability are less than standard.

4.   Prepare supervisors for their tasks. Persons who supervise field participants, student teachers, and interns should be highly competent and possess skills of supervision which will allow them to communicate effectively with their protégés and to assist in their formative growth. Supervision is a special skill that not all teachers have. Schools do not trust their athletic, music, and drama teams to a teacher who is not skilled in coaching or directing. By the same token, those who work with field participants should

also develop expertise in supervision. Teachers need to be trained in such domains as effective teaching, models of supervision, human relations, conference skills, and teaching analysis. In a study at Stanford Copeland (1977) found that student teachers lose the microteaching skills that were taught to them in college unless they were reinforced by the supervising teachers in the field. Training must focus on those areas in which field participants need growth.

5. <u>Examine the basic concepts and assumptions about student teaching</u>. Student teaching has always been the stable component of a teacher education plan. Generally, it has worked to the satisfaction of all, but it has not been examined. The typical scenario is for a student teacher to assume responsibility for the majority of a cooperating teacher's classes for a period of several weeks. The cooperating teacher (who, as indicated, probably has had no training for the role) is left to provide supervision and to turn classes over to another person for a lengthy period during the school year. There are problems with this that need to be considered. A good teacher has been displaced for a number of weeks. Students have to become accustomed to a new person with a different style and with less ability. A student teacher is limited in responsibility. Some liken or compare student teaching to cooking in someone else's kitchen. The arrangement must be looked at to provide for the amelioration of some of these difficulties that undoubtedly prevent maximum growth for all involved.

6. <u>Limit the number of schools that have field participants</u>. Not every school should necessarily be a training site for future teachers. In a teaching center, personnel could be more easily trained, resources could be concentrated, and university supervisors could spend more time in professional matters. Model programs could be established, developed, and evaluated, and new innovations, such as simulation laboratories and interactive learning could be put in place for use in the field setting. Teaching centers could be demonstration sites for various educational programs and displaced supervising teachers could

channel some of their time and energy to the professional endeavors of the centers.

7. Increase and improve the university-public school
    linkage. Goodlad (March 18, 1987, *Chronicle of
    Higher Education*) stated, "The most significant
    changes occur when two cultures bump up against
    one another, and that is why I want the universities
    and schools to work together. They are different
    cultures." When these two institutions work
    together things will be done that cannot be done in
    the university or in the school districts. Field experi-
    ences are the most likely target for this increased
    linkage.

8. Minimum competencies should be identified and
    demonstrated by field participants. The accountabil-
    ity movement cannot be ignored. Colleges of educa-
    tion will establish minimum competencies that must
    be met by students. Students will have to convince
    their supervisors that they know and can demon-
    strate competencies required of each clinical experi-
    ence before they can move to the next one. In short,
    students will have to demonstrate certain basic skills,
    knowledge, and attitudes to both enter and exit each
    clinical experience (Abrell 1982).

9. Establish an internship as the culminating field
    experience. As indicated, the internship has
    appeared throughout educational history in various
    forms, including a way to hire teachers when there
    was an oversupply and to secure people for class-
    rooms when there was not a sufficient supply. The
    possibility exists now that with creative leadership,
    an internship can be incorporated into teacher
    education which is the capstone experience and
    provides a link that has long been missing in teacher
    education–systematic supervision while a teacher is
    learning to teach independently. An internship
    would include support, skill development,
    acculturation, monitoring from the university as
    well as the public school, and formative evaluation.
    Studies have shown that a well-designed internship
    improves teaching skills and reduces teacher
    dropout. A professional internship program can

perhaps be the biggest step to making teaching a legitimate profession.

Conclusion

The legacy of teacher education is that improvements in teaching have been synonymous with field experiences. From Flowers through the social advocacy movement to the reform reports of the 80's, field experiences have played a key role in educational change. Better field experiences will not solve all the problems in the educational world but moves can be made which will certainly enhance the ability of the profession to prepare teachers.

In the middle 60's, the author and his family were traveling in Nebraska and toured an historical exhibit which traced the progress that has been made in rural society. We saw the evolution of wagons to automobiles, simple reapers to combines, crude utensils of all descriptions to more useable wares. Eventually we went into the courtyard and toured a one-room school. My twelve-year-old daughter had been more observant than I thought. When we entered the foyer of the school building, she looked at the lunch boxes on the shelves and commented, "Lunch boxes have not changed." Then we went on into the main room. She looked around and exclaimed, "Blackboards have not changed and seats have not changed much either." It was very obvious to a twelve-year-old that schools were not changing as rapidly as the rest of the objects we had seen that day.

Change in education is slow. Once again we have experienced a series of proposals for improving teaching–most of them not from the people who know best about the complex nature of the act; a series of proposals virtually all of which advocate a "top down" mentality instead of broad participation from persons who are equally concerned about the effectiveness of schools and the abilities of the teachers who run them.

The competency examinations and the GPA's will get the publicity, but field experiences will be the key to improved practice. If we are to get away from the one-room schoolhouse mentality and to improve rather than repeat past practices, we will have to do it through field experiences as a primary vehicle for delivery.

References

Abrell, Ron. 1982. Clinical experiences in the 21st century. *Clearinghouse* 55 (February): 284-286.

Ashburn, Elizabeth A. 1986-87. Current developments in teacher induction programs. *Action in Teacher Education* 8 (Winter): 41-44.

Provides an overview of the induction scene from the need for induction programs to sources for existing induction programs and the need for comparative analysis of different types of programs.

Bennie, William A. 1982. Field-based teacher education–a reconsideration? *The Teacher Educator* 17 (Spring): 19-24.

A review of empirical evidence concerning field experiences in the classroom that suggests that field experiences are not as significant in effecting change as is generally assumed.

Brooks, Douglas, ed. 1987. Teacher induction: A new beginning. Reston, Va.: Association of Teacher Educators.

Carnegie Forum on Education and the Economy. 1986. A nation prepared: Teachers for the 21st century. New York: Carnegie Forum on Education and the Economy.

Cheney, Lynne. 1987. American memory. Washington, D.C.: National Endowment for the Humanities.

Report of a survey of student knowledge of dates and periods in American history. Stresses that the schools should emphasize information rather than how to learn.

Conant, James Bryant. 1963. *The education of American teachers.* New York: McGraw-Hill.

Summary and recommendations based on an extensive study of teacher education practices in the United States. Includes specific recommendations for practice teaching experiences for elementary and secondary teacher education candidates.

Cooperman, Saul, and Leo Klagholz. 1985. New Jersey's alternate route to certification. *Phi Delta Kappan* 66 (June): 691-695.

Describes the New Jersey plan for offering teacher education to college graduates while they are in their first year of teaching. Describes how the idea relates to the reports, especially the Carnegie Report, outlines essential professional knowledge for beginning teachers, and describes how the program was implemented in a field setting. Concludes with a statement of anticipated results.

Copeland, Willis D. 1977. Some factors related to student teacher classroom performance following microteaching training. *American Education Research Journal* 14 (Spring): 147-157.

Describes the results of a follow-up study on the retention of microteaching behaviors in student teaching. Concludes that unless supervising teachers have experienced training in teaching skills, the student teacher will not continue to use the skills learned from microteaching training.

Cross, K. Patricia. 1984. The rising tide of school reform reports. *Phi Delta Kappan* 66 (November): 167-172.

Summarizes the content of the reports and urges a rational consideration of their meaning and of the solutions for improvement that are suggested.

Dewey, John. 1904. The relation of theory to practice in education. In *Teacher education in America: A documentary history*, ed. Borrowman, Merle 1965. New York: Teachers College Press.

States the position that some form of practice teaching in public school classrooms is essential.

Feistritzer, Emily. 1987. America's changing workplace. *Teacher Education Reports* 9:20 (October): 6-7.

Presents data concerning the future of the American work force and summarizes the projected need for new teachers in the next decade.

Flexner, Abraham. 1910. Medical education in the United States and Canada. Bulletin #4. New York: Carnegie Foundation for the Improvement of Teaching.

Report of the status of medical education at the turn of the century. The report served as a watershed for reform in medical education.

Flowers, John C., ed. 1948. School and community laboratory experiences in teacher education. Washington, D.C.: American Association of Teachers Colleges (now AACTE).

Summary of a subcommittee study of standards for field experiences. Concludes with a series of recommendations for improving field experiences.

Frymier, Jack. 1987. Bureaucracy and the neutering of teachers. *Phi Delta Kappan* 69 (September): 9-14.

The author studied a large urban system that had been reorganized and concluded that the increase of bureaucracy has a detrimental effect on teachers.

Goldberg, Milton, and James Harvey. 1983. A nation at risk: The report of the national commission on excellence in education. *Phi Delta Kappan* 65 (September): 14-18.

Two staff members of the National Commission on Excellence in Education discuss the report.

Gray, William A., and Marilynne M. Gray, 1985. Synthesis of research on mentoring beginning teachers. *Educational Leadership* 43 (November): 37-43.

Summarizes the findings concerning desirable mentor characteristics and presents a five-level helping relationship model for working with first-year teachers.

Griffin, Gary. 1983. Clinical preservice teacher education: Final report of a descriptive study. Austin: The

University of Texas at Austin: Research and Development Center for Teacher Education.

The executive summary of the final report of a study of a multi-site, multi-method, semester-long study of student teaching.

Griffin, Gary. 1982. Student teaching: Problems and promising practices. ERIC ED223 571.

Report of a working conference on student teaching. Under discussion was the student teaching process and the nature of research that might contribute to its better understanding and improvement. Papers on pertinent issues are presented by several scholars.

Griffin, Gary, and Suzanne Millies. 1987. The first years of teaching: Background papers and a proposal. Chicago: The University of Illinois at Chicago.

Grissmer, David W., and Sheila Kirby. 1987. Teacher attrition: The uphill climb to staff the nation's schools. Los Angeles, Calif.: The Rand Corporation.

Conclusions based on analysis of attrition data. Predicts that teacher attrition will rise over the coming decade.

Harris, Louis. 1986. The Metropolitan Life survey of the American teacher. New York: Metropolitan Life and Affiliated Companies.

Henry, Marvin A. 1986. I like it just the way it is: Dare we change the most popular component in teacher preparation? *Tennessee Education.* 16 (Fall): 28-31.

Describes factors affecting the future of field experiences in teacher education and presents an agenda for change in field experiences.

Henry, Marvin A. 1987. **Final report of project CREDIT.** Terre Haute, Ind.: Indiana State University.

Final report submitted to the Indiana Department of Education. Summary of an experimental intern program, including results of internal and external teacher retention, teacher skills, and stress levels, all favoring the experimental group.

Holmes Group. 1986. Tomorrow's teachers. A report of the Holmes Group, East Lansing, Mich. The Holmes Group Inc.

Recommendations of representatives from "major research universities" concerning revision of teacher education programs. Makes 13 recommendations including the development of clinical experiences in the schools as opposed to apprenticeships.

Ishler, Peggy, ed. 1986/1987. *Action in Teacher Education* (Winter): 41-85.

Special section on teacher induction. Several articles relating to teacher induction are included.

Johnson, Jim. 1968. *A brief history of student teaching.* DeKalb, Ill.: Creative Educational Materials.

Traces the history of student teaching from its European beginning to recent times. Concludes with a look at student teaching in retrospect.

Lasley, Tom, ed. 1986. *Journal of Teacher Education* 37 (January-February): 2-41.

Murray, Frank B. 1986a. The complete teacher. *Change* 18 (September-October): 21-25.

Discusses the reform movements and notes that "reforms" one hears talk about are not, by themselves or together, likely to improve teacher education because either they focus on factors that are largely irrelevant to the education of teachers or because they do not realistically take into account demographic constraints and the need for large changes in teacher education.

Murray, Frank B. 1986b. Goals for the reform of teacher education: An executive summary of the Holmes Group report. *Phi Delta Kappan* 68 (September): 28-31.

Murray, Frank B. 1986c. Teacher education. *Change* 18 (September-October): 18-21.

> Recommends further scrutiny of the standard prescriptions for reforming undergraduate teacher education. Includes more clinical experiences as one of the recommendations.

National Commission on Excellence in Education. 1983. *A nation at risk.* Washington, D.C.: Department of Education.

> Summary of the study of the President's select committee on the condition of education in America.

National Council for Accreditation of Teacher Education (NCATE). 1985. NCATE redesign. Washington, D.C.

Parker, Linda. 1986. The efficiency of a teacher instruction program in providing assistance and support of first-year teachers. Ph.D. dissertation. The University of Wisconsin, Madison.

> A study of the teacher intern program at the University of Wisconsin-Whitewater. The results showed a decrease in teacher dropout and more positive attitudes about teaching.

Rossetto, Celeste R., and Judith K. Grosenick. 1987. Effects of collaborative teacher induction: Follow-up of graduates of a teacher induction program. *Journal of Teacher Education* 38 (March-April): 50-52.

> The authors investigated the perceptions of graduates of an induction program in teacher education. Results indicate that the majority of graduates continued careers in education after program completion.

Sandefur, J. T. 1985. Competency assessment of teachers. *Action in Teacher Education* 7 (Spring): 1-6.

Saunders, Robert L. 1985. Memphis State University's new five-year program for the instructional preparation of teachers. *Tennessee Education* 15 (Fall): 26-29.

Summary of the new program for teacher education at Memphis State indicating the increased role of field experiences in teacher preparation.

Shanker, Albert. 1986. The Carnegie Report: An endorsement for teacher education. *Change* 18 (September-October): 8-9.

Emphasizes that teacher educators need to embrace the Carnegie report's intellectual and professional approach to what teachers   ought to know, and its endorsement of the legitimacy and significance of teacher education.

Sikula, John. 1986. Visions of reform: Implications for the education profession. Reston, VA: Association of Teacher Educators.

Report of the ATE Blue Ribbon Task Force. Reviews and analyzes three reform proposals: NCATE Redesign, Holmes Group, and the Carnegie Forum. Summarizes the implications of these recommendations for state education agencies, bachelor's level institutions, state colleges and universities, and research-oriented universities.

Tamashiro, Roy T. 1982. Evaluating the impact of new priorities in teacher education. Paper presented at the annual meeting of AACTE, February. ERIC ED 215965.

Describes the evaluation study of a program of early field and clinical experiences in preservice teacher education. Surveyed cooperating teachers involved with a core program for sophomore teacher candidates. Results suggested that cooperating teachers believe that more practice is better for prospective teachers. Cooperating teachers also endorsed the idea that these field experiences should be structured and well supervised.

Tyler, Ralph. 1985. What we've learned from past studies of teacher education. *Phi Delta Kappan* 66 (June): 682-684.

Summarizes the results of the Commonwealth Teacher Education Study and The Study of the Commission of Teacher Education. The results of the studies, which were made in the late 1930's, identified the value of early field experiences.

Williams, E. I. F. 1942. *The actual and potential use of laboratory schools.* New York: Teachers College, Columbia University.

Claims that student teaching was a feature of early schools operated by Franciscan friars in New Mexico in the early 1600's.

Zeichner, Kenneth. 1978. The student teaching experience. *Action in Teacher Education* 1 (Summer): 58-61.

Technology and Teaching: Trends for the Future

Rhonda S. Robinson
Peter C. West

A hesitancy to innovate, coupled with inadequate research, has kept schools from tapping the new technologies' full potential to radically advance the instructional process.

William Snider
Education Week, Oct. 14, 1987

Introduction

One of several major forces and shifts affecting higher education today is the technological imperative (Keller 1983). New and emerging technologies such as the microcomputer, laser disc, and interactive systems are altering the way students learn and teachers teach. A recent report by the American Association of Colleges for Teacher Education (1987) confirms that the "expansion of technology in education has been rapid." If teacher education institutions are going to be effective in shaping the school of the future they need to begin addressing this technological imperative. It is therefore critical that these institutions begin examining how they can better incorporate technologies into program areas.

It is no secret that colleges of education have been criticized in recent years. Bush (1987, 13) writes that "never before have teachers and teacher education so captured the American public's concern about the quality of education." This criticism has focused on aspects from the quality of students to the lack of innovation by the faculties. Elementary and secondary schools have not escaped criticism either. The 1980's have indeed been a trying decade for those involved in education, and in particular in teacher education. To resolve some of the problems confronting education, and address some of the criticism facing the education community, educators need to begin considering ways of implementing ideas suggested in reform reports. Substantive change as suggested in these reform reports will not be easy.

Corrigan (1985) believes that "changing schools and teacher preparation programs involves political, economic, social, and educational reform." Teacher education programs according to Corrigan have not changed significantly during the past 20 years due in part to a failure to conceptualize teacher education adequately. Reform in teacher education will not be an easy task. On the contrary, it will be an extremely complex task involving shifts in philosophy and budgetary decisions.

Palaich (1985) has identified four goals that need to be met if the teaching profession is to be enhanced. They are:

1. improving teaching and learning,
2. improving the school as an organization,
3. changing certain characteristics of the teacher work force, and
4. strengthening community confidence in the school.

If these goals are to be addressed adequately it will require a collective effort by all segments of the education community. Educational technology is one of these segments that needs to respond, especially as it relates to the first goal listed above.

The field of educational technology according to Valdez (1986) has reached a "turning point." Its use is no longer viewed as a curiosity or fad, but as an extremely useful tool for improving curriculum and instruction. Valdez describes this metamorphosis as a technological turnaround. *Newsweek* (1984) reports that "technology is a big part of the educational revolution." It reports that with teachers using technology to teach old courses and new job skills, the education boom will be one of ten forces shaping America into the twenty-first century.

Instructional equipment (hardware) and related resources (software) are now commonplace in universities and schools. The question of whether or not educators are using available technologies effectively in attempting to address concerns of recent education initiatives remains. While technology is by no means a panacea, it can provide educators with viable solutions if used properly.

Evangelauf (1987) indicates that in the years ahead the teacher education curriculum will begin to see a good deal of restructuring. He reports:

> A survey of campus trends conducted by the American Council on Education this year found widespread attention to the topic: Nearly half of the baccalaureate colleges and comprehensive universities surveyed and over one-third of the doctoral universities reported that they had recently undertaken new approaches to teacher education or were considering doing so. (A48)

These new approaches could include technology as a basis for delivering portions of a teacher education or school based curriculum. Several successful technology based projects have already been implemented at both the K-12 level and the post-secondary education level (Heinich et al.1985). The use of technology in education is not new however. Technology has been utilized in education throughout the century. The following two sections will describe the history of technology in education and lessons that educators should have learned regarding educational technology as it is applied to curriculum and instruction.

A Brief History

The use of technology, or instructional media, for educational purposes has a relatively brief and fairly unremarkable history. Tracing that history quickly can help illustrate the current problems with the application of technology for education. The introduction of new technologies into the classrooms of our country has always been accompanied by high hopes, and followed by disappointment. The reasons for that disappointment are a part of the history.

At the beginning of this century, textbooks, slates, chalkboards, bulletin boards, charts, feltboards, and classroom collections of realia all were the "media" of instruction available for teachers and students. As early as the 1920's, film began being investigated as an educational tool. Research in the 1920's and 1930's (Saettler 1968) showed that film had merit as an instructional aid, especially when concept attainment, psychomotor skills, or attitude formation were the goals (Schramm 1977). Educators were encouraged to employ films in the classroom, and new teachers were given instruction in projection and utilization.

The same basic research, promotion, and training pattern followed the introduction of other new media during the 1950's to the 1970's (Schramm 1977). Television, and later local video production, programmed instruction, language laboratories, and the "smaller" media such as slide programs, filmstrips, audiotapes, and transparencies were introduced, researched, promoted, and adapted by public schools and teacher education institutions (Saettler 1968; Schramm 1977).

The benefits of using media have sometimes been questioned by the education community and the public. Educators from the elementary to the university level have quickly adopted and espoused new media in their search for solutions to difficult problems. Film, television, and now the computer have all been introduced as an aid to teaching which could assist, or possibly replace, the teacher. This might be termed "the media as savior" approach.

This was especially true of television in the 50's and 60's, and is even more true of the microcomputer today. But technology is expensive, and the public, and parents, often question its usefulness. While technology has not yet solved the problems of education, with this unpromising history, what can be learned for the future of technology in education? Looking at lessons learned can give us guidelines for the next decade. There have been several common problems regarding educational practice and the promotion of technologies.

Lessons Learned

The first problem learned has been that technologies have been traditionally introduced by the manufacturers involved, rather than by educators. The educational value has been promoted only after an entertainment (film, television) or engineering/business (computers) application has been tested and been successful. So, educators had to quickly discover the ways in which technology could aid instruction. Educational design always followed the development of hardware. Classroom film (traditionally 16mm) is an example of this educational adaptation of technology. As early as the turn of the century, film was making its way into the entertainment areas in the United States. By 1920, film was a silent but popular entertainment in our major cities. It was, after all, language free, at a time when inexpensive entertainment was needed and enjoyed by many recent immigrants who spoke little or no English. The popularity of film grew rapidly, and entertainment films were increasingly produced throughout the 1920's. By the late 1920's, educators had begun to investigate the use of the new medium for instructional purposes. For example, a film series was developed at Yale to test the effectiveness of film as an instructional aid to the teaching of history (Saettler 1968). These films recreated historical battles in a very realistic (for the times) way, and were found to be an effective and enjoyable aid to instruction. In many ways the films resembled the famous D.W. Griffith battle film sequences such as those in *Birth of a nation*. The studies showed film to be a reliable history lesson (Saettler 1968). Many other research studies followed, involving many subjects and various universities. The research results were encouraging, and an educational medium was "born" out of one originally thought just for entertainment (Saettler 1968).

A second issue was that technology was constantly being heralded as an aid to teaching. No real change in educational philosophy was researched or promoted. Television, film, and the microcomputer have been considered almost like sophisticated chalkboards. The attributes of an individual technology, like slow-motion and close-ups, make each technology a unique tool for educators. Teachers have traditionally planned instruction regardless of technology, using it only to reinforce, rather than introduce new concepts and skills. They do not use the attributes of media to their best capabilities. Many teachers are not prepared to select the most appropriate medium for a specific objective or goal. Some rely on the school media specialist or librarian for selection. Most, however, are more or less at the mercy of the media collection to which they have access–local or regional. For any given topic and objective, the teacher has limited and sometimes not appropriate or best choices of media. For example, there may be only a filmstrip available on a topic which requires motion, or a slide series on a difficult concept which would be better presented through video. Often teachers have no choice, or are not sure how best to select.

In addition, many teachers have little or no training in the utilization of media for instruction. Teachers may model utilization as it was presented when they were in classes, but have never actually taken a course on the preparation and utilization of media for education. Many states have no such media course or requirement for teacher preparation and certification. Consequently, these teachers have no background in the production and utilization of media. Without familiarity with such media vocabulary, teachers are at a loss to incorporate the attributes of the media themselves into their lessons. Even such simple visual literacy concepts as a zoom in or a close-up in a film or videotape may miss the attention of students if not reinforced by a media literate teacher.

Third, planning for the use of technology implementation was not based on curricular goals and student needs, nor on teacher abilities. So, the technology was often purchased, software selected, and implementation required, all without the support of the staff or the needs of the curriculum in mind. Using 16mm film as our example again, imagine being a classroom teacher in 1935 asked to use a new "teaching film" in your classroom presentation. The school would have had to build a special non-inflammatory projection booth into a special viewing auditorium. The teacher would then have to reserve the space, obtain the services of a professional projectionist, and obtain the film from its distributor. Previews and teacher discussion guides were not available, of course. The films available were not even necessarily related to the classroom lessons or to the specific objectives the teacher had for their lesson plan. But film was a novelty and a proven classroom aid, and so it was recommended.

From this historical example, a practice was unfortunately set. Often, materials and hardware (media equipment) have been purchased because they are currently being advocated in educational journals or by manufacturers. Educational administrators are under pressure to stay current and sometimes purchase materials or equipment in response to that pressure from parents, community, or school boards. In retrospect, we have learned that film was an excellent addition to the classroom but it may not have seemed so when it was first introduced. The fear is that the pattern of pressured adoption or availability causing need may be repeated with each new media, including microcomputers and interactive videodisc.

And finally, the introduction of each technology, regardless of how beneficial, was hindered by the lack of teacher education. Teachers would use technology to enhance the education of their students only after extensive training in the selection, utilization, and evaluation of appropriate media.

Teachers need long term financial, training, and curricular support in order for media to be utilized beneficially. Without (1) preplanning; (2) effective utilization of technologies attributes; (3) thorough integration through curricular design; and (4) teacher education, it is unlikely any technology will ever be introduced that changes education for the better. These four common problems can serve as guidelines for technological change in teacher education.

What are the technologies being developed or introduced that could change the course of education? Which new technologies will be implemented following guidelines to ensure their success? Much depends on financial support and the leadership of educators. As the twenty-first century approaches it appears two basic technologies might prove most useful for teacher education programs. They are various video technologies and microcomputer technologies.

Models of Successful Technology Applications

Four examples of appropriate utilization of these technologies (interactive cable television, satellite television, microcomputers, and laser discs) should provide direction to educators in teacher education and school based programs. Many schools are employing current technologies and have utilized the necessary planning, promotion, and training discussed earlier to make the adoption of technology a success.

Interactive Television

Live, interactive television is used for high school and college instruction in several states. In Carroll County, Illinois, three school districts are cooperatively using their common cable television system to enhance curricula by offering low enrollment or advanced level classes via live television instruction. The teacher in one building is interactively connected to the students in all other schools, and each building can see and hear the other. The system, which has been in place since 1983, has successfully offered advanced math and science courses to small classes, and has made the introduction of a third and fourth year of Spanish and French I and II possible.

The Carroll County Instructional Television Consortium actually started as a series of conversations between the superintendents of small rural school districts in Carroll county. These districts were being encouraged to try new programs in a cooperative manner. The state of Illinois made monies available to small districts for such cooperative ventures. In their conversations, the administrators identified common problems shared by the neighboring districts. Of these, the shrinking class sizes and lack of adequate student enrollment for efficiently offering advanced level courses emerged as a common concern. It was out of these meetings, and the state's call for proposals, that the plan for an interactive television system linking all schools was initiated. The preplanning stage also included talks with the state television office coordinator, visits to other interactive television teaching sites in Wisconsin and Iowa, and much discussion. Teachers were included on the "field trips" and were exposed to the technology as early as possible. Once the system idea was deemed a probable solution to the districts problem, the administrators of the four districts worked together to form a consortium board for advisory control, and to identify courses and schedules that would satisfy all districts. The preplanning stage included, then, much discussion, a grant proposal to the state, visits to similar teaching sites, and teacher involvement.

The second stage involved planning for the effective utilization of the media chosen. In this case, interactive television teaching was chosen as a substitute for limiting courses offered in any one building. Interactive television can be established through regular hard wire cable television, as it was in this case, or by microwave transmission. Either way, each school must be interconnected. In this example, the schools were wired by the local cable company used by all communities. Two-way cable was laid, with a control signal heading the system at the cable company's offices. Each school received its own channel, so it could broadcast programming from its own building, like a mini television station available only to those with cable television.

The state grant helped each district remodel an existing classroom and equip it with the necessary technology. In addition to the cable "drop" each room needed four television monitors, three television cameras, several microphones, a special effects generator, and a video cassette recorder player. Most classrooms were carpeted, and needed air conditioning as well as sound proofing. The state also required a two way viewing mirror or window, so students could be observed by teachers or visitors from outside the studio classroom.

This set-up created a very effective use of the technologies capabilities. Two-way television linked classrooms so that the teacher in any one building could be seen and heard by the students on the monitors in their classrooms. The special effects generator (SEG) allowed the teacher to show his/her own class on the system, or to use overhead transparencies, chalkboards, or other notes. These could be shown independently, or on a split screen with the teacher or the students. In addition, audio or videotapes could be shared, as could other visual materials. The television technology provided all the variety necessary for the instruction of upper-level courses in high schools.

The courses taught included advanced math, Spanish I - IV, French I and II, and frequently chemistry, physics, shorthand, and history. These courses were taught by experienced teachers qualified to teach advanced level courses. The subject matter required some of the essential attributes of televised instruction, attributes that make television the appropriate medium of instruction. These include the close-up, which can be of students asking questions, the teacher, or of visual material or objects; the motion capability; and the ability to show any kind of media or visual on the screen, such as film, three dimensional objects, or charts and graphs. So, the system employed was chosen well, and was adapted to utilize the most valuable attributes of the technology.

A third stage of the implementation involved integration through curricular design. Many of the problems teachers and students encountered in the first year of the program were a direct result of lack of time for curriculum planning and implementation. During the first year, students were in newly formed classes containing students from four different school districts. Because the districts had rushed to get this project into place, they had not spent an advance year assuring themselves that their curricula were comparable. As a result, students were not at the same level of competence in vital areas of math, science, or foreign language. During the first year, curriculum committees were formed of teachers from all the schools to set goals and objectives, course expectations, class text selection, and other cooperative agreements. Students in each school would then be skilled at the same levels, and would have a greater chance of success with material taught via the system by a teacher in another school. This curricular planning was essential to the success of the project and to the continued progress of the students involved. By the third year, curricular problems had all but disappeared, and students entered advanced classes with the same entry level abilities and skills regardless of the district in which they were taught.

The fourth aspect of this technology adoption was the teacher education involved. Prior to the school year's opening, teachers who had been selected for television teaching were given three days of inservice training. The goals of this training were to familiarize the teachers with the operation of the television equipment, to examine communication and coordination practices that the system would require, and to provide practice in these areas. Teachers were given several hours training on television camera, special effects generator, and recorder operations, and were given practice assignments. The communication problems that distance teaching can create were presented and discussed, and teachers were provided several examples of classroom management and communication skills which could enhance their teaching over television. Each teacher was expected to "produce" one short televised class, with appropriate visuals, use of the overhead camera to replace the chalkboard, and communication techniques as demonstrated.

With this preliminary training, teachers started the school year. Consultants from the university continually visited classes to troubleshoot problems with the equipment and offer suggestions to the teachers. This observation and consultation has continued, to a lesser degree throughout the five years of the project. Teachers were provided with oral and written feedback on their progress, and a short newsletter to project participants was used for the first two years as a vehicle for idea sharing. Two or three inservice training days were held each year to continue development of skills and to orient new teachers added to the system.

After five years, this technology implementation has been evaluated and found to be a success. Final exam scores, attitudinal surveys, and interviews have all revealed a fairly high degree of satisfaction with the technology and its ability to enhance curricula for these small schools. Other school districts in the Midwest have modeled themselves on this project and have so far experienced similar success.

The Carroll County Television Consortium is not a unique project. Many others exist around the country with similar objectives and equivalent equipment. Interactive televised instruction has been shown to be a technology that is effective for classroom instruction. The Carroll County project can, however, be an example of how important the four previously described aspects of technology implementation really are. This project and others like it are successful because they have utilized preplanning, effective and appropriate use of the chosen technology, thorough curriculum design, and effective teacher education and evaluation.

Evaluation has shown that the early involvement of the community, the pre-service training of selected teachers, the preparation of students, and the careful and cooperative planning of the school administrators and curriculum committees made this a successful application of technology. The students are learning course material, and have shown very few behavior or learning problems. The lack of face-to-face interaction is countered by the availability of the teacher by telephone. The students report that they enjoy the system classes and getting to know new students as well as the course material.

Satellite Transmission

Satellite television is a technology that shows promise for education. It has the potential for providing schools and universities with access to programming that only a few years ago was not available. Additionally, it has the capability of transmitting live instruction to distant sites. According to Benson and Hirschen (1987) satellite television has already been used successfully in educational settings. Three states actively involved in using satellite television are Oklahoma, Texas, and Illinois.

Professors at Oklahoma State University teach courses in a variety of subjects to high school students via satellite. The high schools these students attend would not otherwise be able to offer these courses. The Texas Education Agency in cooperation with TI-IN, Inc., provides instruction and staff development opportunities to educators in Texas and other states.

The Illinois Education for Technology Employment project began using satellite technology as a means of bringing instructional programming directly to consortium sites. Five public school districts, one community college and one vocational school were involved in the project. These institutions were, as a result of budget limits, beginning to become increasingly unable to provide their students with instruction in select disciplines. Satellite technology offered one solution. It would, on occasion, be able to provide live interactive instruction on selected topics, and it would always be able to provide supplemental programming on a pre-recorded basis.

This consortium has taken the first step in applying technology to meet a need. They can now receive programming. The next step will be for these schools to begin broadcasting instruction to member sites. While that step at this time is still somewhat expensive, it is hoped the cost of transmitting instruction will be within financial reach in the near future. What is important is that these schools recognized the potential of technology and made the decision to utilize it.

Microcomputer Technologies

The microcomputer has established itself as an innovative and extremely useful technology in education. An example of the microcomputer as a teaching and learning tool is currently in place in the Palatine, Illinois, school district. In 1981 the Board of Education established a committee to explore the possible uses of microcomputers in the schools. Again the four aspects (planning, selection, teacher education, and evaluation) of technological implementation were utilized to help ensure success. Preplanning was started by this committee long before any computers were introduced into the classrooms, and the equipment selection followed a great deal of curricular planning and redesign. Teachers were included in every step of this planning, and the training required for a new technology was also planned at this early stage.

First, this committee drafted a plan that would incorporate three levels of computer competencies into the curriculum. Those competencies are (1) awareness, (2) literacy, and (3) proficiency. Each level was defined and specific goals and objectives were set. Classes were redesigned or initiated in business education, math, and computer science.

With the goals agreed upon and the course curricular outlined, the computer program grew each year as teachers became more proficient and equipment and software purchases were made. Over $200,000 was dedicated to the implementation of the curricular goals, used in five high school buildings for over 11,000 students. Equipment, primarily Apple, was purchased *after* software appropriate to the goals was selected.

The curriculum in each subject area was designed by teams of teachers from all the buildings cooperating in a summer curriculum project. Each summer, the district supported curriculum design and development projects as new courses or units were added. Teachers were also supported in their training needs. The district provided training in several ways: after school, inservice programs, in-school inservice sessions, and tuition support for university coursework in computing. All teachers were expected to achieve at least the first level of computer awareness, and were offered a four-hour course to assist them. Teacher education continues for new staff in the district.

So, to effectively use technology, the district first set curricular goals based on educational need. They trained teachers, cooperatively wrote curricula, and selected software all prior to equipment purchases. Finally, they routinely offered training and rewarded further coursework.

All this has led to a successful implementation of microcomputer use for teaching and learning. All students (100%) achieve level one, awareness. Over 50% of the students achieve level two, literacy. And between 25 and 40% of the students achieve level three, proficiency, learning to program in two or more languages. The curriculum innovation has been successful because of prior planning, informed purchases, and continued teacher education and involvement.

Laser Videodisc

The laser videodisc is an emerging technology that has been available since the late 1970's. This technology has only recently begun to show promise as an educational tool.

Two basic videodisc systems are available. One is a stand alone system. This system only requires a player and a monitor to view the disc. A second type of videodisc system is computer assisted. This requires the videodisc player be connected to a computer. The educator now has a computer assisted videodisc instruction system, or CAIV, and has the potential for accessing a variety of media formats including television, slides, and computer software. If this technology is to be used effectively in teacher education programs though, careful thought must be given to how it will be used, what attributes of the technology will best serve the instructional needs, and finally how it will be integrated into the curriculum.

The use of this new technology is virtually limitless. One videodisc can hold up to 54,000 images per side and any one of those images can be accessed in less than two seconds! Still pictures and motion can be combined on videodisc. Various K-12th grade classroom scenarios (on discipline for example) could be stored on a single disc, accessed and viewed in teaching foundations classes. Teaching skills examples (presentation techniques, questioning skills, non-verbal communication techniques, etc.) could be stored on disc for easy access and discussion in teaching methods classes.

Because the videodisc has the capability of combining various media, its attributes are tailor made for educators. It is easy to use, is relatively inexpensive, takes up very little space, and a good selection of software is beginning to be marketed by educators.

One final consideration before videodisc technologies can be effective in teacher education programs is that of curriculum integration.   A report (1987) by the American Association of Colleges for Teacher Education (AACTE) suggests that if new technologies are to be used effectively in public education, then training in the use of that technology needs to be incorporated into teacher education programs. The AACTE report (1987) further states there are "valuable uses of technology for programs in counseling, physical education and special education."

While laser disc may sound high tech, it is really simple to use and can provide teacher education programs with experiences in observation and evaluation of teaching skills and techniques.   Van Horn (1987) suggests all educators should become familiar with this technology.

Conclusion

With these four technologies as samples, a model of current technologies can be developed. This model includes (1) curricular needs analysis; (2) student and community needs analysis; (3) curricular objectives; (4) intra-district planning at all levels; (5) cooperative training of teachers prior to initiation; (6) regular evaluation and feedback; and (7) careful coordination of schools, schedules, software, and materials.

What role will teacher education programs have in making projects like these a reality? How will new technologies impact education? History, as has been shown, provides us with the problems and benefits of technology, the current examples show us what can be done now. The future will depend on learning from all these lessons and incorporating that learning into teacher preparation programs. Teacher education programs should lead the way if technology is going to be an effective change agent in schools.

In order to become an effective change agent teacher education programs need to adopt the following plan of action:

1.   Provide schools with research that supports the use of technology as a learning and teaching tool. This research should precede adoption of technology by educators.

2.   Adopt the use of these new and emerging technologies themselves. Teachers have a tendency to teach the way they themselves have been taught. If teacher education institutions are using technology

effectively then it follows elementary and secondary teachers will do the same.

3. Design teacher education programs that get away from the traditional text-book based lecture method. Snider (1987) agrees that the "biggest block in the use of technology is changing the current format of education."

Teacher education institutions need to begin taking the lead in technology utilization. Too often these institutions wait to see how or what society will do, or what the business community will do, or even what the public schools will do. This "wait and see" attitude needs to change. Universities and school districts need to encourage innovation rather than follow it.

It seems clear that technology has the capability to alter markedly the methods in which teachers are trained and students learn. What remains to be done is for educators to become active in bringing about this necessary change. Failure to do so will result in teacher education programs remaining static. Many of today's technologies have the potential to provide teacher educators with new and unique strategies for learning. It is important we begin incorporating these strategies into our programs. It serves no useful purpose to maintain the status quo.

The technological future of education does not have to repeat the lessons of the past. Instructional technologies have repeatedly shown educators the benefits and supportive attributes of the various instructional media. Recent projects involving technologies such as interactive and satellite television, laser discs, and microcomputers have all shown that technologies can be used to help students learn and teachers teach. The role of the teacher in all this must be defined and refined during the teacher education program. In order for technology to be adopted and to be beneficial, the teachers involved must be committed to the use of, and skilled in the operation of, the various technologies. Most importantly, a philosophy must be developed that encourages teachers to plan for and use all means, technological and methodological, to help students learn in ways that will prepare them to live and work in an increasingly complex, interdependent world.

References

AACTE Task Force on Technology. 1987. The challenge of electronic technologies for colleges of education. *Journal of Teacher Education* (November-December): 25-29.

Adams, Dennis M., and Mary Hamm. 1987. Artificial intelligence and instruction: Thinking tools for education. *T.H.E. Journal* (August): 59 -62.

Seeks to put AI in perspective. AI researchers have not developed machines that think, but have given us a tool to help us think. Classroom instruction can be aided by AI but we must still depend on humans for judgement, wisdom, and common sense.

Benson, Gregory M., and William Hirschen. 1987. Distance learning: New windows for education. *T.H.E. Journal* (August): 63 -67.

Distance learning (where the instruction occurs at a point distant from the learner and uses an interactive audio and/or video component) can be an innovative and inexpensive resource which can provide equitable learning opportunities for all people. The article examines several technologies useful in providing distance learning opportunities.

Bush, Robert N. 1987. Teacher education reform: Lessons from the past half century. *Journal of Teacher Education* (May-June).

Clark, R.E., and G. Salomon. 1986. Media in teaching. In *Handbook of research on teaching*, ed. M.C. Wittrock, 464-478. New York: Macmillan.

Reviews and critiques the media comparison research in instructional media. They analyze the results of past research and describe current changes in the research questions. The authors then discuss the way lessons of past media research effect future directions. Meta analysis studies are discussed. The authors recommend that before any technology is employed, the question "why this technology now" should be answered.

Corrigan, Dean. 1985. Politics and teacher education reform. *Journal of Teacher Education* 36 (1): 8-12.

A dozen noted proposals and models for teacher education reform have gone unimplemented, and he warns that if improved teacher education cannot be used in the workplace/schools, we will simply be producing more unhappy teachers. He provides suggestions for incentives to attract and keep high quality teachers. Among them are bonuses rather than merit pay; reduced class sizes; implementing new uses of technologies and others.

Evangelauf, Jean. 1987. School-reform drive spotlights colleges' education of teachers. *The Chronicle of Higher Education* (September 2).

This article examines the current state of teacher education in the United States and provides suggestions as to future direction. He indicates that nearly half of all teacher education institutions are undertaking new approaches to teacher education, and may expect major restructuring efforts in the next 3-5 years.

Gross, Lynne S. 1983. *The new television technologies.* Dubuque, Iowa: Wm. C. Brown.

While texts on new technologies age very quickly, this is still a useful explanation of the various television delivery media available in the 1980's. Chapters on cable T.V., satellites, videodiscs, videotext, lowpower T.V. and other technologies such as fiber optics and video games are included. A brief overview on economic and social concerns concludes the chapters. This is a clear and precise explanation of these technologies, with history and current issues for each technology discussed. A short glossary is included, and brief notes give references for further reading.

Heinich, R., M. Molenda, and J. Russell. 1985. *Instructional media and the new technologies of instruction.* New York: Wiley and Sons.

A comprehensive textbook designed for an introductory course in instructional technology, this text includes chapters on most commonly found media and their design and production. Included are audio, photography, multimedia, film, video, computers and new technology systems. The book takes a very systematic approach, and outlines each chapter, providing objectives and appraisal checklists for students as they read. Special features include examples of media, various "how-to" sections, flashbacks to the past, and a current lexicon of specialized vocabulary terms.

Keller, George. 1983. *Academic strategy: The management revolution in American higher education*, Baltimore: The Johns Hopkins University Press.

This book examines how colleges and universities can more effectively manage their programs. It suggests new strategies for administrators, and proposes an agenda for the future.

Kirman, Joseph M., and Jack Goldberg. 1981. Distance Education: Teacher education Via Live Television and Concurrent Group Telephone Conferencing. *Educational Technology* (April): 41-42.

Teacher education via live television and telephone conferencing is probably the ultimate in "distance education." It seems to be as effective as face-to-face instruction and can accommodate small groups at conveniently located centers. This article presents some realistic advice on preparations necessary for using live television as a training medium. The authors conclude that this mode of instruction is effective, but warn that the use of the technology must be weighted against costs.

Newsweek. 1984. Why teachers fail. Vol. CIV (September 24): 64-70.

Palaich, Robert. 1985. State actions to improve the teaching profession: What are the implications for teacher education? *Journal of Teacher Education* 36 1 (January-February): 50-51.

Robinson, Rhonda S. 1985. An investigation of technological innovation: Interactive television. Proceedings of the Annual A.E.C.T. Convention, Anaheim, Calif.

This article discusses in more detail the inquiry methods used to evaluate an interactive television project currently being used by four school districts to share classes. Included are several evaluation data collection methods appropriate to technology projects. The paper also discusses the successes of the project in its third year.

Saettler, Paul. 1968. *A history of instructional technology.* New York: McGraw-Hill.

This text reviews in some detail the history of instructional media, its research and its introduction into schooling. Each common media, from audio and radio to television, is discussed. Government support, federal research projects, and outcomes are all uncritically examined. This is an excellent historical review for an introduction to media in education.

Schramm, Wilbur. 1977. *Big media; little media.* Beverly Hills, Calif.: Sage Publications.

In this book Schramm presents the historical, pedagogical, and experimental evidence supporting the use (and misuse) of media in instruction. Research is summarized, projects are discussed, and the differentiation between "big" and "small" media is drawn. The author supports the use of less expensive and less "glamorous" technology for effective instruction, and provides his argument.

Simonson, Michael R., and Robert P. Volker. 1984. *Media planning and production.* Columbus, Ohio: Charles E. Merrill Co.

This text was designed to assist instructors and preservice teachers in their own planning and production of educational materials. Proceeding from simple to more complex, the text clearly explains the use, production, and delivery of instruction via audio, photography, film, video, microcomputers, and other media. Special features of the text include goal statements for each chapter, followed by objective, instructions on operation of equipment, production how-to's and examples.

Snider, William. 1987. March of school technologies proceeding–but slowly. *Education Week* (October 14).

Sununu, John H. 1986. Will technologies make learning and teaching easier? *Phi Delta Kappan* (November): 220-222.

Effective technologies for classroom use have been created but as a nation, we have not invented enough in research and development to learn how to make that technology useful to students and teachers. We don't know what works best. The article includes a variety of recommendations for technology use by the National Governors Task Force on Technology.

Valdez, Gilbert. 1986. Realizing the potential of educational technology. *Educational Leadership* 43 6 (March): 4-6.

Van Horn, Royal. 1987. Laser videodiscs in education; endless possibilities. *Phi Delta Kappan* 68 (9): 696-700.

Van Horn enthusiastically convinces us that laser videodisc technology is a medium that will play an important role in the education process. Ease of use, cost, life of disc, space requirements, depth of available resources and capabilities as a "computer peripheral" are among the advantages of the laser.

West, Peter, Rhonda S. Robinson, and Keith Collins. 1986. A teaching and telecommunications partnership. *Educational Leadership* 43: 6 (March): 54-56.

A brief article explaining one of the many local district uses of innovative technologies. Four school districts in rural Illinois connected via cable television teach several subjects live, interactively to high school students unable to receive these classes otherwise. The article explains the project, the equipment, and discusses the positive and negative aspects of this use of technology. Goals, planning, and the necessary teacher education are all highlighted.

A Futurist View:
Forces Framing the Future of Teacher Education Programs

Robert Alley

Teacher education students today are confronted with two realities as they look forward to their careers. First they will spend the majority of their professional lives working in the twenty-first century. Second, during the next decade the society and its attendant social, political, and economic institutions, including education, will change as much or more than as they did during the entire previous century. Such dynamism behooves teacher educators to address changes occurring in society to better prepare their graduates to cope and ultimately to be successful professionals.

Fortunately, help is available to teacher educators to analyze society, chart its expected trends, and to describe their effects upon the educational system. This relatively new science was developed by people from various disciplines, principally economics, sociology, anthropology, education, and the sciences. The collective work of these scholars has enabled a new discipline, futurism, to emerge.

The Trends

Eight selected trends from among many that have been identified by futurists as likely to have major impact on society will be highlighted. Following the discussion of the selected trends, and their implications for our educational system, especially for schools and teachers, the problems and opportunities teacher education programs will face will be explored.

Trend #1: Change from Industrial to Information Society

As far back as the early seventies, most futurists agreed that a fundamental change away from the industrial society was underway (Theobald 1976). Indeed, this change to an information or communications based society is often referred to as a revolution. Toffler (1980) described this revolution as the "third wave" in his book by the same name. More recently, the concept was popularized through the term "high tech" (Naisbitt 1982). Key elements of the revolution described by futurists include the following.

Communication systems. The revolution that futurists describe can easily be observed in our everyday lives. Contemporary communication systems such as the telephone, the television, the computer, or a combination of the three are used for such diverse activity as radar weather reports on television or interactive video disc learning materials for the classroom.   Other concrete evidence of the communications revolution can be seen around us in the form of neighborhood computer, video, or telephone stores which have replaced the corner gasoline station and the neighborhood grocery store of earlier eras as major influences in our lives.

Robotics. Robots are another example of the dominance of electronic systems in our lives. It is possible, for example, to buy a robot to do housework, or to deliver food from the central kitchen to a patient's room in a hospital. Robots, however, are most rapidly increasing in the manufacturing sector. Some 80,000 or more robots are expected to be in our manufacturing force by 1990. More than 60,000 of these will be in the auto industry (Naisbitt 1982, 48, 75). Robots in industry can be seen daily via television commercials where they are shown turning on and off an automobile's windshield wiper, opening and closing car doors, welding auto bodies, or doing other routine manufacturing tasks.

Job change. The communications revolution also means that in the 1970's only five percent of new jobs created in our economy were in manufacturing, whereas 90 percent were in the information, knowledge, or service areas (Birch 1981). Currently, about twelve percent of our work force is engaged in manufacturing (Naisbitt 1982, 5) down from twenty-eight percent in 1980 (Cetron 1983); at the same time 3.5 percent of the American work force is expected to be engaged in some form of education or training preparatory to the constantly evolving new jobs (Cetron and Appel 1985). The percentage of persons employed in manufacturing is expected to continue to decline.

   The electronic cottage.   More directly related to education, the electronic cottage has become a reality as a result of the communications revolution   (Wolfram 1984).   A computer can be available in virtually every home along with a television set. A linking of the two to the telephone system, and its satellite based transfer of information, permits instantaneous communication by voice, printed word, and/or picture throughout a society. Electronic mail systems are already a reality among universities, corporations, and public agencies. Gradually, the concept is being adapted for home use. Anyone with a home computer can subscribe to a service to receive specific information through a telephone-connected home computer. Stock quotations, catalog ordering, personal messages, sports news, and other information can now be exchanged via this process. Schoolwork or library services can also be available in the home through electronic mail systems.

Trend #2: Ever More Rapid Change

   Early in the last decade Alvin Toffler (1970) coined the term "future shock."   Second only to the communications revolution in its importance, the phenomenon he described continues to be evident in numerous ways. Some examples follow. One-third of the shelf items in the local supermarket were not there ten years ago. Nearly a thousand new books are published each day. There are nearly a quarter of a million words, out of a total of 450,000, in our present English language which Shakespeare did not know. Finally, fifty percent of today's factual, scientific knowledge is expected to be obsolete in ten years (Toffler 1980).

   Telescoping. Toffler also points out that this rapidity of change is further exaggerated by a telescoping effect. To illustrate the point, if the 50,000 years of man's recorded history is divided into average lifetimes of sixty-two years each, there have been approximately 800 such lifetimes (Toffler 1970, 14). Of these lifetimes the first 650 were spent in caves. Only in the last seventy lifetimes has it been possible to communicate from one generation to another by writing to one another. Only in the last six lifetimes did humans learn to use the printed word. Measuring time accurately has been possible only during the last four lifetimes. Only in the last two have humans used the electric motor. Finally, the overwhelming majority of the material goods we use in daily life today have been developed within the present, the 800th, lifetime (Toffler 1970, 14).

Further, it is expected that the next ten years will bring as much change as did the last forty years. This compression of change into ever shorter and shorter time spans is expected to continue.

Trend #3:   Rapidly Changing Institutional Roles

An important concept called "high tech" received a great deal of attention from both the press and the public in the early 1980's. Of special importance to educators, its corollary, "high touch," was also described but received less attention (Naisbitt 1982, 35-52). The point of the "high touch" concept is that wherever technology is developed, and flourishes, there is a counter-demand for more personalization of services. Witness the popularity of Leo Buscaglia (1972, 1982); his writings, personal appearances, and television programs about love provide solid evidence of the demand for high touch.

Self-Reliance. A second illustration of change in our institutions is found in the increasing emphasis on self-reliance in society (Naisbitt 1982, 143-174). Cottage industries are thriving. Midwives have grown in prominence, and natural childbirth is a common practice. At the same time, the "wellness movement" has become popular. In education there has been a growth in the home school movement. Credentialling of all types is being assaulted by those who demand a role within the system. Alternative certification proposals dramatically reducing or eliminating teacher preparation as a requirement for certification illustrate the point.

Decentralized government. Finally, there has been a decided move to decentralize and to further democratize government. Toffler (1975, 224-229) and Naisbitt (1982, 175-210) both describe this shift. Power and decision making are clearly being transferred from Washington to the state capitals and from the state capitals to the local community. Within the local community, the decentralization trend has been further extended to neighborhood groups which have received increased attention and power.

Decentralization is evident in education, too. Clearly, most states have reasserted their power over education matters vis-à-vis Washington. In Washington, reform of education has been largely rhetorical with little concrete action and too few dollars to support reform proposals. In contrast, although their performance to date is uneven, several states have taken steps to assure that reforms do occur in their educational systems.

Trend #4: Demographic Shifts

It is well documented that a significant population shift from the Northeast to the Sun Belt occurred during the past decade. What is less well understood is that the population expansion was primarily in the Southwest, on the West Coast, and in Florida (Bureau of the Census 1987). States and cities in those regions are experiencing a pattern of especially rapid growth although this trend has been slowed in some states by the current economic downturn for the petroleum industry. These demographic shifts tend to parallel the decline of the industrial society and its areas of primacy in the Northeast.

Mega-states. The large, growing states have sometimes been referred to as "super-states" or "mega-states." Specifically, California, Texas, and Florida have been so labeled (Naisbitt 1982, 244). These states are unique in that they are becoming increasingly independent of the remainder of the country for economic growth, trade, etc.   They also tend to develop policies counter to, or different from, other states.   The remaining forty-seven states tend to follow their lead in these matters.   The increase in size, power, and influence of the "mega-states" is accompanied by companion trends of population decline, aging population, and loss of power and prestige of the industrial states of the Northeast (Naisbitt 1982, 248).

Aging population. Another important demographic change is the graying of the population of the United States. Our population, in spite of the current "baby boomlet," is an increasingly older one. Today we have more people over fifty-five than we do in the school-age population (Bureau of the Census 1987). This also means that the population groups responsible for maintenance of the society through its taxes, leadership, etc. are a continually shrinking percentage of the citizenry as the over fifty-five group ages and moves to retirement. In the early 1980's, for example, the Social Security System had 3.2 workers per beneficiary as opposed to a 5.5 workers/beneficiary ratio in 1960 (OASDI 1985). As recently as 1950, by contrast, a ratio of 35:1 existed.   The figures demonstrate that this is a continuing trend.

Trend #5: A Multi-Option Society

Increasingly, options and variety in all facets of life are demanded by people in our society. The United States has become what is often described as a multi-option society. Nowhere is this trend more evident than in the marriage vs. career issue confronted by women in recent decades. Two decades ago women were thought to have made great strides when society acknowledged that they had the right to choose whether they would have a marriage or a career. Today that choice is not the issue. The demand among young women today is for a third option, both marriage and career.

Our multi-option society, sometimes referred to as the "Baskin and Robbins Society" (Naisbitt 1982, 260) because everything seems to come in thirty-one flavors, is clearly evident at the local supermarket. It can be enlightening to analyze the supermarket shelves in the breakfast cereal and hand soap sections. An astounding array can be found. Basically there is only one product in each section, cereal or soap. Yet society demands a proliferation of options in taste, texture, and color in breakfast cereals as well as the options of skin conditioning, smell, and bar vs. liquid among the hand soaps.

Trend #6: Changing Life Styles

Examples of the change in life styles abound. For example, a majority of children live in homes where the parent or parents work away from home. In 1985 54.5 percent of all women were working outside the home (Bureau of the Census 1987). More startling, seven of ten women in the seventeen to forty-five age group work outside the home (Education Week 1986, 22). Presently, only four percent of the family units in the United States fit the traditional pattern of homemaking mother, working father, and two children. As a result of the above factors, sixty-five percent of the children in the United States are "latch-key" children (*Education Week* 22, 1986). Each weekday morning, often long after the parents have gone to work, a van or bus picks up these children to whisk them off to a day-care center or school. In the afternoon the same vehicle returns the children to a house where no parent is present. These children spend several hours each day with no parental or adult supervision. The trend toward more "latch-key" children will continue with 58.9 percent of the women in the United States expected to be working outside the home by 1995 (Bureau of the Census 1987, 376)

Job changes. Other changes of a more revolutionary nature are expected in our future life styles. Only a small percentage of people will be in paying jobs outside the home shortly after the turn of the century. Entire industries and businesses will disappear from the scene. Millions of persons in our population are expected to shift roles and become self-employed entrepreneurs in one- or two- person cottage industry businesses (Wolfram 1984, 34). As an example, a person developing computer software for sale to others can now develop, copy, package, and distribute those programs at home. Such persons are excellent examples of the combination of the cottage industry concept of the past with the communications revolution of the present to create new forms of employment for the future. Made possible through communication links incorporating the computer and the telephone, the net result of these changes is that increasing numbers of adults will turn to schools, job-training programs, or community resource programs for education or training to make career changes and/or to enhance their life styles.

Trend #7:   Link-up of Medicine and Education

Although we are in the early stages of this particular trend, the most significant effects are probably still in the future. Potentially it could be the most significant of the changes in terms of impact upon our educational system. Three examples are especially noteworthy.

Chemical transfer of knowledge. Experimentation of a crude nature wherein chemical injections are utilized to transfer knowledge from one animal to another has been carried out with lower animals as subjects (Pines 1973). Rats were taught to find their way through a maze. Then chemicals were taken from their brains and injected into other rats thereby enabling the second set of rats to more easily find their way through the maze to demonstrate the feasibility of such a learning process. Early excitement regarding the possibility of transference of memory from organism to organism by chemical injections was not justified, and such research has largely been shelved. Current research has gone in other directions although limited research similar to that discussed by Pines continues (Smith 1985, 72). Memory transfer research utilizing chemical injections is presently mostly limited to the immunobiology field with researchers attempting to determine the processes by which immunity is transmitted from cell to cell following immunization.

Biochips. A second research front has been established because it is now recognized that the brain functions through electrochemically transmitted neurons (Haddon and Lamola 1985) leading the more recent research to be directed toward understanding the electrochemical processes by which electrical impulses in the brain may be utilized to transmit memory. Under development is a microchip or so-called "biochip" which can be implanted in the human brain permitting the instant transfer of knowledge from computer storage banks to the human brain (International Resource Development, Inc. 1984). Early experimentation on this brain/computer link is now under way through use of laser-guided weapon systems in the military.

Increased life span. Finally, the education/medicine linkup, as represented by the development of the bionic man or woman who may have numerous artificial and/or transplanted organs or body parts, or who may be immune from many current diseases, may well result in an increased life span that extends far beyond anything we now envision. For example, some believe the life expectancy for a newborn in the late 1990's may be as much as 150 years (Cornish 1984).

Trend #8:   Increasingly Pluralistic Society

The number of people from our minority cultures is rapidly increasing. We are nearing the time when a majority of the population in the growth states will be from minority cultures. Indeed, certain cities in the Southwestern United States already find that to be true among the school-age population (Cetron, Soriano, and Gayle 1985). Increased numbers of Hispanic and Asian immigrants and differential birth rates among various ethnic groups are the principal reasons for the present minority growth pattern. Indications are that the pattern will continue and become stronger in the future.

Implications for Education

Futurists tell us that our future is determined by the choices we make today. This axiom must be understood by teacher educators so that they will realize that their future is not predetermined. At no time in our history have teacher educators had a greater array of choices. In simple terms, they can decide to support and actively develop certain trends thereby increasing the chance that those particular ideas will become reality for the future, or they can oppose them and decrease the likelihood of their development. For example, teacher educators could decide to consciously employ more technology in delivering future teacher education programs and thus promote the information revolution. Some universities are adopting such strategies for the future by developing computer-based curricula or using satellite delivered, interactive television courses. But neither society nor education, as a whole, has yet made the necessary commitment to take an active role in shaping future trends. Presently education is responding to the trends rather than planning the direction of the trends themselves.

Changes Projected for Education

Educational changes resulting from technological, economic, and social changes can be projected to include many new forms of education, awareness of individual needs, new strategies for motivation, and life-long education among others. The most important changes are discussed below.

Values. To respond to revolutionary changes in a responsible manner a society must determine if these changes are consistent with the values of its majority. Consequently those persons who oppose value-oriented curricula in schools are destined to fight a losing battle. For a democratic society there really is no alternative to a curriculum which helps students formulate their own values if the society is to make intelligent decisions concerning its future (Burdin, Nutter, and Gips 1984).

Life-long education. With a projected increase in human life-span, a decline in employment outside the home, a rapidly increasing older adult population, and rapidly increasing minority and immigrant populations, a birth-to-death educational system designed to serve the needs of all segments of society becomes a necessity. The current practice of treating education as though it is merely schooling for ages 5 to 18 and little else is outmoded as is the notion that education only occurs between 8:00 a.m. and 5:00 p.m., nine months of the year.

Day care centers and preschools along with adult learning centers will become public functions central to the educational process because society will insist upon an educational system where anyone, at any age, can find the education and/or training necessary for a productive life. An increasingly technological society demands a better educated, better trained, and periodically retrained populace to succeed.

New forms of education. Some have suggested that nothing short of razing school buildings will permit society to restructure education and to develop an educational system adequate to meet the future needs of the society. Others have argued that educational systems are incapable of making the needed adjustments to survive in the twenty-first century (Faure 1972). However such extremes are likely to give way to less radical views of the current condition. According to more moderate thinking new environments, new institutions, and new strategies make education more responsive to the needs of twenty-first century youth. Educators, assisted by leaders of other professions and business, may well generate wholly new approaches to teaching and learning in response to the need for a reformed educational system.

For example, as the electronic cottage with its computer, interactive video system and/or other electronic media becomes more common, it will be imperative that the society recognize that education is more than those experiences for which the school is responsible. Educational opportunities are everywhere in the community. With teleconferencing the community can be the whole world. There is no reason to restrict learning to the "school" or to the typical 9 a.m. to 4 p.m. day in the educational system of the future.

Schooling practices developed to meet the needs of the dominantly agrarian society of the seventeenth and eighteenth centuries in the United States will give way to other forms of schooling as citizens continue to demand learning options. Time, i.e., school is 9 a.m. to 4 p.m., five days per week for 36 weeks per year; place, i.e., school is a specific set of rooms in a specific building; delivery mode, i.e., teachers are supposed to impart knowledge; and rigidly structured schedules, i.e., students all study math at 9:30 a.m. and social studies at 10:00 a.m., will all give way. Such practices will be replaced by an educational system which is need-specific for students, learner driven, based upon learning options developed to meet individual student goals and, above all, flexible. The challenge to teachers will be to assist their students in sorting out the knowledge which can be most effectively learned through electronic systems from that which requires the presence of a teacher in a classroom setting. As a first step, a delivery system where students learn basic knowledge through electronically-based instruction thus permitting personal contact with faculty to be reserved for those times when discussion of significant ideas, synthesis skills, counseling, or other forms of direct contact is necessary (Hoyle and Johnson 1987).

In the educational system of the future the central teaching function may change dramatically. At the extreme, through the teaching/medicine link described earlier the knowledge imparting function of teaching may give way to brain implants or "bio-chips" (International Resource Development Inc. 1984) or to chemical injections to transfer memory from one person to another (Pines 1973). Through such processes students could almost instantaneously acquire the knowledge and skills which now take months or years to learn. Teachers would at last be freed of the drudgery of teaching low-level cognitive skills. But even if these radical changes do not take place, a number of other significant changes are occurring as a result of our interaction with technology. These changes will afford teachers time to concentrate on more advanced cognitive skills such as application and synthesis of knowledge or to focus on the affective aspect of learning (Burdin, Nutter and Gips 1984).

"High touch." In describing the "high touch" concept Naisbitt (1982, 35-52) calls our attention to the fact that technology isolates people from one another. Others have pointed out that contemporary cultural trends such as certain types of dancing, use of walkman radios, television, and video games do the same thing. The point of the "high touch" concept is that technologically based activities create a need for human interaction. The need is for warmth, support, and physical contact. Providing for this will entail fundamental changes in the schools. As pointed out earlier, knowledge and low-level cognitive skills will be transmitted to students through computer programs, interactive video systems, etc. Direct teacher-to-student interaction will be reserved for the development of high-level cognitive processes such as synthesis or evaluative skills, improved communication skills, and enhanced thinking skills as well as affective processes which enhance the development of self-worth, understanding, empathy, and other traits best gained through direct human contact (Goodall and Bunke 1980).

To summarize, futurist thinking suggests that schools will continue to exist and to serve the society as will teachers, but both schools and the role of the teachers will undergo radical changes over coming decades.

Changes Produced by Economic Factors

A second set of revolutionary changes in the educational system will be produced by the economic impact of technology. As the information revolution continues, manufacturing will be restructured and millions of people currently holding jobs in the industrial sector will be replaced by robots (Cetron and O'Toole 1983, 243). Unless these workers are retrained or have otherwise acquired the skills necessary to be productive in an information society their chances for finding new jobs will be slim.   Some will become self-employed entrepreneurs delivering services to individuals, businesses, or industry from small shops or often from their homes; others may be unemployable because of their inability to adapt to the changes. As expected layoffs and job eliminations occur, millions of adults will seek retraining for new jobs, counseling to adjust to the disruptions in their lives, and perhaps to explore avenues to more profitably use the increased time they find they have available.   Talk in the past was of the retooling of American industrial plants.   "Today the talk is of retooling American workers, American schools, and American Training Systems" (Cetron and Appel 1985, 116).   As a result, renewed interest in and a vastly increased emphasis upon adult education appears likely for the future.

Motivation. Educators would do well to remember that the children of the adults described above will also need an educational program adapted to the radical changes posed by the communications revolution.   Teachers will find themselves increasingly challenged by students who hold fatalistic attitudes because they see little value in education when it cannot be tied directly to a future vocation.   The result may be a decreased emphasis upon the work ethic and a corresponding rise in antisocial behavior as the work place changes.

Motivation will become an increasingly important concept. Teachers who are capable of engendering high levels of motivation for learning by means other than the traditional "carrot-and-stick" approach   will be sought.   Grades as motivators may be deemphasized or perhaps, come to an end. The current emphasis on behaviorism may become outmoded, or at least reexamined and refined.   Motivational strategies based upon sensitivity to individual needs and learning styles with an emphasis on self-reliance will be demanded.   Self-motivation will become the goal for students.

Life-styles. One positive effect of having fewer people employed away from home is the possibility of the emergence of new life styles. If the economy of the United States continues to grow as expected, some families may have the luxury of establishing life styles very different from present practice (Best 1980). For example, when children are small, both parents may have the opportunity to stay home to devote significantly more time to rearing children. Later, either parent may go back into the work force on a part-time or full-time basis while the other continues to rear the children and perhaps do volunteer work in the community. Similar options will be open to single parents. An intermittent pattern of work, nonemployment, and further schooling may well become the norm for the future (Best 1980).

Diverse Cultures. Schools of the future must also face the need to extend past efforts to successfully teach culturally different children. The need is illustrated by a case in point from the school system of a medium-sized city in the Midwest. In that school system a survey of the first languages spoken by the 40,000 plus students in the system was conducted in the early 1980's. It was found that forty-two different languages or major dialects were spoken. Such cultural diversity is an asset to society, but both society and schools in the United States need to recognize this. As American society continues to diversify, multicultural curricula and teaching materials will become increasingly important components of the educational process.

Futurism as curriculum. The ability of people to understand and cope with change and with the future itself is critical if society is to respond effectively to the trends described earlier. Curriculum materials and teaching specialties to foster understanding of and adaptation to the rapidity of change and the ideas of futurism are likely to gain in importance. Fortunately, some school systems have already begun to develop such curricula and the necessary teaching materials to accompany them. However, developmental activity may be needed.

The Futurist Teacher Education Program

Forward-looking teacher educators can take the various social, economic, and educational trends previously discussed and project them into the future. From such projections an accurate picture of teacher education in the United States, as it can be expected to emerge a decade or more hence, can be developed. Through such a process teacher educators can determine needed revisions in both preservice and inservice programs in preparation for what might be appropriately described as the Futurist Teacher Education Program, one specifically designed to best serve society in the twenty-first century.

Much of the change in futurist teacher education programs will be in adjusting to the fundamental trends described earlier. But certain basic processes within teacher education programs themselves will also change. Both types of projected changes are described in the remainder of this chapter. They are discussed in no particular order.

Certification practices. The rise of "mega-states" which are so strong as to be able to ignore national or federal trends (Naisbitt 1982), combined with the drive for options and self-reliance (Naisbitt 1982) and a trend toward localized control of government (Toffler 1975), will impact teacher education programs through certification and accreditation practices. The so-called "bellweather states" (Naisbitt 1982) provide a glimpse of likely certification practices for the coming decade or beyond. The "mega-states," Florida, Texas, and California, are particularly influential states for studying the future of teacher education. From their lead the following projections provide prudent guidelines which futurist teacher education programs might follow.

The attempt by the Carnegie Forum on Education and the Economy (1986) to establish a process for national certification of teachers has received considerable attention, but it is a development counter to contemporary political trends. Those trends suggest that it is highly unlikely that the "mega-states" will give up their constitutionally granted control of certification to adopt a set of national certification standards, much less give up their power to directly certify and thus control those who may become teachers for their schools. However, the Carnegie group has substantial resources at its command to promote a national plan for certification as well as to develop it. What is presently unclear is whether they can overcome the chauvinistic tendencies of the various states and create a true national certification process or whether their effort will result in, at best, another voluntary national accrediting agency competing with the present National Council for the Accreditation of Teacher Education (NCATE). That the Carnegie group is a major threat to NCATE is very clear. NCATE may not survive as the national accrediting agency for teacher education.

The most reasonable projection would be that there will probably be a mix of state plans. Some states will adopt the Carnegie standards as their own and accept certificates from one another on a reciprocal agreement basis. Others, most notably the "mega-states," are more likely to continue with their own certification standards and accreditation processes, perhaps borrowing liberally from the Carnegie group's research as well as from elsewhere, but continuing to insist that their requirements are superior to those of the Carnegie states. To assume that individual states will give up control of their educational system, as expressed through certification and accreditation, is somewhat naive. The practices which resulted from fear of federal control of education in past decades when substantial sums of money were at stake provide a clear picture of the extremes to which the various states will go to protect their sovereignty.

Teacher shortages. Projected shortages of teachers may have more influence upon certification practices than either research data or the efforts of the Carnegie Forum, especially when combined with the twin demands for personal options and self-reliance. The net result of the interaction of this particular combination of factors is likely to be the further development of so-called alternative certification programs. The argument that teacher education programs are excessively rigid and more interested in producing credit hours than in developing quality teachers provides a beguilingly simple solution to the teacher shortage. Reduce the credit hour requirements for professional education, and more liberal arts graduates will choose to become teachers, it is argued. The widely heralded New Jersey alternative certification plan (Cooperman and Klagholz 1985) and the mandated 18 credit hour limit on professional education courses in teacher education programs in Texas (SB 994 1987) are examples.

For futurist teacher education programs three considerations will be of particular importance and perhaps will even determine which programs survive. First, a careful balance must be struck between the essential concepts needed to prepare quality teachers and the number of professional education credit hours required in teacher education programs. Second, teacher educators will more and more need to sell their programs as necessary preparation for a successful career in teaching as opposed to relying upon the state certification process to set requirements which demand that students enroll for extensive professional education credit. Careful attention to the expectations of school administrators and to the needs of students in the program will be necessary. Increasingly, teacher education programs may find themselves in the same position as private schools. Just as private schools must convince parents that there are clear and compelling reasons to enroll their children with them, future teacher education programs must convince college students that clear and compelling reasons exist for completing a non-required teacher education program prior to becoming a teacher. Third, formal teacher education programs may not be required. In response, successful teacher education programs will very probably develop a series of alternative programs so that potential students may select a program which best suits their needs. Alternative teacher education programs such as those developed in recent years by Memphis State University (Center for Excellence in Teacher Education 1987) provide a model for futurist programs to emulate.

It is clear that the next decade will be one of great turmoil for both certification and accreditation processes. Teacher education programs will be thrown into the political arena as debate regarding issues of control, quality, and even the very existence of teacher education continues.

Teachers of diverse ages. Increased numbers of preschool teachers will be needed in the future to accommodate the growing numbers of children attending day care centers or preschools. Parents will insist upon the opportunity for their children to have structured learning experiences while they are employed outside the home or are pursuing further education or training for themselves. On the opposite end of the age spectrum an ever expanding adult population will also create a demand for more teachers. The reasons are twofold. First, increased numbers of adults will have significant free time and will seek educational programs to prepare for constructive use of their time. Second, large numbers of adults may seek job retraining to cope with layoffs and job eliminations that result from the "high tech" revolution. As a result of these factors many more adult educators will be needed for the future. And, contrary to current practices, these adult educators will need education and skills that go far beyond the vocational skills typical of today's adult and vocational programs. Skills in human relations, counseling, and motivation will be in demand for adult programs.

To summarize, it can be projected that a significant increase in numbers of professionals prepared to teach either the very young or adults will be needed by the educational system as society demands more and varied learning situations. Developing quality teachers for such an educational system will provide futurist teacher education programs with a significant challenge. The current practice of treating both early childhood education and adult education as appendages to the main body of teacher education must cease. Preparing teachers for elementary and secondary classrooms will continue to be central to teacher education, but far-sighted teacher education institutions will redesign their programs to also prepare significant numbers of new teachers for both preschool and adult programs.

Redefined teaching. It can be projected that the previously discussed trends will free teachers from much of the drudgery of teaching for knowledge transmission and permit them to concentrate on other badly needed human skills and attributes such as those identified by Goodall and Bunke (1980). These include enhanced communication skills, quality interpersonal relationships, and improved thinking skills.

As part of this redefinition of teaching, students in schools of the future will be permitted to acquire their basic knowledge at home, elsewhere in the community (world), or in the school itself at virtually any time of the day or night through the application of the electronic cottage concept to schooling. With such a schooling concept learning is neither site nor time bound. It can literally take place anywhere at any time (Ishler 1980).

The task confronting futurist teacher educators will be to develop programs which provide teachers with the ability to separate those parts of human learning which can be most efficiently transmitted to students through technological processes from those which demand human interaction. Teacher educators of the future will seek to prepare their students in such a manner that their skills and abilities become those associated with "high touch" and/or other forms of teaching which demand face-to-face interaction between a teacher and students. Teacher educators will be expected to help their students learn to teach such skills as human warmth, motivation development, values clarification, moral development, and higher order thinking. The redefining of teaching away from knowledge transmission to higher order thinking and affective learning will be a basic challenge for futurist teacher education programs. Unfortunately those teacher education programs that do not make such radical changes will leave their graduates as vulnerable to displacement by electronic processes as today's assembly line workers are to robots. Simply stated, in the future those teachers who can be replaced by electronic gadgets will be!

One additional note on redefining teaching. An important function of the futurist teacher education program will be the modeling of traits and skills that teachers are expected to exhibit. Empathy, critical thinking and motivation development are examples. Teacher educators will be expected to model these traits for their students. Modeling will be a major responsibility for teacher educators whether they are school-based or are in the colleges and universities.

Use of time. Wise use of leisure time has been a major goal of the American educational system for decades; future projections suggest an even greater need for productive use of time, leisure or other. The twin realities of fewer people in traditional jobs and longer life spans will permit, or perhaps even force upon people, increased time available for activities other than those related to making a living (Best 1980). As society seeks to cope with this change, leisure time specialists, recreation promoters, life-style specialists, or possibly other education-related occupations may emerge. Such possibilities provide teacher educators with the opportunity to create an entirely new set of education professions not unlike the library/media specialist or the counselor who represent new professions that emerged in the past due to the changing needs of society (Burdin, Nutter, and Gips 1984).

Redefined curriculum. An educational system reflecting societal needs of the twenty-first century will produce a number of changes in curriculum (Shane 1973, 1977). A dramatically expanded use of the community (world) as a learning resource, increased utilization of volunteers to assist with the teaching process, and the teaching of theories of change and futurism as curriculum concepts will be three important changes that can be expected. For teacher education programs, the most vital point is that these changes will demand skills of teachers that current programs do not teach at all or, at best, to which too little attention is given. In response to these demands it can be projected that teacher educators will develop components within their programs to assure that future teachers possess the skills and knowledge necessary to more effectively use the community as a source of curriculum along with the ability to effectively use community volunteers to enrich and strengthen the curriculum. They will also develop materials and teaching strategies designed to enable teachers to work with students to help them understand societal change and its impact upon their lives.

Student teaching sites. In current teacher education programs the environment in which student teaching takes place is most often determined by faculty convenience, the quality of cooperation that the teacher education institution receives from the local school system, the availability of cooperating teachers nearby, or cost and level of inconvenience experienced by the student teacher, factors which have little to do with the quality of the learning environment. With a high percentage of student teachers placed in suburban or rural areas under current practice, student teaching sites which guarantee that student teachers will have an opportunity to work in a multicultural, multiethnic environment are the exception rather than established practice. Future teacher education programs must reverse this trend. Every graduate of a futurist teacher education program should be prepared to successfully teach in a school where the student body reflects the increasing diversification society is now experiencing. Redesigning student teaching to assure experience working in multicultural environments is necessary for teacher education if it is to be relevant in the future. Here is a very real opportunity for teacher education programs to positively influence the quality of the educational system of the future.

Summary

This chapter began with a description of eight trends identified by futurists as influencing today's society and schools. The resulting changes present and will continue to present both challenges and opportunities to teacher education programs. However, the teacher education profession still has time to help shape or influence many of the trends and/or their resultant impact upon the education system or upon schools in particular. The question is whether or not the teacher education profession will be successful in meeting this challenge. If successful, it will be because teacher educators study the trends and their impact upon society and take steps to influence twenty-first century education. Waiting for the arrival of the new century will be too late.

References

Bell, Daniel. 1973. *The coming of the post industrial society.* New York: Basic Books.

Best, Fred. 1980. *Flexible life scheduling.* New York: Praeger.

Subtitled, <u>Breaking the education-work-retirement lockstep</u>, this work encourages individuals to treat their time as though it belonged to themselves instead of someone else. It is essentially a compendium of possible schedules for education, work, and leisure in options for future lifestyles which may emerge as the economic and social structure of American society changes.

Best, Fred. 1973. *The future of work.* Englewood Cliffs: Prentice-Hall, Inc.

Birch, David L. 1981. Who creates jobs? *The Public Interest* 65 (Fall): 3-14.

A summary of Birch's study in which he used the computer to analyze millions of individual companies to determine their job creating patterns. Because he did not use more conventional macro-analysis of employment patterns, his data is considered more reliable. He also has a new work entitled: *Job creation in America: How our smallest companies put the most people to work,* published by Macmillan, 1987.

Burdin, Joel, Norma Nutter, and Crystal Gips. 1984. Inventing the future: Options and strategies for educators. *Action in Teacher Education* 6 (Fall-Winter): 7-13.

These educational futurists have pointed to the necessity to teach values if we are to realistically confront the future. This particular work also suggests a number of possible new education-related occupations and roles for teachers which may emerge in the future.

Bureau of the Census. 1987. *Statistical abstract of the United States.* Washington, D.C.: Government Printing Office.

Burgliavello, George. 1984. Hyperintelligence: The next evolutionary steps. *The Futurist* 18 (December): 6-11.

Buscaglia, Leo. 1982. *Living, loving, and learning.* New York: Fawcett Columbine.

Buscaglia, Leo. 1972. *Love.* Thorofare, N.J.: C.B. Slack.

> Preaching a steady gospel of love in print, on television, and in personal appearances Buscaglia has become a faddish, almost cult-like leader for millions who have come to agree with him that human problems are solved best by loving one another more fully.

Carnegie Forum on Education and the Economy. 1986. *A nation prepared: Teachers for the 21st century.* Report of the task force on teaching as a profession. Washington, D.C.: The Forum.

> See this report for the basic Carnegie proposals.

Center for Excellence in Teacher Education. 1987. *Graduate level teacher education programs.* Memphis: College of Education, Memphis State University.

> In the wake of the excellence movement the College of Education at Memphis State began developing a series of programs to serve the needs of diverse populations seeking to certify as teachers. This particular work is a description of two graduate-level programs, one an MAT and the other a certification only program.

Cetron, Marvin, and Marcia Appel. 1985. *Jobs of the future.* New York: McGraw-Hill Book Company.

> Subtitled, The 500 best jobs and where they'll be and how to get them, this work analyzes trends in the job market within American society, the impact of technology on those jobs and the outlook for basic job categories. The authors also give tips to be followed in job searching in today's high tech oriented market.

Cetron, Marvin, Barbara Soriano, and Margaret Gayle. 1985. Schools of the future. *The Futurist* 19 (August): 19.

Cetron, Marvin. 1983. Getting ready for the jobs of the future. *The Futurist* 17 (June): 15-22.

Cetron, Marvin, and Thomas O'Toole 1983. *Encounters with the future*. New York: McGraw-Hill Book Company.

Clarke, Arthur C. 1973. *Profiles of the future*. New York: Harper and Row.

Commission on Population Growth and the American Future. 1971. *Population and the American future*. New York: New American Library.

Cooperman, Saul, and Leo Klagholz. 1985. New Jersey's alternate route to education. *Phi Delta Kappan* 66 (June): 691-695.

  An explanation of the intent and implementation plans for the New Jersey certification plan by the authors of the plan itself.

Cornish, Edward. 1984. Undernutrition may be key to longevity. *The Futurist* 18 (June): 63-64.

Cornish, Edward. 1979. The future of the family. *The Futurist* 13 (February): 45-58.

Cornish, Edward. 1977. *The study of the future*. Washington: World Future Society.

de Brigard, Paul. 1970. *Some potential societal developments 1970-2000*. Middletown, Conn.: Institute for the Future.

Dede, Christopher. 1985. The future of school libraries. *School Library Media Quarterly* 18 (Winter): 18-22.

Traditional families–A dying breed? 1986. *Education Week* (14 May): 22.

  This particular article describes contemporary family patterns as well as the continued changes in family structure in the United States.

Enzer, Selweyn, Dennis Little, and Frederic D. Lazar. 1972. *Some prospects for social change by 1985 and their impact on time money budgets*. Middletown, Conn.: Institute for the Future.

Fitch, Robert M., and Cordell M. Svengalis. 1979. *Futures unlimited*. Washington: National Council for the Social Studies.

Goodall, Robert, and Clinton R. Bunke. 1980. Planning the future of teacher education: Reflections and projections. *Action in Teacher Education* 2 (Summer): 25-30.

Gordon, Theodore, and Robert Ahment. 1969. *Forecasts of some technological and scientific developments and their social consequences*. Middletown, Conn.: Institute for the Future.

Haberman, Martin, ed. 1986. Evaluating alternative certification. *Action in Teacher Education* 8 (Summer): 1-74

Haddon, P.C., and A.P. Lamola. 1985. The molecular electronic device and the biochip computer: Present status. In *Proceedings of the National Academy of Sciences*. 1985. Washington, D.C.: National Academy of Sciences.

Hoffer, William. 1986. Taking social security private. *Nation's Business* 74 (July): 30-34.

Hoyle, John R., and Glenn R. Johnson. 1987. The 21st century professor. *The Futurist* 21 (December): 26-27.

  The authors detail projected changes in the delivery system for higher education at the turn of the next century and beyond

International Commission on the Development of Education. 1972. *Learning to be: The world of education today and tomorrow*. Faure, Edgar, ed. Paris: UNESCO.

  This study points to rapidly increasing costs to maintain the world's education systems combined with steady learning rates as the basic problem which may cause educational systems throughout the world to collapse early in the twenty-first century. The Commission recommends the development of educational technology to save the educational systems.

International Resource Development, Inc. 1984. *Non-keyboard data entry*. Norwalk, Conn.: International Resource Development, Inc.

Ishler, Richard, ed. 1980. A look at education in the year 2000. *Action in Teacher Education* 2 (Summer): 24.

In this work a number of teacher educators speculate upon the direction of teacher education to the year 2000. Ishler summarizes key points regarding the future of teacher education programs.

Kahn, Herman, William Brown, and Leon Martel. 1976. *The next 200 years.* New York: Morrow.

Naisbitt, John. 1982. *Megatrends.* New York: Warner Books.

Summarizing and focusing the work of many other futurists into a very readable yet provocative description of the radical changes occurring in our society. Naisbitt examines what he calls the ten major transformations taking place in society. He argues that the ten trends are so powerful that they actually create other trends. Therefore they are megatrends.

Old-Age, Survivors, and Disability Program (OASDI). 1985. *Annual report of the board of directors.* Washington, D.C.: Government Printing Office.

Pines, Maya. 1973. *The brain changers.* New York: Harcourt Brace Jovanovich, Inc.

This book summarizes decades of brain research including the works of James McConnell and others on transmitting memory from the brain of one animal to that of another.

Rocks, Lawrence, and Richard P. Runyan. 1972. *The energy crisis.* New York: Crown Publishers, Inc.

SB 994. 1987. Texas Legislature (June).

Shane, Harold. 1973. *The educational significance of the future.* Bloomington: Phi Delta Kappa Educational Foundation.

Shane, Harold, ed. 1977. *Curriculum change toward the 21st century.* Washington, D.C.: National Education Association.

Smith, Roberta. 1985. Memory transfer in planaria. In *The Ohio Journal of Science*. Columbus: Ohio Academy of Science.

Theobald, Robert. 1976. *Beyond despair*. Washington, D.C.: New Republic Book Co.

> One of the earliest scholarly works to clearly describe the social phenomena now known as the communications revolution or the information society.

Toffler, Alvin. 1980. *The third wave*. New York: Morrow.

> The first wave was agriculture; the second was the industrial revolution. The world is now in the middle of it third great wave or revolution in which the industrial civilization is dying to be replaced by a new form of civilization where technology and information are the sources of power.

Toffler, Alvin. 1975. What is anticipatory democracy? *The Futurist* 9 (October): 224-229.

Toffler, Alvin. 1970. *Future shock*. New York: Random House.

> Probably the most significant piece of popular literature written about the future; in it Toffler calls attention to change as a major force in our lives through discussion of concepts such as the death of permanence, transience, and novelty. He also discusses human adaptability and suggests strategies appropriate for coping with the future.

Wolfram, Tammara H. 1984. Working at home. *The Futurist* 18 (June): 31-34.

> At the time of publication of this article Wolfram was project director of the National Association for the Cottage Industry (NACI), headquartered in Chicago. In the article she discusses the many obstacles entrepreneurs face as they develop home-based businesses. The electronic cottage is one type of cottage industry discussed.

Where Have All the Futurists Gone?

Linda S. Tafel

As the First Global Conference on the Future opened in Toronto in July 1980, those who gathered acknowledged the two themes that would guide dialogue throughout the rest of the decade. On the one hand, futurists described the emergence of a new civilization in which humanity and institutions would take a quantum leap forward. Change was seen as positive and manageable. On the other hand, careful observers of social institutions predicted an accompanying "paralysis of imagination and will" which could lead to the confident expectation that change was temporary and that the future, by and large, would continue the present (Toffler 1980, 10-11).

As the decade draws to a close and the reform movement in teacher education is analyzed, the significant role that futurist thinking has played in shaping reform may be overlooked. However, both the initial and somewhat awkward embrace of futurists' thinking and the subsequent rejection of fundamental futuristic assumptions were important benchmarks in determining what the eventual focus of the reform movement would be. The purpose of this chapter is to examine the tensions between futurists' thinking and the thrust for reform in teacher education and to address the question, "Where have all the futurists gone?"

The Rise of the Futurist Movement

The futures movement traces its origins to the time of the emergence of a uniquely different Western Civilization at the beginning of the sixteenth century. The tradition of attempting to reconcile opposite or contradictory images of what the world might be lies at the center of the futures movement at its inception. Following World War II, the field of technological forecasting broadened from a consideration of military problems to a concern for societal futures in general.

Beginning in the late 1960s, "think tanks," futures organizations, and journalists recorded worldwide interest in futures research.

Certain leaders of the futures movement in the United States (Toffler 1971, 1974, 1980; Ferguson 1980; Harman 1979; Theobald 1981) extended the optimistic vision of the future to include a reexamination of the purposes and practices of schooling and education. Since the primary focus of futures research is image-formation and the analysis of long-term alternative futures, possibilities for educational endeavors for the twenty-first century were clearly a "hot topic" among futures scholars as the 1980's began.

There was initially much support for this timely exploration of "alternative futures" related to education. Futurists were predicting a fundamental shift from an industrial to an information society (Toffler 1980). The implications of an accompanying paradigm shift, a fundamental change in the way we view the world, was explored by Ferguson (1980). In addition to the works of scholars, popular writers such as John Naisbitt (1982) presented a compelling argument for a reexamination of institutions in light of changing technological and human advances. The mismatch between current schooling practices and the needs of learners in the next century were made clear. Criticism for current schooling practices in light of future considerations was abundant.

Several futurists presented cogent criticism directed at educational institutions and their approaches to learning. Kauffmann provided an overview of these criticisms:

> Futurism questions traditional education on two grounds. First, traditional methods of education tend to produce individuals who are psychologically ill-equipped to cope with a society undergoing continual rapid change. Second, the content of the traditional curriculum is designed to fit the student into the existing society, in spite of the fact that the society more accurately the succession of societies which the student will live in will be quite different--a case of trying to hit a moving target by aiming at it where it is now, rather than where it will be. (1976, 8-9)

Extending this argument, Botkin and others defined learning as the "process of preparing to deal with new situations" (1979, 8). Hence, the type of learning appropriate for the twenty-first century could be characterized as "innovative learning" which has the key characteristics of anticipation and participation (Botkin et al. 1979, 10-13).

The Role of Reconstructionism in Futurist Thought

As the decade of the 1980's dawned, futurists were examining how existing models of school, teacher education, and learning could be altered to more nearly reflect a futuristic perspective. Those futurists who proposed to restructure society through education reclaimed the philosophy of reconstructionism as articulated by Theodore Brameld. By 1956 Brameld was already convinced that America and the world were "passing through one of the greatest periods of transformation in the history of mankind" (1956, 3). Our deepest problem, Brameld suggested, was to learn how to move forward toward the future rather than backward toward the past. For twenty years, from the mid-1950's until the mid-1970's, Brameld continued to articulate his reconstructionist philosophy which he claimed was "distinctly future-looking" (1971, 23). The time had come, he claimed, to reinterpret and respond to contemporary problems through schooling: "the reconstructionist throws in his lot unequivocally with those who believe . . . that only thoroughgoing transformation of principles and institutions is any longer possible or suitable" (1971, 357).

Brameld's reconstructionist philosophy found its roots in the strong traditions of the progressive movement. Dewey, Counts, and Brameld all attempted to define the fundamental purposes of education. Early on in his career, Dewey outlined what he thought was the integral relationship of the school and society: "I believe that education is the fundamental method of social progress and reform" (1974, 457). Later, he articulated the appropriate role for the school in a democracy:

> As a society becomes more enlightened, it realizes that it is responsible not to transmit and conserve the whole of its existing achievements, but only such as make for a better future society. The school is its chief agency for the accomplishment of this end. (1916)

Extending Dewey's philosophy in the 1930's, Counts asked whether the school would remain reactive to the whims and wishes of society, or whether the school would be the

primary force in building a new social order. He saw the
school as a potentially effective instrument for giving
expression to social forethought and wisdom (Counts 1930).

These important earlier ideas were expanded by
educational futurists in the late 1970's and early 1980's who
wished to carry out the work of educational reconstructionism.
There seemed to be a consensus about the role of the school in
bringing about fundamental social change. Dede concluded
that "While futurists may differ on their views of desirable
programs and the use of technology, all agree that education is
the most crucial, central force in shaping what the future will
be" (1979, 15).

Educational futurists initially set about examining
existing schools. They criticized the "transmissive" design of
school which, they claimed, had resulted in "spectatorism,
consumption, and competition in the classroom," all of which
reinforced "an industrial, middle-class myth of deferred
gratification" (Bowman et al. 1978, 71). Not only did they offer
criticism, they proposed new paradigms of learning,
broadening education beyond the context of the school
(Ferguson 1980, 279-321). Bowman and others presented a
model for education which attempted to implement the
reconstructionist philosophy. This conceptualization reflected
the following key ideas:

> Education must be an institution for planning
> desired change . . . . The traditional dual role of
> education is as a source of manpower allocation
> equated to life itself and not considered preparation
> for life. Education is, therefore, synonymous with
> lifelong learning. Learning must also be
> participatory--social change priorities and parameters
> of choice must be part of the the 'curriculum' of the
> future. (Bowman et al. 1978, 136)

Futurists not only applied the reconstructionist
principles in their analysis of schools, but also questioned the
appropriateness of teacher education programs.

Futurists and Teacher Education

An earlier analysis (Tafel 1982) revealed that there was a
fundamental contradiction between the goals for education
identified by the futurists and those reflected in models for
teacher education. An examination of the typical teacher
education program at the beginning of the 1980s indicated that:

1. The thrust of teacher education programs had been and continued to be that of socializing preservice teachers into the profession and perpetuating the status quo.

2. The elements of the typical teacher education sequence–subject matter, pedagogy, practice teaching–had remained relatively unchanged since the Normal School era.

3. The fundamental goals for teacher education had remained unsettled and ill-focused (Zeichner 1983); however, the profession had become increasingly standardized in its approach to credentialing. The controlling agencies were effective gatekeepers for the profession.

4. The profession had studied itself, been studied by others, and been severely criticized. However, the preoccupation with maintaining the status quo seemed to override any significant attempts to make fundamental changes in either the form or substance of the teacher education curriculum.

As the 1980's began, the opportunity to explore a fundamental reconstruction of teacher education programs existed. Futurists were urging a close look at programs and those within institutions were seeking clarity about the purposes of teacher education. Zeichner, for instance, provided a strong argument for exploring alternative paradigms of teacher education. He urged a reexamination of the "beliefs and assumptions about the nature and purposes of schooling, teaching, teachers and their education" (1983, 3).

How did the profession respond to the challenge to think futuristically? There is clear evidence that the teacher education profession continued to dwell on issues related to "which procedures and organizational arrangements" were most appropriate–the "whats" and "hows" of teacher education rather than the "whys." The "questions of which educational, moral and political commitments ought to guide" teacher education remained unanswered (Zeichner 1983, 8). The old debates over the amount of liberal arts background for education majors, the role of clinical experiences as part of preparation programs, the sequence and arrangement of course

work, and the length of preparation programs continued
(Corrigan 1982). Two crucial questions were ignored: What
should be the goals for schooling in the twenty-first century?
How can teacher education programs prepare teachers to meet
these goals?

By 1984 the opportunity to discuss fundamentally new
directions for teacher education had passed and teacher
educators were seemingly overwhelmed by a perceived need to
respond quickly to the public outcry for reform. Rhetoric
shifted toward admitting shortcomings and offering "quick fix"
proposals for reform. Clark's "modest" proposal for "basic
structural reform" stressed many of the Holmes Report
recommendations, namely the requirement of a bachelor's
degree with a subject-matter major prior to pre-service study
and practice leading to a master's degree in education and the
revamping of pedagogy based on "research on teaching and
teacher effectiveness" (Clark 1984, 120). The perspectives of
futurist thinking with regard to both schooling and teacher
education had been consumed by present concerns to react,
respond, and retreat to old ways. Any possibility for
reconstruction of education seemed doomed.

Schooling, Teacher Education, and Change

In his book, *Schooling in America*, Seymour Sarason
notes, "it is one thing to become aware of alternatives; it is
another to examine them seriously" (1983, 148). He continues
by saying, "whether one is dealing with an individual or an
organization, the pressure to change, to consider unfamiliar
alternatives, is on a collision course with the quest for
certainty" (152). What is it about alternatives, about change,
about unlimited possibility which caused those associated with
schooling and teacher education to become "stuck . . . as
nostalgic anachronisms who hunker down and cling to the
past" (Deal 1985, 323)? Perhaps a partial answer lies in an
examination of the culture of schools and teacher education.

In 1930 Barnard described culture as a "social friction"
created by people to give meaning to work and life (cited in
Deal 1985, 301). Deal adds that culture "provides stability,
fosters certainty, solidifies order and predictability, and creates
meaning" (301). An examination of the culture of schools
reveals that they are remarkably similar in both context and
content and that the culture of teacher education assumes that
teachers will continue to be prepared for schools as they
presently exist. As Sarason notes, "the traditional way of
viewing schools requires the assumption that it is impossible

to achieve the goals implied . . . except through schools as we know them" (1983, 149). It is difficult to imagine something other than schooling as schooling because this would mean transcending the barriers of the past and present to create a hypothetical culture which would provide the same supporting network as the one we have always known. While the "universe of alternatives is greater than [we] customarily think," "to consider [the] unfamiliar is on a collision course with the quest for certainty" (Sarason 1983, 148, 152).

The retreat in the face of the possibility of reconstructing schooling and teacher education is not surprising. Deal (1985) discusses change as a "loss" concept. Since change shatters reality and alters our relationships with people and objects, we deny the existence of change. We bring control to bear by looking for structure. Sarason says we "desire . . . to judge any uncertainty by the criterion of certainty or predictability, i.e., the degree to which it provides a blueprint, or a road map that clearly tells how things will look and how one will be able to go from here to there" (1983, 152). Since "what if" models or scenarios often cannot stand the test of instant practicality, they are often dismissed as unworkable. This was precisely the challenge which futurist thinking offered. The measure of a "good" idea was one which was based squarely on shared beliefs and values. Measures of practicality and do-ability were to be secondary considerations. Nonetheless, the "presentists" and pragmatists prevailed; the reconstructionist agenda was replaced by a revisionist outlook.

The Restructuring of Schooling and Teacher Education

Revisionists, those persons in the futures field who worked within institutional structures and programs, subscribed to the notion that while teaching and learning would be occurring in some changing contexts, schools, as we know them, would remain–at least for the short term future. In theory, revisionists felt that working to make small changes during the larger transformation of society was better than making no changes at all. Revisionists were criticized by reconstructionists in the futures movement for bringing past and present values into the future. Reconstructionists feared that revisionists would be dangerous in offering cosmetic rather than fundamental change within present institutions.

In order to determine if the changes in schooling and teacher education have, indeed, been as "fundamental" as the reconstructionists would have advocated, we need to look beyond the buzzwords of reform: phrases such as "fundamental restructuring" (Schlechty 1987) and "basic structural reform" (Clark 1984). Such rhetoric seems to indicate significant change–but a closer look reveals several "old" assumptions about schooling and teacher education.

About schooling:

*learning content and acquiring knowledge is the student's most important role
*learning is measurable and demonstrable
*a prescribed curriculum is best
*skill training is important to meet the needs of business and industry
*in academics, more is better

About teacher education:

*teacher is transmitter of "dominant" cultural values and subject matter
*there is a prevailing "most appropriate way to teach"
*liberal arts work is separated from the professional sequence
*there is a hierarchical, top-down power structure in the profession
*credentialing is the goal

These examples demonstrate that revisions in schooling and teacher education have resulted in little change that is either fundamental or basic. Traditional assumptions about both schooling and teacher education remain firmly in place. A consideration of "the matrix of beliefs and assumptions about the nature and purposes of schooling, teaching, teachers and their education that gives shape to specific forms of practice in teacher education" (Zeichner 1983) has not been accomplished. Instead of engaging in "critical rationality" which is "characterized by wide-ranging skepticism as well as grounding in logical argument and empirical data," the thrust of teacher education programs will continue to be "technocratic rationality–a mode of reasoning, investigation or planning that gives priority to considerations of procedure or technique" (Cornbleth 1987, 515). Unfortunately, the reform movement has effectively narrowed the focus of thinkers to the content and substance of existing school and teacher education programs. "The irony . . . is that, by deflecting attention from questions of purpose and substance and their social and political implications, [technocratic rationality] precludes the institutional reform that it claims to further (Cornbleth 1987, 515).

Sarason has said, "We can never underestimate two processes . . . the effectiveness with which we have been socialized to view the world in particular ways and the extraordinary difficulty in taking distance from the consequences of our socialization" (1983, 152).

Toward a More Optimistic Future

In the tradition of the futurists, it is important to take a stance of hopeful realism about the current reform movement. Sarason (1983) has noted that "We dearly want to believe that the problems of schools have solutions . . . " (153). However, he continues, we are recognizing "that we have reached the point when what's learned in school and what's needed to live life is unbridgeable" (162). Our problems–with schooling and with teacher education–lack clear-cut, sure-fire solutions.

While we look for signs of stability, we are surrounded, as the futurists declared, by increasing complexity and diversity. Schooling is not schooling anymore. The ideal of the teacher education program must not ignore the reality of today's classrooms. As Patterson, Purkey and Parker note, the old assumption that there is one best way to teach for maximum educational effectiveness has to be replaced with the new assumption that there are a variety of situationally appropriate ways to teach that are optimally effective (1986, 8). These authors offer a helpful perspective for those involved with schooling and teacher education in a "nonrational" world. Their admonition that we need to accept "change, ambiguity, and crisis . . . [as] a normal state of affairs" (111), represents a proactive stance toward change and planning.

More important than "what we know" about schooling and best practice may be "what we see" when we visit schools today. Futurists warned us about taking our past with us into the future. The best way to plan for the future is to look closely at the present. The danger of thinking we <u>know</u> something for sure about <u>how</u> to teach ignores the fact that <u>who</u> we are teaching will change dramatically in the next few decades. Multiple models of teaching, experiences within a wide variety of carefully chosen clinical settings, and a careful, reflective analysis of teaching styles and strategies are crucial if the aim of teacher education is to shift away from socialization. Teachers in preparation need, as the futurists claimed, to anticipate change and participate in changing programs to meet their needs. While research reveals some answers, it also raises questions about whether what "worked" with third graders in a hand-picked suburban elementary school will "work" as well or is even appropriate for other groups of students in suburban, urban, or rural settings. The teacher education student must, like the futurists, link what one finds out to what she already knows, sort out the inconsistencies, make connections, and raise questions. In short, the teacher education student must think--about our profession, about change, and about possibilities.

Where have all the futurists gone? At a recent professional meeting the answers to this question were varied. Some discussants pointed to themselves and say, "We're still here!" Others thought that futurists were hard at work, subverting efforts to "standardize everything about schooling and teacher education." Still others claimed that all futurists headed for California and were never heard from again. As the discussion became a bit more serious, there was a consensus that futurism is alive and well–especially in the hearts and minds of those who are actively involved in both schooling and teacher education–learning and using new strategies for setting goals, making decisions, planning, distributing power, structuring organizations, leading organizations, and thinking about teaching (Patterson, Purkey, and Parker 1986).

References

Botkin, James W., Mahdi Elmandjra, and Mircea Malitza. 1979. *No limits to learning.* Oxford: Pergamon Press.

The authors identify the "human gap" as the distance between the growing complexity of life and our capacity to cope with it. They offer a new definition of learning-- a new approach to both knowledge and life that emphasizes human initiative. The book offers a convincing argument that our conventional patterns of "maintenance/shock" learning are inadequate.

Bowman, Jim, Fred Kierstead, Chris Dede, and John Pulliam. 1978. *The far side of the future: Social problems and educational reconstruction.* Houston: Education Section of the World Future Society.

The reconstructionist view toward the future of education is documented in this volume. The authors dismiss present schooling models and sketch possible alternatives which question the basic assumptions of present-day schooling models.

Brameld, Theodore. 1971. *Patterns of educational philosophy: Divergence and convergence in culturological perspective.* New York: Holt, Rinehart and Winston.

Brameld, Theodore. 1956. *Toward a reconstructed philosophy of education.* New York: Holt, Rinehart and Winston.

Brameld's work raises fundamental questions about the relationship between schools, society, and individuals. Critical elements of the reconstructionist philosophy are presented here.

Clark, David L. 1984. Better teachers for the year 2000: A proposal for the structural reform of teacher education. *Phi Delta Kappan* 66 (October): 116-120.

Among the first to call for "basic reforms," Clark's proposals contain many of the themes of the Holmes and Carnegie reports. His perspectives are valuable in illustrating the focus on debates about form rather than substance of teacher education programs.

Corrigan, Dean C., ed. 1982. *The future of teacher education: Needed research and practice.* College Station, Tex.: Texas A & M University, College of Education.

Cornbleth, Catherine. 1987. Knowledge in curriculum and teacher education. *Social Education* 51 (November-December): 513-516.

  A lively discussion of knowledge as discussed in the Holmes and Carnegie reports. The author offers alternative conceptions of knowledge that seem to offer more possiblity for substantive reform of education.

Counts, George S. 1930. *The American road to culture.* New York: John Day.

Deal, Terrence E. 1985. Cultural change: Opportunity, silent killer, or metamorphosis? In *Gaining control of the corporate culture,* eds. R. Kilmann, M. Saxton, and R. Serpa, 292-331. San Francisco: Jossey Bass.

  Many of Deal's ideas about change as "loss" are developed in this article. His vivid descriptions of typical "coping" strategies are excellent examples of what happens when a school culture is affected by major change.

Dede, Christopher J. 1979. Educational technology: The next ten years. *World Future Society Bulletin* 8 (November-December): 1-8.

Dewey, John. 1916. *Democracy in education.* New York: Macmillan.

Dewey, John. 1974. My pedagogic creed. In *John Dewey on education,,* ed. Reginald D. Arhambault, 437. Chicago: University of Chicago Press.

Ferguson, Marilyn. 1980. *The Aquarian conspiracy: Personal and social transformation in the 1980s.* Los Angeles: J.P. Tarcher.

  The author's compelling treatment of learning raises many important questions about what schools and teacher education programs do to encourage or retard students' ability to think futuristically. A rereading of the book nearly a decade later reveals enormous "advances" in some social areas, but not in education.

Harman, Willis W. 1979. *An incomplete guide to the future.* New York: W.W. Norton.

Kauffmann, Draper L., Jr. 1976. Futurism and future studies. Washington, D.C.: National Education Association.

Naisbitt, John. 1982. *Megatrends.* New York: Warner Books.

Both this book and his 1985 *Reinventing the corporation* (with Patricia Aburdene), written in journalistic style, encourage the reader to further explore futures research. Emerging ideas about what positive approaches to change can achieve are highlighted in the second volume.

Patterson, Jerry L., Stewart C. Purkey, and Jackson V. Parker. 1986. *Productive school systems for a nonrational world.* Alexandria, Va.: Association for Supervision and Curriculum Development.

A theoretically sound, yet wonderfully practical book about "educating in an era of change." Excellent perspectives on how use change to make needed reforms in schooling.

Sarason, Seymour B. 1983. *Schooling in America: Scapegoat and salvation.* New York: The Free Press.

A thoughtful, reasoned treatise on the rising criticisms against education. Sarason's indictments of present schooling practices can provide a focus for planning for change.

Schlechty, Phillip C. 1987. Schools for the 21st century: The conditions for invention. Unpublished manuscript.

Tafel, Linda S. 1982. A curriculum design for teacher education programs based on futures research. Unpublished doctoral dissertation. DeKalb, Ill.: Northern Illinois University.

Theobald, Robert. 1981. *Beyond despair*. Cabin John, Md.:
Seven Locks Press.

   The closing chapter, "Creating change" provides a
helpful primer for all who seek to make changes from
the "grass roots." The authors suggestions for redefining
the roles of teachers and for de-credentialing the
teaching profession are compelling.

Toffler, Alvin. 1971. *Future shock*. New York: Bantam
Books.

   A rereading of Toffler's classic indicates the value of
forecasting and prediction. Relatively few of the
sweeping changes which deal with education have
"come true," however. Provocative, even today.

Toffler, Alvin. 1974. *Learning for tomorrow: The role of the
future in education*. New York: Random House.

   Philip Werdell's chapter on the reform of higher
education is especially pertinent as we assess changes
which have occurred as a result of the reform
movement.

Toffler, Alvin. 1980. *The third wave*. New York: William
Morrow.

   Toffler's analysis of changes in Second Wave
institutions is particularly revealing as we "take stock"
almost a decade later. While homes have not become
"electronic cottages," the author's discussion of schools
as institutional dinosaurs is amazingly accurate, given
the response of public schools and higher education to
the challenges of the eighties.

Zeichner, Kenneth M. 1983. Alternative paradigms of teacher education. *Journal of Teacher Education* 34 (May-June): 3-9.

The author describes the assumptions and priorities which distinguish four paradigmatic approaches to teacher education from one another. This is a useful article for exploring where programs are and where they might be. The author poses five questions to guide debate about the proper content and focus of teacher education programs.

PART II.

REFORMING TEACHER
EDUCATION: NEW DIRECTIONS

New Directions In Teacher Education: Which Direction?

Walter C. Parker

Common sense is not so common after all. If it were, the *National Enquirer* would have no audience and as many people would turn out for local elections as for ball games. And were it more common in teacher education, teacher preparation programs would not enroll more students than they could educate well, their faculties would be composed of model teachers, and longitudinal data on their students would be abundant.

My subject in this chapter is common sense in teacher education. Its apprehension is no small task. Assistance was found in cultural anthropology where common sense is treated as a *cultural system*. As such, it shares attributes with other cultural systems (values, myth, art, epistemology). Like them, common sense is constructed socially, has a history, and can be questioned, disputed, affirmed, formalized, and taught. What distinguishes common sense from the other systems is the unspoken premise from which its authority obtains–that it presents reality in a nutshell; that it is an account of things which strikes at their heart.

Geertz (1983) specifies several properties of common sense, and three of them were applied to a search for common sense in teacher education. The first is *naturalness*. This is the matter-of-fact quality of common sense: People with their head screwed on straight can see that such and such is true. Naturalness provides the confident tone that marks assertions of common sense, like those that opened this chapter. Such statements could be (and often are) preceded by "of course" or "obviously," phrases that match verbally common sense's subverbal conviction.

A second characteristic of common sense is *practicalness*, not in a pragmatic and utilitarian way, but as in the everyday, fend-for-yourself, street-smart heuristic. Common sense tells the novice to wise up: "to be prudent, levelheaded, keep his eye on the ball, not buy any wooden nickels . . ." (Geertz 1983, 87). A third characteristic is *literalness*. The supposed wisdom of common sense is not regarded by those espousing it as anything at all esoteric. Rather, it is just simply there, written on the surface of things and concealed only from those too dumb or too clever for their own good. Geertz illustrates:

> It takes a while (or, anyway, it took me a while) to absorb the fact that when the whole family of a Javanese boy tells me that the reason he has fallen out of a tree and broken his leg is that the spirit of his deceased grandfather pushed him out because some ritual duty toward the grandfather had been inadvertently overlooked, that, so far as they are concerned, is the beginning, the middle, and the end of the matter: it is precisely what they think has occurred, it is all that they think has occurred, and they are puzzled only at my puzzlement at their lack of puzzlement. (89)

By applying this analysis of common sense to teacher education, I was not attempting to treat teacher education as though it were a culture but to help ferret out from the literature on teacher education modal ways of thinking about problems in that field. Developed first in a subfield, social studies teacher education (Parker 1988; Banks & Parker in press), they are here refined and extended to teacher education across subject areas.

Those who write on teacher education in the United States generally have concluded that it remains in a very sorry state. I have not found a writer who takes issue with the claim that teacher education is "largely arbitrary, technical, fragmented, and without depth" (Lanier & Little 1986, 554). But this conclusion generally is put forward as reasoned judgment, not as common sense. Advanced as common sense, however, are the *explanations* given for the sorry state of teacher education, particularly the often unstated normative claims, or ethics, in teacher education.

Three are elaborated and illustrated here. Briefly they are: teachers should study the academic subjects they will teach (the ethic of cultural initiation); teachers should study methods for bringing about student learning of those subjects (the ethic of effective pedagogy); and, teachers should scrutinize the activity of teaching (the ethic of critique). Others were found, but their presence in the literature was slight and they will not be considered here. In the descriptions that follow, I endeavor to preserve the common-sense tone of each ethic.[1]

The Ethic of Cultural Initiation

Education has been called an initiation into the great human conversation--an initiation into a partnership of knowing and inquiring (Oakeshott 1962). While occurring the world over, this conversation is bound by culture. Education conceived as cultural initiation is thus an introduction of a culture's new members to its traditions of knowing–its inventory of ideas as well as its ways of understanding and inquiring (Kerr 1987).

If this is the purpose of schooling, then what is the purpose of schooling *everybody*, as this society aims to do? The argument is a moral one: A society that holds the ideal of democracy as its basic organizing principle must educate everyone. In a society seeking to maintain and enhance democracy, universal education is no frill. It is a condition of survival. Government of, by, and for the people presupposes a people who are knowledgeable and who are committed to democratic ideals; it presupposes a citizenry that is, in a word, virtuous. Lacking virtue, citizens are better suited to totalitarian rule where they are expected only to obey public policies, not make them. The moral argument for universal education in turn is embedded in a cultural one, since what a people value, whether the ancestral justice of the Javanese family or the due process of law cherished in the United States, assumes a cultural context in which those particular values are comprehended and shared. To have values, indeed to have a mind, as Richard Peters put it, "is not to enjoy a private picture-show or to exercise some inner diaphanous organ" (cited in Kerr 23); rather, it is an achievement of cultural initiation.

This vision of initiating all children into a common democratic conversation has been sharply undermined in recent decades. Who or what is the culprit? Chairwoman Lynne Cheney (1987) of the National Endowment for the Humanities has been explicit. Citing evidence on the deplorable state of high school students' knowledge of history and literature (Ravitch & Finn 1987), Cheney blames what she calls *process*. Process is a code word for "the belief that we can teach our children *how* to think without troubling them to learn anything worth thinking about." It is the belief "that we can teach them how to understand the world in which they live without conveying to them the events and ideas that have brought it into existence (1987, 5). What has gone wrong with education in the United States? Immersion in process has replaced cultural initiation as the aim of education.

It is not difficult to trace the spread of this belief to education professors and their philosophies: instrumentalism and formalism. What are these, and how did they arise? It should be helpful first to consider what they replaced. Gone is the mental discipline model, according to which the act of studying certain subjects was itself good for the intellect. Study basket weaving and the mind goes to mush; study Latin, Plato's *Dialogues*, and Euclid, and it becomes lean and facile. Once this belief was overturned empirically (Thorndike 1913), advocates of classics education had lost a primary rationale for an education that had students study a common curriculum. The door was thus opened for John Dewey's (1910, 1916) progressivist mischief: instrumentalism.

Instrumentalism provided curriculum planners with a new selection criterion–a new answer to the question, What knowledge is of most worth? It diverted their attention from the knowing into which all children should be initiated and focused it instead on contemporary social conditions and the present life interests of the individual child. Core curriculum patterns established by blue ribbon committees of arts and sciences scholars in the late 1800's were overturned by committees of educators in the early 1900's (Ravitch 1985). Overturned was the earlier commitment to democratizing knowledge by distributing it to *all* children, and the consequence was the fragmented curriculum that today typifies the American public school. Captured well in phrases like ability grouping, child-centered education, and the smorgasbord curriculum, the new curriculum was devoted to tailoring education to the perceived real-life needs and wants of individual students. This is a philosophy that reveres relevance, electives, and Rousseau's romantic notions of childhood made notorious in Neill's *Summerhill*. It is sacrosanct in schools of education today.

The new curriculum priorities have become so popular with education professors that those who argue for a common knowledge base are "dismissed as reactionaries, out of touch with the times and with the findings of modern pedagogical science" (Ravitch 1985, 128).

Instrumentalism was not the only weapon used against a common cultural initiation for all. Another was the exaggeration of the importance of skills instruction–what

Hirsch (1987) calls *educational formalism*. This philosophy conceives of cultural knowledge not as specific content but as "a set of techniques that can be developed by proper coaching and practice" (p. 110). Promulgated in our schools of education, the skills fad has overtaken a proper consideration of the content on which these skills are to be put to use. It is accompanied by a pejorative view of memorizing facts which has arisen from the popular worry over the "Third Wave" and the "information age" (e.g., Toffler 1980). This view, which pervades rhetoric on teaching higher order thinking skills (e.g., Baron & Sternberg 1987), holds that the world beyond the schoolhouse requires not factual recall but inventive thinking; consequently, little is to be gained by sentencing students to twelve years of trivial pursuit.

But the view is wrong. Educators' distaste for memorizing facts is "more pious than realistic" (Hirsch 1987, 30). One cannot think without information, and participation in cultural discourse requires a storehouse of *common* information. Life is no private picture show; literacy is a *social* phenomenon. Without a common network of background knowledge, children cannot make sense of what they are asked to read and think about in school. Without that knowledge, they are initiated not into a common culture but into a cycle of failure. Prevented from acquiring the very information that would enable them to make further progress in reading and thinking, they are summarily dismissed from the human conversation. Begun early in the primary grades, the amassing of the common storehouse of cultural content is most manageable and lays the foundation needed for academic success in later years; not begun early, critical cultural bonds are dissolved, democracy is threatened, and the disadvantaged are kept where they are—down in the lower tracks of the school and, later, the labor force.

The sort of teacher education needed, therefore, is one that prepares teachers to convey to their students a common body of knowledge and ways of knowing needed to participate in and contribute to the culture of the society where they live. It follows that this preparation should be concentrated on the rigorous study of the academic subjects they will teach. Time spent in schools and departments of education—especially in pedagogy courses—is time wasted on the very philosophies that caused the mess we now face: students who know far too little about the important cultural content that is needed to be partners in the great human conversation, *and a fragmented curriculum that promises more of the same.*

Teacher education faculties should wise up to their fixation on child-centered education, reading and study skills, higher order thinking, individualized education, learning styles, and the rest of this content-void shibboleth. What matters, and what future teachers need most, is not the piling on of pedagogic knowledge, but of academic knowledge that is itself the content of the needed initiation.

The Ethic of Effective Pedagogy

To the contrary, it is the cultural initiators' who are fixated. Their attention is centered on academic knowledge, which they treat with the awe and mysticism normally reserved for precious stones and deities. It is a fixation afforded by not having spent much time in schools.

Educators' knowledge base (pedagogy) is not thought to amount to much by those who suffer "physics envy" (Gould 1981)–those whose idea of epistemic integrity is drawn from the ivy towers of the physics hall. Hirsch's field is English, Ravitch's is history, and their disparaging view of pedagogy is wholly consistent with the historically low regard academic faculty have for faculty in the applied fields on campus, such as nursing, social work, and education (Judge 1982). Nevertheless, pedagogy **is** a field in its own right, complete with a knowledge base built up with empirical data, theorizing, canons of inquiry, and wisdom of practice. Accustomed to snubbing by their colleagues in the arts and sciences, pedagogues understand that education entails far more than the selection of content.

Recent responses to Hirsch by pedagogues are illustrative. Tchudi (1988), for example, notes that Hirsch confuses content and learning. He "seems to take the existence of texts themselves as evidence that youngsters actually learned the material in them . . ." (73). This is a glaring error and, Tchudi adds, one that few teachers, administrators, or others who actually work in schools are likely to make. In his response, Yinger (1988) uses linguistic analysis to explain how the initiators' argument falls short. To be culturally literate, they (the initiators) argue, is to have the culture's vocabulary. But just as the acquisition of words is necessary but not sufficient for speaking a language, so is the acquisition of a people's vocabulary insufficient for participation in their conversation. Conversation is more than words. Needed too are semantics and pragmatics–a shared network of meanings and an intricate sense of when, where, and how to use words in a way that is culturally appropriate. I know very well that enchiladas should be smothered in a tomatoless sauce made primarily of ground red chiles, preferably from the Chimayo Valley in New Mexico. Moreover, I know how to make an enchilada sauce that isn't bad. But I also know not to launch into this discussion here. Non sequiturs are at the heart of incompetence; as Whitson (1985) reminds, nothing is quite so incompetent as an algorithm that is executed competently in the wrong time or place.

In short, content is necessary but not sufficient. Pedagogues are well aware that material "taught" is very often not "caught." And for this reason they know that treating low scores on examinations simply as a *curriculum* deficiency undermines any sober attempt to deal with the problem of low scores. Pedagogues' attention thus shifts, as it must, to where the problem lies–to learning and instruction. Their attention turns from the question, 'What content should be taught?' to a companion question 'What instructional practices might increase student learning of that content?' Pedagogues are not naive about the content-selection problem. As Yinger notes, initiators are on target as far as they go, but they do not go far enough. They are helping us figure out what knowledge is of the most worth, but not how to help children learn it. Pedagogues know that educational problems cannot be reduced to a content problem in spite of Cheney's attempt to do precisely this.

The logic of effective pedagogy is perhaps best expressed by Goodlad (1984). Like Ravitch, Hirsch, and Cheney, Goodlad laments the little attention paid to K-12 content in recent years, and he spells out the effects: large school-by-school variation in children's access to knowledge rather than the democratic distribution of a common curriculum on which democracy relies. Unlike the initiators, however, Goodlad's analysis does not end here. He examines also the unequal access to knowledge *within* schools and thereby takes up the pedagogues' "taught but not caught" concern. Instruction *does* make a difference, but only a portion of our students have access to the better instruction. Making matters worse, most likely to be denied access to the better instruction are poor and minority students (see also Cummins 1986 and Oakes 1985).

The priority of the ethic of effective pedagogy is thus the propagation of instructional practices that are likely to increase student learning of the selected content. Clearly, differences abound within this ethic: compare Hunter's (1982) controversial model to Shulman's (1987) wisdom-of-practice studies. But the concern for effective instruction is the theme that binds them together. Let us examine three variations on this theme: mastery learning, wisdom of practice, and favorite method.

The central question of the mastery learning approach, according to Bloom (1984), is "What methods of group instruction are as effective as one-to-one tutoring?" Pedagogues who are interested in this question are impressed by data indicating that the many students who do not learn well the selected curriculum suffer from unfavorable conditions of learning, not from low intelligence. The proof offered up for this claim is that the average student in a tutorial setting, where conditions of learning are optimal, outperforms 98% of the students in a conventional classroom, where conditions are typically least favorable. By any measure, this is a striking difference, with an effect size of two sigma.

These pedagogues focus on empirical studies that spell out just what these favorable conditions are, and then endeavor to convey them somehow to future teachers. Being realistic, they understand that the favorable conditions that easily obtain in a one-to-one teacher-student ratio cannot be reproduced in the one-to-thirty ratio of a classroom. But they can be *approximated*, and there the promise lies. Specific instructional practices that make tutorials so successful can be, to a degree, transferred to the classroom: frequent and specific feedback and correction, clear cues and explanations from the teacher, and high levels of student participation and time spent on learning tasks. Furthermore, powerful instructional practices can be developed in classrooms that take advantage of the group setting, for example, cooperative learning. Used in combination, these favorable conditions can transform the conventional classroom into what Bloom calls a mastery classroom. There the average student outperforms 84% of the students in the conventional classroom. The point is that more students can learn more than they are now, and the difference lies in the alteration of classroom conditions by teachers. As Brophy put it, "the key to improvement has been to concentrate on developing knowledge about effective teaching and translating it into algorithms that teachers can learn and incorporate in their planning prior to teaching" (1980, 3).

Pedagogues of the wisdom-of-practice orientation are less sanguine about the desirability of identifying powerful instructional practices and then training teachers to implement them. It is not, they argue, that such conditions cannot be specified, but that teachers are not empty conduits through which research findings can be delivered unadulterated to classrooms. Teachers are subjects, not objects. Like everybody, they have interests and and inventory experience, neither of which are inert. Their professional practice is thus best consid-ered a *craft*–a practical arena where reflection and action, not dutiful obedience to research findings, help them work through the immediacies of the day. While Schon (1983) has been most persuasive on this view of professional practice, Tom (1984) and Shulman (1987) have brought it most force-fully into teacher education. Emphasized is a teacher's knowl-edge-in-use, which is built up through trial and error as well as academic coursework. It is often tacit, usually complex, and, consequently, not reducible to the transmission of specified teaching skills that have been stripped of their contexts by researchers. Such teaching skills (rather like Hirsch's vocabu-lary) do not add up to competence.

According to this variation, when teacher educators endeavor to install a list of algorithms in novice teachers, little is gained and much is lost.   Most noticeably lost, argues Shulman (1987), are the *knowledge base* of teaching and an appreciation for the ways by which that knowledge base is brought to bear on, and refined in, particular teaching situa-tions. "Those who hold with bifurcating content and teaching processes have once again introduced into policy what had been merely an act of scholarly convenience and simplification in research" (6). An unfortunate and widespread example of this list-to-policy fiasco is the supervision checklists used by more than a few principals enamored with the Hunter (1982) model.

Perhaps most egregious of all has been the failure of so many teacher educators, principals, **and** researchers to notice that the content objectives to which the mastery learning research is most relevant are concerned with learning skills, not understandings and dispositions. Yet the latter are very often the type of objectives in social studies, literature, and the arts. Even Rosenshine (1986), a prominent researcher of the mastery learning bent, has recognized this. A proper teacher education curriculum should endeavor not simply to install pedagogic algorithms in novices but to shed light on the inter-action of teaching methods, experience, and interests with characteristics of the particular content and learners at hand. Then, proper attention may be paid to the intellectual base of teaching–to the pedagogic reasoning needed to manage that extraordinary interaction in real, flesh-and-blood classrooms.

While mastery-oriented pedagogues emphasize process-product research findings, and wisdom-of-practice pedagogues emphasize the craft of teaching in real-world classrooms, a third group of pedagogues turn to those methods that for various reasons they have come to favor. Teacher educators in this group are less concerned with the question, "What works?" than with the question, "What is truly needed?" These teacher educators believe, with Dewey, that education is indeed a moral undertaking that can and should transform society. They compare and contrast methods with that end in mind and then advocate their favorite methods, sometimes with fervor. Examples are abundant. Consider the tremendous push toward discovery or inquiry learning in the 1960's (Taba 1963; Suchman 1961), moral education in the 1970's (Kohlberg & Mayer 1972), and the whole language approach (Goodman 1986) and cooperative learning (Johnson, Johnson, Holubec, & Roy 1984; Slavin 1986) in the 1980's.

Their differences notwithstanding, the three groups of pedagogues are sufficiently alike to warrant their treatment in one category. Their intent is to prepare teachers who can and will engage in particular instructional practices, and this intent is precisely what sets them apart from the cultural initiators. While initiators lament the time wasted by preservice teachers in methods courses–time that could have been spent learning more about the subjects they are trying to teach–pedagogues lament the dismal record of methods courses to propagate desirable ways and means of teaching. If practiced, those techniques are the gateway through which students gain real access to the curriculum so valued by the initiators. Without them, the curriculum will remain beyond the grasp of but a small percentage of the K-12 population, which is "a crime against humanity" (Bloom 1987). While the initiators have argued well for democracy's mandate to educate *everybody*, their failure to apprehend the critical role of pedagogic knowledge in that mission weakens their argument to the point of collapse.

The Ethic of Critique

As these characterizations suggest, the common senses of cultural initiation and effective pedagogy are defined against one another. Beneath appearances, however, the two are more alike than different. Their similarity, seen by neither, is a central tenet of yet a third ethic, the ethic of critique. The apprehension of this third common sense in teacher education begins with an historical analysis of the birth of mass schooling, and then mass teacher education earlier this century. That analysis reveals that the dominant way of thinking and knowing–the *rationality* or *discourse*–with which teacher education is pervaded was drawn not from the utilitarianism and formalism of Dewey, as initiators are wont to believe. Nor was it the consequence of reform-minded educators who wanted only to increase students' access to knowledge and, thereby, create a better world. Rather, the dominant rationality of teacher education was derived from, of all places, the business community–from corporate management. What was good for the market economy also was considered good for the schools. In 1916 Cubberley was straightforward:

> The specifications for manufacturing come from the demands of twentieth-century civilization, and it is the business of the school to build its pupils according to the specifications laid down. This demands good tools, specialized machinery, continuous measurement of production to see if it is according to specifications, the elimination of waste in manufacture, and a large variety in the output. (Cubberley 1916, cited in Kliebard 1975)

This manufacturing philosophy might be good for the production of automobiles (though history has shown it was not good even for that), but it is certainly not good for the education of children. And this is doubly true when these children are expected to take on the ambitious task of sustaining and enhancing democracy. To treat democracy's children like raw material in a widget factory prepares them for docility, tedium, and obedience–for days at the assembly line and evenings at the television screen–not for the challenging project of creating and recreating democracy. Teacher education's central challenge then, according to this ethic, is to free teachers' minds from the disabling grip of corporate rationality so that they might create schools that likewise free their students. The challenge, in a word, is emancipation.

Critique is valued within this ethic because it is the gateway to emancipation. Without it, teacher educators will not scrutinize what is now taken for granted–the conditions and assumptions of the existing education regime. And without scrutiny, preservice and inservice teachers alike will be inclined simply to accept the status quo whether it emancipates them or functions to reproduce the status quo for the benefit of those whose interests are best served by it. Those people, scrutiny reveals, are typically of a particular race, class, and gender.

Liberal pedagogues deny this because they are convinced that schools are politically autonomous agencies that are set apart from the broader society–neutral, depoliticized zones where dominant groups do not hold sway. Similarly, teachers and teacher educators are considered neutral actors in the system, not advocates of particular groups' interests. Such a view, the critics note, is naive and potentially antidemocratic. Between initiators' fixation on the right content and pedagogues' fixation on the right teaching methods, there is, without critique, no opening through which it can be seen that schools are deeply political places that are embedded in the institutions and power conflicts of the broader society; that they generally cater to whatever social groups and ideologies are dominant at the time; and that prospective teachers typically are not encouraged to examine the "implicit contradiction between the promise and reality of American education" (Wood 1984) nor to envision alternatives that are more democratic and just.

Nonetheless, teacher education manages to appear apolitical and value-free. It accomplishes this feat by concentrating on one, and sometimes two, questions: What content should all students learn? (the initiators' question) and What teaching methods should teachers use? (the pedagogues' question). At first glance, these are questions that do not favor particular interest groups; at second glance, they are deeply political. Consider the first question. Analyses have shown the content question to be pervaded by a particular conception of knowledge in which knowledge is considered certain, neutral, and detached from the historical settings in which it was constructed (e.g., Beyer 1988). That it is not discovered but made is not seen; nor that its construction manifests the interests of dominant groups living in particular times (Apple 1982). It is for this reason that the content question is embedded in this particular conception of knowledge--the conception allows the asking of the content question without scrutinizing the underlying social dynamic. It keeps the question well within the centrist boundaries set up to protect the status quo.

As well, the "methodology madness" (Giroux 1980) rampant among pedagogues is not an emancipating but a conserving force. By focusing narrowly on the question, "What teaching methods should teachers use?" attention is fixed on the means of teaching and kept away from questions that could illuminate the status quo: Not only *what* knowledge (the initiators' question) but *whose* knowledge, is of most worth? *Whose* interests are served by the school's hidden curriculum? If tracking is for remediation, then why do so few students escape the tracks to which they are initially assigned? Why does "culture deprivation" theory, learned in the 1960's, but shown in the 1970's to be little more than an apology for wealthy white male dominance, persist? Why are community involvement curricula so steadfastly unsuccessful? Why is family income a highly reliable predictor of school success? As long as teacher educators assess their primary responsibility as propagating effective teaching methods, attention is diverted from questions whose consideration could make a real difference in school effectiveness. In a statement often quoted by the critics, Smith (1980) baldly admits the pedagogues' conservative intent:

> The preservice student should not be exposed to theories and practices derived from ideologies and philosophies about the way schools *should* be. The rule should be to teach, and to teach thoroughly, the knowledge and skills that equip beginning teachers to work successfully in today's classroom (23-24).

Giroux has done much to advance the ethic of critique in North America.[2] He argues that teachers are intellectuals, as is everybody. "Although one can speak of intellectuals, one cannot speak of non-intellectuals, because non-intellectuals don't exist" (Gramsci, cited in Giroux 1985b, 84-85). That this claim is provocative supports the very argument he puts forward: Teachers' practice as intellectuals has been made largely technical and clerical (that is, vocational) by the material conditions of their work–a corporate-style division of labor that separates conception from execution and expects little more of teachers than the carrying out of plans made by higher-ups in the school, the central office, universities, and the legislature. Treating teachers as mere technicians whose job is to teach the special content conceived by wise academics like Ravitch and Hirsch, using the special teaching methods conceived by the leading pedagogues of the day, makes of them dulled functionaries, not the creative and critical professionals to which so much lip service is paid in the current reform movement.

Regarded as dulled functionaries, teachers' intellects are given over to serving the present education regime. Giroux (1985a, 1985b) specifies four categories of teacher-as-intellectual, only one of which manages to break free of that service. That one category is the *transformative* intellectual. These teachers join critique with political action, and use their intellects to envision and build forms of schooling that do not systematically sacrifice women, the poor, and minorities of color. That is, they function intellectually to democratize schools and to engage their students in the ongoing endeavor to create a better world. Transformative intellectuals are not fooled by schools' pretense toward neutrality; rather, they are keenly aware that schools are political sites which are very much implicated in "the way things are."

Critical intellectuals, the second category, are one step removed from reality. While also opposed to extant forms of schooling that systematically dominate some groups and empower others, they manage to avoid stepping into the fray, arguing that this would distort their performance as intellectuals and teachers. They prefer to remain on the sidelines (though no sidelines actually exist) where they scrutinize the status quo and encourage their students also to think critically. They relish criticism, yes, but not activism.

The third category of teachers-as-intellectuals would do neither. *Accommodating* intellectuals "generally stand firm within an ideological posture and set of material practices that support the dominant society and its ruling groups" (Aronowitz & Giroux 1985, 58). These teachers are perhaps the most common. Unlike the first two categories, they do not perceive the inherently political nature of their work; indeed, they suppose themselves to be objective actors in the educational process. This false sense of objectivity functions to accommodate dominant groups while appearing to accommodate no one but the children's best interests.

In the fourth category are teachers whose critical ability has been turned over altogether to various dominant groups. These educators, the *hegemonic* intellectuals, literally and self-consciously work for the present regime. They identify themselves personally and professionally with dominant groups; consequently, their interest in preserving the regime are straightforward and unapologetic.

Why view teachers as intellectuals? There are a number of clear advantages. Foremost among them is that seeing teachers as intellectuals shifts the analysis of teaching from a position that assumes teachers are objective workers in a neutral agency to one that recognizes that position as an exercise in avoidance. Viewing teachers as neutral actors invites teacher educators to overlook the patterns of social domination expressed in the legitimation of particular curricula and teaching practices. In short, that view invites teacher educators to overlook the fact that schools are terrains of political struggle.

On the other hand, construing teachers as intellectuals invites teacher educators to understand teaching as a form of labor that, like all other forms, is implicated in the way things are. It is inevitably political; consequently, every act of teaching functions to protect current social arrangements or to rethink and transform them. This is an extremely empowering view of teachers. Far from being simple conduits of others' plans, or what Giroux (1985c) calls "clerks of the empire," they are agents who mediate those plans according to their own political sensibilities.

How should teacher preparation proceed according to the ethic of critique? It should concern itself with the development of a critical perspective in teachers. It should help them to probe beneath surface appearances–beneath the daily practices of classrooms, relationships among school and community groups, the apparent autonomy of schools, and conventional educational wisdom of all sorts. This means linking together the study of the social foundations of education with the study of teaching methods so that means can be linked with ends. And it means deemphasizing the role of educational psychology. Its preoccupation with the individual (which new developments in cognitive science have done little to correct) has only fueled the methodology madness, adding geometrically more methods as new groups of students (vis-à-vis learning styles, learning disabilities, etc.) are discovered and labeled. In short, teacher education ought to liberate preservice teachers from the frantic, unreflective, buzzword world of *remediation, excellence, competencies,* and, worst, *theory versus practice.* Instead, it ought to introduce them to a practice of education where interests are acknowledged and put first, where skepticism is considered fundamental, and a narrow preoccupation with what is "practical" is considered wrong.

Discussion

I have endeavored to sketch three common senses in teacher education. These sketches have centered on the particular conception of the good–the normative vision–which distinguishes one from another. Two general comments are in order, followed by a recommendation.

First, a caveat. This is a descriptive taxonomy of broad orientations within the field of teacher education. Its limitations include the clustering of highly diverse perspectives (e.g., grouping together Taba, Shulman, Bloom, and Goodlad).

Clustering errs by skirting differences as it pursues similarities; naming the clusters gives them a solidity they do not actually possess.

Second, it will be necessary to compare the common senses described. But this task requires criteria, which in turn depend upon interests. We can imagine that the three ethics will not agree to the same criteria for comparison: Initiators will suggest that the three be compared in terms of their contribution to cultural coherence; pedagogues will suggest their contribution to enabling students to learn the curriculum; and critics will suggest their relative contribution to revealing political interests in education. As the critics argue, standards vary with interests because knowledge itself is embedded in interests.

As a case in point, consider Zeichner's (1983) attempt at a taxonomy of orientations in teacher education. After laying out four "alternative paradigms," he sets about comparing them on "the most salient dimensions along which one can distinguish one conception from another" (7). The dimensions he considers "most salient" are the *received-reflexive* dimension and the *problematic-certain* dimension. The first of these refers to the degree to which the teacher education curriculum is specified in advance. On that dimension, the initiators and pedagogues consider beginning teachers to be relatively passive recipients of a teacher education curriculum that has been developed by people who know what beginning teachers need to know. By contrast, the critics view them as relatively active subjects in their own education: Beginning teachers will have to scrutinize their own taken-for-granted beliefs about school and society—an activity that cannot be predetermined by their education professors. The problematic-certain dimension refers to the degree to which "a conception of teacher education views the institutional form and social context of schooling as problematic" (7). On this dimension, the initiators and pedagogues both accept as given the present education regime; they accommodate it and are to varying degrees at the service of "the empire." On the other hand, the critics want to foster in prospective teachers a critical attitude toward the status quo.

While Zeichner claims to save for another time *his* position, he in fact reveals is plainly by advancing these two dimensions for comparison. Neither would be advanced by initiators or pedagogues. Indeed, they are at the very heart of the critics' ethic. My point here certainly is not to chastise Zeichner for lack of neutrality, for I concur fully with the critics on the matter that neutrality is not possible. Rather, my point is that these ethics are indeed fundamental: they not only dictate what teacher educators should be concerned with and how teacher preparation should proceed; as well, they dictate the very categories by which they might be compared.

So, let me turn from comparison to a recommendation. In what direction should teacher education move? Rather than recommend that it move toward one of the three ethics presented here, I shall recommend that it move toward greater self-consciousness of its ethics–toward an understanding of teacher education as an inherently moral and multilogical terrain. This should complement the common practice in the field of debating only *within* a single ethic, and it should allow prospective teachers, even if only at the awareness level, access to an array of ethics. Such access should be helpful for the same reason that the quest for truth generally is aided by knowledge of alternative claims: reasoning is opened to a dialectic and thus to possibilities that lie beyond the horizons of any one group's common sense. Ignorance of alternatives not only shuts off dialectical reasoning but, more crippling still, it is likely to be accompanied by unknowing obedience to the rules of thought that support the particular common sense within which one perceives and reasons. These rules may or may not serve the aims of education in a society that is striving to sustain and enhance democracy. The clear advantage brought by awareness of alternative rules of thought is the apprehension of those governing one's thinking at present (cf. Cherryholmes 1983).

As for the three ethics predominant in the field today, none in my judgment has alone the standard to which the field ought to move. Initiators and pedagogues alike are often naive about the nature of knowledge, ignoring its social mooring and its political bases. This undermines their work in a most fundamental way, obscuring their participation in the construction of the very categories in which they do their thinking. Moreover, as pedagogues charge, initiators typically ignore *learning*. Preoccupied with the search for worthy content, they display a pitifully poor grasp on the reality of classrooms–of teaching to culturally different children, of facing widespread student disengagement, and of dealing with the many teachers who either cannot or will not conduct their classrooms in a way that enables most of their students to achieve the curriculum. Meanwhile, the pedagogues, as initiators charge, have consistently slighted the central curriculum question, what knowledge is of most worth? Preoccupied with rendering an education that is child-centered, they have failed to exercise their responsibility for deciding what these children really need to learn given the sort of society we want to create.

And for their part, the critics have succeeded in displaying to the field the problematic nature of much that it had taken for granted or conveniently ignored. Especially, they have revealed content selection and teaching methods to be not neutral at all but value-loaded and deeply political activities. This has been important work. However, they have done little more than this. Their work so far has been long on ends but short on means; consequently, they have provided an opposite, and equally extreme, pole to the pedagogue's immersion in practical techniques. Neither extreme is very helpful. Moreover, the critics have tended toward the "true believer" pattern, producing too little *self*-critique and behaving too much like a sect in which affiliation is the main goal. While the initiators and pedagogues have together performed the singular disservice of constructing the false dichotomy of content and pedagogy, the critics have, ironically, dichotomized theory and practice.

Let me be clear that I am not recommending that teacher educators waffle in "open-mindedness" and indecision, endlessly debating alternative ethics and trying to get it "just right" before taking any action. To the contrary, because they must act they must do what they think at present is best. Yet they owe it to their students, to the intellectual livelihood of the field, and to the construction of better forms of teacher education to know and declare what they are about—to reflect upon their present ethic, revise it as they judge necessary, and strive to articulate it to their students and to one another. In short, a teacher education program should know and reveal its mission: It should bring to the surface and communicate its vision of the good, thereby opening its common sense to scrutiny, affiliation, and rejection, as the case may be.

Notes

1. I am grateful to Bill Stanley, Don Bragaw, Mary McFarland, Margit McGuire, and Larry Strickland for comments on an earlier version of this chapter.

2. This section on Giroux draws heavily from an earlier work (Parker 1987).

References

Apple, M.W. 1982. *Education and power*. Boston: Routledge & Kegan Paul.

Aronowitz, S., & H.A. Giroux. 1985. *Education under siege*. South Hadley, Mass.: Bergin & Garvey.

> Drawing on the works of Dewey, Gramsci, and Freire, the authors provide a radical critique of current trends in public education. Their goal is Dewey's: schools that are in fact "laboratories of freedom."

Banks, J.A., & W.C. Parker. In Press. Social studies teacher education. In *Handbook of research on teacher education*, ed. W.R. Houston. New York: Macmillan and Association of Teacher Educators.

Baron, J.B., & R.J. Sternberg. 1987. *Teaching thinking skills: Theory and practice*. New York: W.H. Freeman.

Beyer, L.E. 1988. *Knowing and acting: Inquiry, ideology and educational studies*. London: Falmer.

> This is a radical critique of teacher preparation programs. It bemoans the wedge that has been driven between educational studies and liberal studies and argues that the former is, indeed, an academic field of inquiry.

Bloom, B.S. 1987. A response to Slavin's mastery learning reconsidered. *Review of Educational Research* 57 (4): 507-508.

Bloom, B.S. 1984. The 2 sigma problem: The search for methods of group instruction as effective as one-to-one tutoring. *Educational Researcher* 13 (6): 4-16.

Brophy, J.E. 1980. *Teachers' cognitive activities and overt behaviors*. East Lansing: Michigan State University, College of Education.

Cheney, L.V. 1987. *The American memory: A report on the humanities in the nation's public schools.* Washington, D.C.: National Endowment for the Humanities.

    Written by the NEH chair during the Reagan administration, this pamphlet gives an explanation for "the erosion of historical consciousness" and recommends ways to reverse that trend.

Cherryholmes, C.H. 1983. Knowledge, power, and discourse in social studies education. *Journal of Education* 165 (4): 341-358.

Cummins, J. 1986. Empowering minority students: A framework for intervention. *Harvard Educational Review* 56 (1): 18-36.

    Cummins analyzes the school failure of some minority students and criticizes previous attempts to remedy the problem. Recommended are interventions that alter the relationship between educated minority students and between schools and minority communities.

Dewey, J. 1916. *Democracy and education.* New York: Macmillan.

Dewey, J. 1910. *How we think.* Boston: D.C. Heath.

Geertz, C. 1983. Common sense as a cultural system. In *Local knowledge*, ed. C. Geertz, 73-93. New York: Basic Books.

Giroux, H.A. 1985a. Critical pedagogy and the resisting intellectual, Part II. *Phenomenology + Pedagogy* 3 (2): 84-97.

    This two-part article argues that teachers are by definition intellectuals, and that intellectuals are necessarily political actors. They help to support or transform, as the case may be, current social inequities.

Giroux, H.A. 1985b. Intellectual labor and pedagogic work: Rethinking the role of teacher as intellectual. *Phenomenology + Pedagogy* 3 (1): 20-32.

Giroux, H.A. 1985c. Critical pedagogy, cultural politics and the discourse of experience. *Journal of Education* 167 (2): 22-41.

Giroux, H.A. 1980. Teacher education and the ideology of social control. *Journal of Education* 162 (1): 5-27.

Goodlad, J.I. 1984. *A place called school.* New York: McGraw-Hill.

Goodman, K. 1986. *What's whole in whole language?* Portsmouth, N.H.: Heinemann.

Gould, S.J. 1981. *The mismeasure of man.* New York: W.W. Norton.

Hirsch, E.D., Jr. 1988. Restoring cultural literacy in the early grades. *Educational Leadership* 45 (4): 63-70.

Hirsch, E.D., Jr. 1987. *Cultural literacy: What every American needs to know.* Boston: Houghton Mifflin.

The bestseller that stirred a nationwide debate on *what* knowledge all students in this nation must share.

Hunter, M. 1982. *Mastery teaching.* El Segundo, Calif.: TIP Publications.

Johnson, D.W., R.T. Johnson, E. Holubec, and P. Roy. 1984. *Circles of learning: Cooperation in the classroom.* Alexandria, Va.: Association for Supervision and Curriculum Development.

Judge, H. 1982. *American graduate schools of education.* New York: Ford Foundation.

This study grapples with the uneasy partnership in graduate schools of education between teacher preparation and research on education.

Kerr, D.H. (1987). Authority and responsibility in public schooling. In *The ecology of school renewal*, ed. J.I. Goodland, 20-40. Chicago: National Society for the Study of Education and the University of Chicago Press.

Kliebard, H.M. 1975. Bureaucracy and curriculum theory. In *Curriculum theorizing: The reconceptualists*, ed. W. Pinar, 51-69. Berkeley: McCutchan.

Kohlberg, L., & R. Mayer. 1972. Development as the aim of education. *Harvard Educational Review* 42, 451-496.

Lanier, J.E., & J.W. Little. 1986. Research on teacher education. In *Handbook of research on teaching* (3rd ed.), ed. M. C. Wittrock, 527-569. New York: Macmillan.

  The most helpful review of the research that has been done on teacher education.

Oakes, J. 1985. *Keeping track: How schools structure inequality.* New Haven: Yale University Press.

Oakeshott, M. 1962. *Rationalism in politics and other essays.* London: Methuen.

Parker, W.C. 1988. Social studies teacher education: Contending visions of the good. Occasional paper No. 2, unpublished manuscript. Center for the Study of Civic Intelligence, University of Washington, Seattle.

Parker, W.C. 1987. Teachers' mediation in social studies. *Theory and Research in Social Education* 15 (1): 1-22.

Ravitch, D. 1985. From history to social studies: Dilemmas and problems. In *The schools we deserve*, ed. D. Ravitch, 112-132. New York: Basic Books.

  One of several essays in a book by a historian critical of the present educational establishment. This essay claims that education professors ruined the proper study of history by reducing it to the vacuous "social studies."

Ravitch, D., and C.E. Finn, Jr. 1987. *What do our 17-year-olds know?* New York: Harper & Row.

Rosenshine, B. 1986. Unsolved issues in teaching content: A critique of a lesson on Federalist Paper No. 10. Paper presented at the meeting of the American Educational Research Association, San Francisco, April.

Schon, D.A. 1983. *The reflective practitioner.* New York: Basic Books.

Shulman, L. 1987. Knowledge and teaching: Foundations of the New Reform. *Harvard Educational Review* 57 (1): 1-22.

   Shulman lays out a new paradigm for studying and preparing teachers. It asserts, against the grain, the importance of teachers' knowledge of the subject they are trying to teach.

Slavin, R.E. 1986. *Using student team learning* (3rd ed.). Baltimore, MD: The Johns Hopkins Team Learning Project.

Smith, B. 1980. *A design for a school of pedagogy.* Washington, D.C.: U. S. Department of Education.

Suchman, J.R. 1961. Inquiry training: Building skills for autonomous discovery. *Merrill Palmer Quarterly of Behavior and Development* 7: 147-69.

Taba, H. 1963. Learning by discovery: Psychological and educational rationale. *Elementary School Journal* 63 (6): 308-316.

Tchudi, S. 1988. Slogans indeed: A reply to Hirsch. *Educational Leadership* 45 (4): 72-74.

Thorndike, E.L. 1913. *Educational psychology.* New York: Teachers College, Columbia University.

Toffler, A. 1980. *The third wave.* New York: Bantam.

Tom, A.R. 1984. *Teaching as a moral craft.* New York: Longman.

   The author critiques the popular assumption that teaching is a sort of applied science and suggests a different metaphor--that teaching is a moral craft and, accordingly, that teachers are moral agents who use power to promote particular values.

Whitson, T. 1985. Truth or competencies. Paper presented at the meeting of the Bergamo Conference on Curriculum Theory and Practice, Dayton, Ohio, October.

Wood, G.H. 1984. Schooling in a democracy: Transformation or reproduction? *Educational Theory* 34: 219-239.

Yinger, R.H. 1988. The conversation of learning: A reaction to Hirsch's Cultural Literacy. *The Holmes Group Forum* 2 (2): 20-21.

In only two pages, the author undermines Hirsch's "cultural literacy" argument. Using linguistic analysis, Yinger shows there is more to a conversation than knowing the words.

Zeichner, K.M. 1983. Alternative paradigms of teacher education. *Journal of Teacher Education* 34 (3): 3-9.

This author examines diverse orientations in teacher education. The criteria on which he compares them, however, are drawn from his own ethic of critique, so the logic of other orientations is not well displayed.

Building A Better Mousetrap for Teacher Education

Michael P. Wolfe
Lawrence Giandomenico

Ralph Waldo Emerson once said, "If a man makes a better mousetrap, the world will beat a path to his door." It is presumed that the goal of building a better mousetrap is to catch more mice or other variations on this theme. The problems of applying the mousetrap analogy to teacher education is our lack of consensus on program goals and outcomes as a profession. Indeed, just as there have been a multitude of mousetraps invented in the past one hundred years, there have been no lack of attempts to reform teacher education in the United States (McCaleb et al. 1987).

Introduction

It has been suggested that much of the effort to reform education in this country has been like rearranging deck chairs on the Titanic (Hart 1981). Perhaps the claim that more than forty percent of American high school students are simply not expending academic effort near their capacity lends support to this contention (Glasser 1986). There is a proliferation of reports calling for continued reform supported by allegations of mediocrity and lower test scores, professional dissatisfaction, lower standards among teachers, and unproductive teacher education programs. Where, then, is the bedrock for improvement? Are we to assume that no well-spring exists to support change? Perhaps we have overlooked one of the most fundamental issues in the entire schema–changing the focus of preservice teacher education.

This chapter will examine some issues in teacher education and suggest redirection based on a growing body of research focusing on four essential factors: the teacher, the school, the curriculum, and the learner. This chapter cannot possibly present the entire research agenda in these four major areas of education; therefore, the discussion will be limited to several areas of teacher education which address the realities of classroom practice.

More than twenty-five years ago, Sarason, Davidson, and Blatt (1962) observed that the preparation for teaching was "an unstudied problem." The problems in teacher education seem to be of an enduring nature. Teacher education is a field whose problems have been widely debated since the turn of the century. Substantial improvement-oriented inquiry combined with related developmental activity, has been undertaken since then, although the troublesome circumstances remain basically unchanged (Lanier 1986).

Troublesome circumstances have surfaced in the 1980's which may be characterized as the "Decade of Reports" on educational reform. The myriad of local, state, and national task force reports written since *A nation at risk* have focused attention on concerns with education in America and have suggested an educational reform movement. Messages of dissatisfaction in education are frequent threads throughout the reports.

While the emphasis in the major Education Reform Reports is on the K-12 public schools, teacher education reform is also prominently discussed. In the K-12 reform agenda items, the focus seems to emphasize recommendations for improving the teaching act while the higher education reform proposals (Holmes Group 1986) reflect a focus on curriculum and program structure changes (Gruesemer & Butler 1983).

An analysis of the major task force reform agenda on teacher education suggests some attention to certification requirements and standards, but much less mention of the substance of teacher education programs or how changes can be initiated.

The reform agenda for teacher education in the 1980's may very likely guide program developments for the next decade. By its very nature, the preparation of teachers must be general. Since the teacher education program cannot predict the characteristics of the particular school, the nature of the students, or even the specifics of the curriculum which a new teacher will be asked to teach, teacher preparation is at a disadvantage in addressing the realities of practice (Ryan 1987).

Schwab et al. (1978) provided a general structure for teacher education which he referred to as the "commonplace of teaching." For teaching to occur, someone (a teacher) must be teaching someone (a learner) about something (a curriculum) at some place and point in time (a milieu or school).

Much current research on the school, the teacher, the curriculum, and the learner presents implications for future practices in teacher education. These four areas provide the conceptual framework for describing essential program outcomes/components in teacher education (Figure 2). In the following section we will address several issues regarding the "at-risk" learner and describe promising practices for enhancing learning in the classroom.

Teacher Education

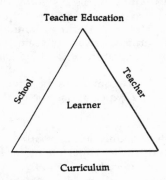

Figure 2. Essential program components in teacher education

The graduating class of the year 2000 presents a significantly different set of demographic factors for the teaching profession. It has been stated that as many as a third of the nation's 40 million school-aged children are, based on their circumstances, "at-risk," either of failing in school, dropping out or falling victim to crime, drugs, teen-aged pregnancy, or chronic unemployment (Patterson, Purkey, and Parker 1986).

Failure in school is expected to increase among children and likely to be based on a confluence of demographic factors. The proportion of children in poverty has increased from 15 to 20 percent since 1970; projections suggest that 60 percent of today's 3-year-olds will live in single-parent homes before they turn 18; immigration has increased and birth rates among poor and minority families are significantly higher than those among middle-class whites. At the same time, the school-age population has declined, from 53 million in 1970 to 45 million in 1986 (Snyder 1984).

The overlap of these trends has wide ramifications for those preparing to work with the graduating class of the year

2000. The nation's schools and its teachers, the first group to encounter the rapidly changing demographics, are society's best–some would argue–and only hope for solving the problems. However, schools at the present time are ill-equipped to meet the challenge perhaps because of the excessive responsibilities already assigned to their mission.

The implications for these changing demographic phenomena are far-reaching.

1. Teacher efficacy, the power to make a difference in children's education, is declining due to reaction of teachers to the rapidly changing student demographics. As Darling-Hammond (1984) states, even the altruistic reward of seeing students grow has declined as the nature of teaching has changed.

2. Families and communities are increasing their demands and expectations for quality and equity in education.

3. The goals for education as contrasted with individual school and teacher expectations for student outcomes may be contradictory.

4. Students are becoming a more diverse group with more complex needs.

5. Students may have to attend to basic needs before quality learning can occur.

6. New teaching/learning strategies matched to changing values of students and society may be necessary.

The success of education depends on adapting teaching to individual differences among learners. In one form or another, this phrase has been included in theories of learning through previous decades to the present (Snow & Sternberg 1982).

Research directed toward some of the issues more closely associated with learners has suggested that schools currently approach teaching with narrow homogeneous methodology. In addition, it has also been suggested that this methodology permits nearly fifty percent of public school students to not attempt to work hard at doing well academically. The ultimate reason may lie in the fact that school activities are not need-satisfying for many of these students. Using a divergent theory of behavior, Glasser (1986) demonstrates that the needs of students can be incorporated into behavior which is both need satisfying and academically productive. One additional promising direction from which conclusions have been derived is the current research on the operation of the human brain.

Research data on cerebral growth and functioning decry the narrow methodology used in most schools. Using cerebral lateralization as the framework for comparison, schools generally require input (processing) and output (production) along similar lines (Goodlad 1984).

Prospective teachers need to understand brain functioning because the field of neuropsychology will likely continue to provide valuable clues for enhancing learning in the classroom. Some of the recent research discoveries of Levy (1983) are as follows:

- Evidence suggests that there are individual differences among people to the extent that one hemisphere is used more preferentially than the other.

- In the majority of predominantly right handers, speech is almost entirely confined to the left hemisphere.

- Right hemisphere processes add emotion and humorous overtones important for understanding the full meaning of oral and written communication.

- The two hemispheres differ in their perceptual roles but both sides are involved in the creation and appreciation of art and music.

- Both hemispheres are involved in thinking, logic, and reasoning.

- The right hemisphere seems to play a special role in emotion. If students are emotionally engaged, both sides of the brain will participate in the educational process regardless of the subject matter.

The realization that the whole brain is actively participating in perception, encoding of information, organization of representations, memory, arousal, planning, thinking, understanding, and all other mental operations whether it be a social interaction, painting a picture, playing the piano, doing mathematics, writing a story, attending a lecture, or seeing a movie, seems to have escaped recognition by many, if not most, popular educational authors (Levy 1983).

Leslie Hart (1981), McCarthy (1980), and Messier (1986) have applied related brain research to classroom instruction and learning. Whether classroom learning is organized using Hart's Proster Theory or McCarthy's 4-MAT system, the focus for teachers is whole-brain learning. The picture emerging from hemispheric research is of a brain specialized for different but complementary forms of learning.

The sound foundation which supports the work of such theorists as Hart and McCarthy affords useful implications in spite of the incomplete nature of the research.

Though the notion of right and left brain thinking is compelling yet speculative, the dichotomous metaphor is one source to encourage prospective teachers to adapt teaching methodologies to individual differences among learners. Learning style/brain research activities hold extraordinary potential to significantly and positively alter the professional behavior and student learning process in our classroom (Gregoric 1982).

Since the learner is the central focus for teacher education programs, teacher behaviors must be developed in order to effectively address the individual differences of student.

The Teacher

The core of what teachers should learn in preparation for their careers should be derived from what is known about effective teaching. This assumption seems to be gaining support among teacher educators (Smith 1983; Egbert & Fenstermacher 1984), though there are few programs of teacher education based primarily on research-based conclusions about teaching and learning (Egbert & Kluender 1984, 4).

The proliferation of research studies on teacher effects suggests a strong need to uncover more specific details about the science/art of teaching (Schulman 1987). The research focus offers replicated connections between teacher behavior and student achievement (Rosenshine 1986). However compelling the findings, they must be interpreted and applied with some caution due to the nature of the suggested subject context where direct instruction is considered to be most effective.

The teacher effectiveness research primarily deals with learning when the goals are clear and the objectives are focused upon basic skills. Other teaching behaviors are necessary when lesson objectives include critical thinking and problem solving domains.

Rosenshine, in a synthesis of research on effective teaching, suggests six teaching functions, which he stipulates are not new (1986). He states that while some of the techniques may be used by all teachers, effective teachers use almost all of them most of the time. Sporadic usage with less rigorous application may be less effective. Specific modifications are also suggested to more closely reflect the particular qualities of the children in a given class. It is important to note that in addition to focused instruction which is well represented in the six functions, the issues of thorough lesson planning and positive classroom management skills are also represented in effective teaching research (Blum 1984).

Six Teaching Functions

1. Daily review. Effective teachers begin with a review of homework, previous learning, and/or prerequisite information needed for the lesson. This effort helps students establish connections between previous content and the present material. It also affords a diagnosis to the teacher concerning students' readiness for the next lesson. Daily review can vary in importance depending on the particular nature of the content and its structure. Content arranged in a sequence of dependent skills or concepts may require rigorous review to avoid gaps in students understanding.

2. Presenting new material. Elements included by effective teachers in the presentation of new material include beginning with a brief statement of the objective. Utilizing small steps, effective teachers model procedures providing examples which clearly convey the critical attributes of the skill or concepts taught. Consistent efforts to check for understanding afford the effective teacher with diagnostic data to determine the need for additional instruction and students readiness to proceed with the lesson.

3. Guided practice. Initial practice is a critical moment in teaching. Madeline Hunter (1986) refers to this point as "wet cement" since it "damages" very easily. Guided practice is the first opportunity for students to practice using the new content or skill under close supervision by the teacher. It is characterized by a high frequency of questions with all students

involved in activities and showing a 70-80 percent success rate. Initial practice continues until fluency is achieved.

4. <u>Corrections and feedback</u>. The guiding principle for this phase of effective teaching is that feedback should be immediate and specific. Corrections provide supportive prompts that help students arrive at the correct answer. Effective teachers strive for longer and improved answers to increasingly frequent and complex questions. This process continues until the teacher determines the need for further feedback is unnecessary.

5. <u>Independent practice</u>. Following guided practice students are expected to be able to complete the steps or skills taught albeit hesitantly. Independent practice is suggested by Rosenshine (1986) as the opportunity for students to develop fluency. It begins in the classroom as an extension of guided practice and concludes with homework which is checked the following day for accuracy and completeness.

6. <u>Weekly review</u>. Rosenshine calls upon the research of Good and Grouws (1979) to support the final step in his six teaching functions. Weekly and monthly reviews and tests provide students additional opportunities to more fully integrate the concepts and skills while affording additional practice. Effective teachers use this opportunity to reteach concepts and skills as necessary.

Research on teacher effectiveness has suggested a pattern of instruction which has produced significant results when content is organized in hierarchial form. The direct instruction format may be less relevant for content which is less structured. Appropriate modifications in the six steps are suggested with variation in skills and background of the learners. Wide discretion in such modifications is suggested to meet the variation in subject matter and the learners. However, Rosenshine (1986) notes that most effective teachers use most of the six steps nearly all of the time. Content specific research may afford more definitive insight as the technology is refined in the future.

The Curriculum

A classic definition of curriculum is a plan or program for all the experiences which the learner encounters under the direction of the school (Oliva 1982). Instead of focusing on this general conception of curriculum, there is a need for preservice teachers to focus on human information processing which integrates content and the interaction of the learner and teacher with the content.

The typical model used to depict information processing includes the short-term memory and its limitations (Case 1985). Active effort by students to review, summarize, or elaborate utilizing new information affords the opportunity for transfer to the long-term memory. Without active use of the information it may be lost in as little as thirty seconds (Dembo 1988). The limitations of the short-term memory are self-evident. Skimming, omitting, and confusion are common effects of short-term memory overload (Tobias 1982). When processing activities are presented with manageable chunks of information, transfer potential to long-term memory is improved.

Relevant implications for teaching are suggested from information processing research. When introducing new material, teachers must be keenly aware of the amount of information presented. Presenting content utilizing small "chunks" with frequent opportunities for practice before introducing additional material is suggested by the research. Suggested teaching techniques that assist students in managing a "chunk" of new information include a review of relevant prior information. When similarities with previously understood information are available, highlighting these assists students in developing cognitive structure. Differences may be underscored by making explicit those critical elements which separate the new from the old learning. These techniques serve to facilitate management of the "chunk" of new information presented in a lesson. Another technique which may help students in this regard is a content outline which assists the learner to connect new information with previously learned content.

The importance of processing activities to transfer information from the short-term to the long-term memory is supported by information-processing research (Chi & Glasser 1981). Active practice facilitates the process of transfer. If all students are expected to learn the skill or material, then practice activities must reflect participation by all students. Guiding students efforts requires close monitoring and specific feedback by the teacher. Efforts to practice the new skill correctly at the beginning of the process are extremely important (Good & Grouws 1979).

Further practice is necessary in order to afford learners effortless recall. The process of overlearning is achieved by such additional practice at the point beyond which significant deliberative effort is required by the learner to complete the task. Overlearning facilitates retention and allows freedom for the short-term memory to fix upon new information.

The research on information processing provides insight into altering conceptions about the design of instructional approaches that integrate processes and coverage of content. Involving the student in unique learning strategies which connect his experiences to the content in meaningful ways will enhance retention and transfer of information. It has been suggested that the emphasis on the improvement of classroom teaching is most likely to achieve results when the entire school is committed to the improvement of teaching and learning as its primary mission.

The School

It seems that if a preservice teacher education program concerns itself with the learner, the teacher, and the curriculum, then one would be equipped with a great deal of essential knowledge and skill for beginning the induction year of teaching. However, in the last 20 years, research and practice focusing on the impact of the school itself has yielded further insight into determining programs and practices in teacher education.

James Coleman and others' (1966) study, *Equality of educational opportunity*, concluded that schools have little influence on student achievement that is independent of socioeconomic status and family background. Congress supported Coleman's work in an effort to illuminate the problem of poor minority children attending segregated schools. Variables held in high esteem at the outset of his work were subsequently found to bear no relationship to the quality of students' achievement. Such variables as quality of facilities, supplies, equipment, experience, and training of teachers were found to be relatively insignificant. The overwhelming conclusion from Coleman's work was that children emerge from 12 years of schooling as relatively disadvantaged as they were when they began.

From this examination of static school characteristics, research was directed toward school operations and processes (Edmonds 1979). Some of the efforts to study differences between highly effective and less effective schools examined the work-culture of teaching. Relationships between school culture and school effectiveness emerged as one explanation for the fact that some schools were more effective relatively than others. Culture has been viewed as a plausible explanation for what otherwise may have been a difference without a distinction (Brookover, Flood, Sweitzer, and Wisenbaker 1979).

Culture has been defined as those aspects of the daily behavior of a school's leadership, faculty, and students that reflect their guiding beliefs (Patterson et al. 1986). The guiding beliefs emanate from values shared by members of the group. The particular characteristics of school cultures vary with the context, composition, and environment of individual schools. The culture of the school may be thought of as its "personality" and the variables which compose its fiber may influence achievement positively or negatively. One of the major functions of school culture is to convey accepted standards of work behavior to its members (Owens 1987). The culture of effective schools is characterized by guiding beliefs which are supportive of academic achievement.

In schools considered to be highly effective certain common characteristics, or more specifically correlates, have been identified. The values reflected in the culture of such schools are deeply supportive of these characteristics (Blum 1984; Lezotte 1982).

1. <u>Importance of learning</u>. All major issues and decisions are considered primarily from their likely effects upon student learning. All students are expected to achieve. The significance of learning in schools is well accepted and reflects the school's mission.

2. <u>Opportunity to learn</u>. Class time is protected from unnecessary disruptions. The importance of learning time is reflected in the organization and operation of the entire building. Classrooms reflect this value with students "on-task" behaviors managed appropriately.

3. <u>Clear and focused curriculum</u>. Learning objectives, instructional activities, and student assessments are closely related, clearly written, and well followed. Collaborative curriculum planning, development, and execution are part of regular building operation.

4. <u>Safe and consistent environment</u>. Written guidelines specify appropriate student behavior. Administrators and teachers follow agreed upon procedures and maintain relationships with parents that reinforce appropriate student behavior. In addition, there are activities occurring within the school which enhance a positive learning environment.

5. <u>Learning is closely monitored</u>. Student performance is monitored by organized and well-accepted procedures for collecting and analyzing relevant information. Decisions following analysis are arrived at cooperatively with objectives designed to meet identified needs.

6. <u>Effective leadership</u>. Leaders work within agreed upon procedures to collaboratively assess needs, define

objectives, and implement changes.   Improvement of instruction is the most significant issue in building operation.
7. <u>Parents and partners</u>.   Parents are involved in providing support to the instructional program.   Frequent two-way communication assures understanding of classroom and home behavior.

Implications for Preservice Teachers

Research on classroom and school effects should play a vital role in equipping the preservice teacher with a deep and meaningful understanding of the environment within which he/she may commit an entire career.   Perhaps the absence of such an understanding contributes to what Jackson (1968) describes as the "conceptual simplicity" of teachers.   He describes teachers as viewing their work from an uncomplicated view of causality, utilizing intuitive rather than rational, opinionated rather than open-minded and narrowness in working definitions.

Unfortunately, current directions in teacher education do not appear to support the most significant research conclusions about classroom and school effects.   Just when real advances in preservice teacher education are possible, several states are dispensing with methods courses and reducing credit hours in teacher education (Berliner 1984).

Logically, during the preservice phase of teacher education, a student should study and experience the deep structure of schooling (Tye 1987) and develop various strategies reinforcing positive school effects.   Effective schools are accomplished classroom by classroom.   Thus, the attainment of an effective school necessitates a participating majority of effective teachers.   Lasting changes affecting student achievement and satisfaction are more likely to result from policies that encourage "bottom-up" action, "top-down" support, and school-specific reform efforts.   Such changes require participation relying on faculty collaboration, cohesiveness, and shared decision-making.   These skills and knowledge are crucial to reform.   Effective practices within a school must be incorporated in a preservice teacher education program.

Conclusion

There is little argument that the time is right for improving preservice teacher education.   We have only recently developed a fresh set of conceptions and supportive research on which to base reformed teacher education (Berliner 1984). This chapter has identified several critical program components which ought to be included in preservice teacher education. The program components implied by Schwab, i.e., the teacher, the school, the curriculum, the learner, and current research and practice within these areas provide teacher educators with program building blocks for the future. Fitting these puzzle pieces into a cogent paradigm for preservice teacher education presents an immediate challenge.

Toffler's (1980) suggestions for humanizing the future appear to encourage a more individualized approach to the design of preservice teacher education. When decisions about such redesign are contemplated, relative data upon which to base such decisions may be useful. A preservice teacher education profile is proposed to serve this need.

The purpose of the following instrument is to assess the match between a present preservice teacher education program and an ideal preservice program of the future as suggested through interpretation of some of the research literature.

The items on this instrument were derived from research concerning the teacher, the school, the curriculum, and the learner. They represent some common elements of a futuristic preservice teacher education program. These elements are as follows:

- Preservice teacher education must focus on outcomes.

- Outcomes must integrate theory and practice.

- The process must include reflection and action.

- Training must involve theory, demonstration, practice, and coaching.

- The learning process models a multi-sensory approach.

- The preparation of a teacher requires a wider involvement of the whole school and the community as learning resources and as supports for learning.

- The program empowers participants to design experiences based upon personal needs and needs of the profession.

These elements are incorporated throughout the instrument which follows.

Preservice Teacher Education

<u>What Is</u>
The extent to which you agree that this item describes your program.

<u>What Should Be</u>
The extent to which you agree that this item describes your program.

0 - Disagree
1 - Agree with reservations
2 - Agree
3 - Agree strongly

0 - Disagree
1 - Agree with reservations
2 - Agree
3 - Agree strongly

I. THE LEARNER

1. Whole-brained learning is a process and outcome for the preservice teacher education program. Participants develop knowledge and skill in utilizing brain research to plan curriculum and instruction for a classroom.   1. _____

2. Preservice teachers practice using a variety of teaching methodologies with adaptations to various learners and groups.   2. _____

3. The common target of the preservice program is the progressive mastery of the learning process both as a learner and as a teacher.   3. _____

II. THE TEACHER

4. The program fosters the connection between effective teaching behaviors and student achievement through practice.   4. _____

5. There are many opportunities for preservice teachers to demonstrate understanding of effective teaching behaviors within a regime of theory, demonstration, practice, and coaching.   5. _____

III. THE CURRICULUM

6. The preservice program focuses on human information processing which integrates content and the interaction of the learner and teacher within the context.   6. _____

_____ 7. Participants actively practice information processing as learners 7. _____
and transfer this process into action in the classroom setting as
teachers.

IV. THE SCHOOL

_____ 8. Participants learn the theory and practice of effective schools 8. _____
and the implications of teacher responsibility within a school
setting.

_____ 9. The impact of school culture on teacher behavior and student 9. _____
achievement is recognized.

_____ 10. Preservice students develop strategies for impacting the school 10. _____
effects phenomenon inherent in all schools.

Although the four major areas representing Schwab's commonplace of teaching model do not fully describe all elements of a teacher education program, they do provide directions for thinking and planning for the future of teacher education.

Since the future is built upon the plans of today, the teacher education community must begin immediately to design a quality preservice program to produce teachers who will serve as learning facilitators and resources, who will become positive community builders, and who will derive renewal and rewards from their inherently valuable roles. Building a better mousetrap for preservice teacher education program responsive to ever-changing demands will be our opportunity and challenge for the future. Practicing what we currently know about the learner, the teacher, the curriculum, and the school provides the base for improving teacher education.

References

Berliner, David. 1984. Making the right changes in preservice teacher education. *Phi Delta Kappan* 53, 10: 94-96.

It is suggested that teacher preparation programs should not omit pedagogy but rather incorporate recent research findings.

Bloom, Benjamin. 1980. The new direction in educational research: Alterable variables. *Phi Delta Kappan* 61, 6: 382-385.

Research directed at analyzing the implications of curriculum, time and teaching methods may afford results which encourage rigorous practice.

Blum, Robert. 1984. *Effective schooling practices: A research synthesis*. Portland, Oregon: North West Regional Educational Laboratory.

A compedium of research based conclusions with perspectives from the classroom, school, and district. This document affords a detailed view of each of these three perspectives.

Brookover, Wilbur et al. 1979. *Social system and student achievement: Schools can make a difference*. New York: Praeger.

Case, Robert. 1985. *Intellectual development: Birth to adulthood*. New York: Academic Press.

Cetron, Michael. 1985. *Schools of the future: How American business and education can cooperate to save our schools*. New York: McGraw-Hill.

Chi, M.T.H., and R. Glasser. 1981. The measurement of expertise: Analysis of the development of knowledge and skills as a basis for assessing achievement. In *Design, analysis, and policy in testing*, eds. E. L. Baker and E. S. Quellmalz, Beverly Hills, Calif.: Sage Publications.

Coleman, J. et al. 1966. *Equality of educational opportunity.*
    Washington, D.C.: Government Printing Office.

A classic study suggesting that socio-economic status is
the most powerful predictor of academic achievement.

Darling-Hammond, Linda. 1985. *Beyond the commission
    reports: The coming crisis in teaching.* Santa Monica,
    Calif.: The Rand Corporation.

Dembo, Myron. 1988. *Applying educational psychology in the
    classroom.* New York: Longman.

Edmonds, Ronald. 1979. Effective schools for the urban poor.
    Educational Leadership 37, 10 : 15-24.

One of the first authors to suggest that commitment to
excellence is a choice that can and does produce higher
achievement for students.

Egbert, Robert, and Gary Fenstermacher, eds. 1984. How can we
    use research in teacher education? *Journal of Teacher
    Education* 35, 4.

Egbert, Robert, and Michael Kluender, eds. 1984. *Using
    research to improve teacher education.* The Nebraska
    Consortium. Washington, D.C.: ERIC Clearinghouse on
    Teacher Education.

Feistritzer, Charles. 1983. *Cheating our children: Why we
    need school reform.* Washington, D.C.: National Center
    for Educational Information.

Glasser, William. 1986. *Control theory in the classroom.* New
    York: Harper & Row.

Students behave in ways which serve to satisfy their
needs. The author suggests a directed effort to develop
classroom activities which are need-satisfying to all
students.

Good, Thomas, and David Grouws. 1979. The Missouri
    mathematics effectiveness project. *Journal of
    Educational Psychology* 71: 143-155.

Goodlad, John. 1984. *A place called school: Prospects for the future.* New York: McGraw-Hill.

Gruesemer, L. J., & C. Butler. 1983. *Education under study.* Chelmsford, Md.: Northeast Regional Exchange.

Hart, Leslie. 1983. *Human brain and human learning.* New York: Longman.

    The human brain operates using pattern recognition as a central means of learning. It is suggested that schools adapt instruction to operate in "brain compatible" ways.

Hart, Leslie. 1981. Classrooms are killing learning. *Principal* 6: 8.

Hodgkinson, Harold. 1985. *All one system: Demographics education, kindergarten through graduate school.* Washington, D.C.: Institute for Educational Leadership.

Holmes Group. 1986. *Tomorrow's teachers: A report of the Holmes Group,* Lansing, Mich.

Hunter, Madeline. 1986. *Mastery teaching.* El Segundo, Calif.: TIP Publications.

    A brief but concise view of direct instruction utilizing a series of twenty video-tapes and corresponding chapters in the text.

Jackson, Philip. 1968. *Life in classrooms.* New York: Holt, Rinehart & Winston.

    A classic view of the institutional pressures upon children as they are inculcated through their classroom experiences.

Joyce, Bruce et al. 1987. Synthesis of research on staff development: A framework for future study and a state-of-the-art analysis. *Educational Leadership* 3: 77-87.

    A comphrehensive view of staff development models and techniques. Emphasis upon the need to consider the process of transfer from training to practice is stressed.

Lanier, Judith, and Judith Little. 1986. *Research on teacher education, handbook of research on teaching,* ed. Merlin Wittrock. New York: Macmillan.

Levy, Jerre. 1983. Research synthesis on right and left hemispheres: We think with both sides of the brain. *Educational Leadership* 1: 65-67.

Lezotte, Lawrence. 1982. Effective schools research and its implications. *Citizen Action in Education* 4, 2.

McCaleb, Joseph, Hilda Borko, Richard Arends, Ruth Garner, and Linda Mauro. 1987. Innovation in teacher education: The evolution of a program. *Journal of Teacher Education* XXXVIII, Number 4: 57-64.

McCarthy, Bernice. 1980. *The 4 MAT system.* Oakbrook, Ill.: EXCEL, Inc.

A comphrehensive system of instruction based upon the processing preferences that students demonstrate on a variety of tasks. Specific adaptations for left and right hemispheric preferences are suggested.

Messier, Paul. 1986. *Expanding mental capacities in education.* Unpublished manuscript. Washington, D.C.: U.S. Department of Education.

National Commission on Excellence in Education. 1984. *A nation at risk: The imperative for educational reform.* Washington, D.C.: Government Printing Office.

Oliva, Peter. 1982. *Developing the curriculum.* Boston, Mass.: Little, Brown.

Owens, Robert. 1987. *The leadership of educational clans.* Alexandria, Va.: ASCD Yearbook.

Patterson, Jerry, Stewart Purkey, and Jackson Parker. 1986. *Productive school systems for a nonrational world.* Alexandria, Va.: ASCD.

Rosenshine, Barak. 1986. Synthesis of research on explicit teaching. *Educational Leadership* 4: 60-69.

Ryan, Kevin. 1987. The care and feeding of the new teacher. *Educator's Forum* 4: 2.

Sarason, Seymour. 1982. *The preparation of teachers: An unstudied problem in education.* New York: Wiley.

Sarason, Seymour, Davidson, K.R., and Blatt, B. 1962. *The preparation of teachers.* New York: Wiley.

Schwab, John, I. Westbury, and N. Wilkof. 1978. *Science, curriculum, and liberal education.* Chicago: University of Chicago Press..

Shulman, L.S. 1987. Knowledge and teaching: Foundations of the new reform. *Harvard Educational Review*, 57, 1: 1-21.

Smith, D.C. (Ed.). 1983. *Essential knowledge for beginning educators.* Washington, DC: American Association of Colleges for Teacher Education.

Snow, R.E. [in collaboration with E. Yalow] 1982. Education and intelligence. In *Handbook of human intelligence*, ed. Robert Sternberg, 493-596. London: Cambridge University Press.

Snyder, David. 1984. *The strategies context of education in America 1985-1995.* Washington, D.C.: National Education Association, Office of Planning.

Tobias, S. 1982. When do instructional methods make a difference? *Educational Research* 11: 4-10.

Tye, Barbara. 1987. The deep structure of schooling. *Phi Delta Kappan* 69, 4.

Moral Education in Reforming Teacher Education: Issues and New Directions

Richard L. Hayes

Issues in Moral Education

Moral education is a particularly difficult area of study because so many questions concerning how one ought to proceed are moral questions themselves. What one teaches arises more or less directly from what one aims to teach; thus, education itself is a moral pursuit. As educational philosopher R.S. Peters (1967, 6) pointed out, "the concept 'education' has built into it the criterion that something worthwhile should be achieved. It implies something worthwhile is being transmitted in a morally acceptable manner." Indeed, educational programs all share the general purpose of preparing the uninitiated to assume their proper role in society. The exact nature of this propriety and the proper means to developing it, however, are at the heart of any explanation for the failure of American education to come to some agreement on a program of moral education. Moreover, if teacher educators have yet to come to some agreement on the proper means to preparing teachers (Schutes 1975), then they are even farther from coming to some agreement on the most appropriate means for preparing moral educators.

Today's classroom teacher is not unlike today's students—overwhelmed with information and underskilled to make the best choices. Moreover, the choices to be made are more often moral ones (Smith 1980). How teacher educators are to prepare a new generation of teachers to enter into the discussion about moral education ought to be a central concern. Consider the continuing controversy over textbook selection, creationism and evolution, humanism and fundamentalism, school prayer, and most recently, school clinics, and sexuality and AIDS education.

Moral issues have once again become the focus of our national attention as sexual exploits and plagiarism by presidential candidates and the unethical, if not illegal, acts of cabinet members and presidential aides raise new questions about the old problem of trusting our nation to its leaders. In a country born of the Enlightenment, education is being called upon once more to solve the problems being raised by a heightened social conscience. Not so surprisingly, calls are being made to re-evaluate teacher education curricula and to initiate broad educational reforms.

As is frequently the case, however, well-intentioned educational programs rest on philosophical and theoretical ground insufficient to provide adequate footing to ensure the desired outcomes. Teachers and teacher educators, hoping to find The Answer to the moral education question, are faced with a complex field of competing models, each promising to be equal to the task (Hersh, Miller, and Fielding 1980).

Which of several competing models of moral education one uses, depends in part upon how one answers several key questions about the nature of humankind: Are people basically good or evil? rational or irrational? self-serving or altruistic? Consider, for instance, that if one assumes that people are basically evil, then a program of moral education should be directed to the development of the necessary external restraints to ensure the social control of the individual. If, on the other hand, people are considered to be basically good, then educational programs should be developed that give expression to people's inherent goodness by providing supportive environments for them. Rational persons will require opportunities to develop their intellectual capacities through solving moral problems, while irrational persons, necessarily in conflict with their neighbors, will need to be brought under the control of a benevolent social order.

In addition, the teacher educator who attempts to introduce a course entitled "The Education of Moral Educators: 101," for example, into the curriculum is confronted by a new set of questions: Should the teacher education curriculum in moral education be a moral education program itself? and if so, should it advocate a "best" approach or a variety of approaches? and what would be the moral justification for selecting not only models and materials, but teacher education candidates themselves?

In order to decide between differing schools of thought on the most appropriate approach to moral education, teacher educators must first decide how to answer these questions for themselves. Further, teacher educators need to understand the assumptions that underlie various approaches if they are to make wise choices from among them. Otherwise they are left with picking randomly to fit this or that situation. If any significant program of moral education is to be found in the maze of alternatives, however, then the moral educator must turn first to the moral philosopher.

Moral Philosophy and Moral Education

Those acts that are moral derive their significance from group sanctions of individual behavior. Not merely a reference to habitual action, the word moral implies a judgment by the group as to the acceptability or rightness of the individual's own judgments and consequent conduct. The concept moral has also come to refer to the disposition or character of the individual act or actor. Moral, therefore, refers to the nature of the individual character, which develops through action in a social setting. What one conceives this nature is and what one conceives that it ought to be are questions for which moral philosophy provides an essential link with moral education.

Chazan and Soltis (1973) distinguish three common assumptions of moral philosophy that may be seen as essential to any discussion of philosophy and education in the moral domain. These common assumptions of contemporary moral philosophy are:

1. the terms moral and morality do not simply refer either to behavior or attitudes but rather refer to a complex of components which encompass at least both of these elements.

2. the concept morality does not simply refer to mores or behaviors deemed acceptable in a certain society, but also refers to the act of personal confrontation with and choice between alternative principles and behaviors on the basis of criteria that transcend the values system of any particular society.

3. moral principles constitute an indispensable component of the moral life and hence of moral education. (Chazan and Soltis 1973, 6)

The importance of these common assumptions lies in their implications for any program of moral education. Specifically, moral education should be concerned with the development of attitudes that are likely to lead to specific and desirable behaviors. Yet, moral education should be education in judgment as well as action. Further, moral education should provide alternative conceptions of morality, rather than the transmission of a specific set of moral values. Finally, and perhaps most significantly, moral education should be moral, that is it should be principled education that provides examples of and opportunities for the application of principled thought to relevant human problems.

These three imperatives for moral education point to three distinct but interrelated elements of morality: caring, judging, and acting. As Hersh, Miller, and Fielding noted, "morality is neither good motives, nor right reason, nor resolute action; it is all three" (1980, 2). Consider these elements when applied to the complex of issues involved in the selection and education of teachers.

Caring applied to teaching suggests that the candidate wants to teach–a sort of unreflective "reaching out" to others. This "social motivation" is coupled with a reflective need to know about others that implies a searching for "social knowledge" (Hersh, Miller, and Fielding 1980, 3). Should candidates only be selected who demonstrate some minimal levels of caring and, if so, how shall it be assessed? and should the curriculum be an attempt to foster caring in the students?

Caring about another is a necessary but insufficient condition for generating moral solutions to moral dilemmas. However deeply one cares for another, the problem remains to make a considered decision about what is right or just or fair. Besides affect, therefore, morality involves intellect. Should teacher education candidates–and their professors, for that matter–be among the most intellectually gifted students or be intellectually adept enough to reason completely through those moral dilemmas that face practicing teachers daily?

Finally, teaching is essentially a moral act (Dewey 1960). Beyond an affective interest in another and some careful reasoning about the rightness of this or that alternative, morality is nothing if it is not an act. Of course, an act is not moral in itself, but rather comes as a consequence of the caring and judging that lead to it. Nonetheless, teachers, teacher candidates, and teacher educators would be something less than moral were they to fail to act on the basis of their own caring judgments. Of what use would be an education that is not put into practice? What sort of moral educators would we be were we not to put into practice the kind of teacher preparation programs that would select, educate, and graduate students who are competent in the caring, judging, and acting required to be effective teachers?

In sum, an effective program of moral education should provide opportunities for students to care for others, to make reasoned judgments about genuinely moral problems, and to act on the basis of their own careful deliberations. Whether, and to what extent, such conditions should be inherent in the selection process and/or fostered in students after their selection, remains an open question.

The function of moral philosophy is to provide a super-structure for building a moral education program. The construction itself, however, demands the labors of other experts. Over the past century, psychology has contributed more than any other field to moral education. The results of systematic, empirical investigations of morality provide today's moral educator with unique pedagogical insight. As might be anticipated, however, differing psychological points of view have left the field in a controlled but muddled state.

Moral Development and Moral Education

Given that people strive for, but rarely if ever attain ideal states, any model of the nature of humankind must include a conception of the nature of developmental change (that is, how one gets from the "is" state of humankind to the "ought" state of the developmental ideal). Three fundamental world views, or paradigms (Kuhn 1962), dominate contemporary approaches to the study of human development (Allport 1962; Dobson, Dobson, and Kessinger 1980; Gardner 1978; Gibbs 1979; Hempel 1966; Kohlberg and Mayer 1972; Langer 1969; Maslow 1970; Reese and Overton 1970; Snarey, Kohlberg, and Noam 1983; Wright 1971). Each of these paradigms is distinguished by a particular emphasis upon the role of the environment or organismic factors on development.

The first of these paradigms, the behavioral, focuses on observable actions and explains development in terms of learning, which is believed to be controlled by environmental conditions. Intrapersonal characteristics are recognized but minimized in accounting for individual differences in behavior. Development is believed to be continuous and to have no particular preferred direction. Developmental stages are viewed as arbitrary conveniences that theorists use to organize the data.

The second of these paradigms, the maturational, attributes the change process to growth and differentiation. Environmental factors are recognized but only as placing limits on individual development, not as directing its course. Maturational explanations depend upon age per se, while development is described typically as a continuous sequence of discontinuous stages.

In the third paradigm, individuals are believed to be producers of their own development through active interaction with the environment. Development is the product of an interaction between maturational, social, and physical factors that are more or less in equilibrium with one another. Because most contemporary theorists view development as interactional, the more restrictive term, structural, is used to call attention to the importance attached to the unity and self-constructive nature of the individual implied in this third perspective. (See Hayes 1986 for an extended discussion of these points.)

Each of these views has a long philosophical and psychological history that bears directly upon the development of a program of moral education. Three different educational ideologies may be derived from each of these developmental perspectives (Kohlberg and Mayer 1972). Each approach employs its own strategy for the generation of research, the assessment of data, and the drawing of conclusions, which are brought to bear in forming educational objectives.

Education as Training Toward Adjustment

The first educational ideology may be identified with the behavioral view (see Aronfreed 1968; Bandura 1986; Skinner 1971). The primary task of education, and of teacher education more specifically, is considered to be the "cultural transmission" (see Kohlberg and Mayer 1972, 452) of the facts and rules of the society to the next generation. Although knowledge and rules are not static but ever-changing, the importance of teacher education lies in the transmission of the facts, skills, and values of teaching. The emphasis, therefore, is on training and skill development with successful achievement determined by the ability of the student to exhibit desirable behaviors.

Teaching machines, micro-teaching, and behavior modification are the latest educational innovations of this tradition. Although the technology changes from one period to another and the specific end behaviors may be modified, the ideology that the aim of teacher education is the training of new teachers in the fixed knowledge of the profession or discipline remains the same.

In the realm of moral education, the cultural transmission ideology takes two positions. The first is that the teacher educator must take the value-neutral position of a scientific investigator. Practically speaking, this means assuming the role of a value free consultant (Kohlberg and Mayer 1972, 464). Although teacher educators may be seen as clarifying the means available to satisfy particular client-defined educational ends, the teacher educator serves many clients.

Given that college faculties, teachers, students, parents, clergy, administrators, state boards of education, and the community at large are unlikely to be in substantial agreement on any educational issue, attempts at a solution lead the teacher educator to the second assumption of this approach, that of value relativity. Teacher educators who take the position that all values are relatively equal no longer work toward the satisfaction of particular ends, but rather have cultural survival as their aim. As Skinner (1971, 128) noted, "Each culture has its own set of goods, and what is good in one culture may not be good in another." Because any non-factual argument about the ends of education, the "goods," is meaningless, moral education must be reduced to the training of the succeeding generation in the values of the present culture. Moral education programs that stress reading the "Great Books" or becoming involved in socially rewarded civic activities are examples of this approach. Taking this approach is likely to encourage colleges of education to become bureaucracies that have as their chief aim the preservation of the existing curriculum.

Education as Freedom to Grow

The second educational ideology derives from the maturational perspective of development and had its first full expression in nineteenth-century romanticism (see Hall 1954; Kohlberg and Mayer 1972; Stafford-Clark 1965; Tice 1980). The aim of teacher education in this view is to allow students the full expression of innate abilities and drives.

The task of the teacher educator, then, is to clear away those encumbrances that frustrate the student's free expression. Students and their inner selves are the focus of the curriculum and efforts are directed toward maximizing the mental and physical growth of students as innate potentialities unfold. Unlike the cultural transmission school, which is society-oriented, and concerned with social control, this view is essentially student-centered and dedicated to maximizing individual freedom.

Like the cultural transmission ideology, this romantic view is founded on the assumption of value-relativity. Because the maturationally oriented educator believes that the student is innately wise and realistic, the student is left alone to pursue his or her own interests. The aim of education, therefore, is "to work joyfully and to find happiness" (Neill 1960, 297).

Although these developmental and educational ends are presumed to be inherent in students, their expression is sought in such traits of character as "honesty," "integrity," "self-confidence," "loyalty," and the like. Participation in the Boy Scouts or school athletics, or involvement in Summerhillian classroom experiments are representative of this approach. The strategy is that teacher education programs aimed at developing these traits will result in promoting mental health as the desired end of moral teacher education. Of course, it is easier to select candidates who already exhibit such traits than it is to develop them.

Nonetheless, a maturationally oriented teacher education curriculum should provide opportunities for the refinement of such moral qualities. Because students in general, and teacher education candidates in particular, are seen as basically good, every effort should be made to maximize their individual freedom as the means to growth, which is the aim of education.

Education as the Stimulation of Development

The third view rests upon cognitive-developmental theories of human development as describing both the course and desired ends of a program of moral education (see Piaget 1932/1965; Kohlberg 1981, 1984, 1987). From this view, development is seen as a progression toward greater adaptation, differentiation, and integration through a universal, invariant, and hierarchical progression of stages (Kohlberg 1969; Piaget 1968). The existence of universal stages of psychological development provides a theoretical framework for educational intervention. The purposes of teacher education should be the stimulation of individual human development to the next higher stage. To paraphrase John Dewey, teacher education "is the work of supplying the conditions that will enable the psychical functions, as they successively arise to mature and pass into the higher functions in the freest and fullest manner" (Dewey and McLellan1964, 207-208).

For the structuralist, the acquisition of morality involves changes in the patterns of one's thinking. Such changes come about through attempts to solve problems of a moral nature that arise from social interaction in situations of social conflict. The structural-developmental approach to moral education finds its most modern expression in the moral reasoning approach of its leading proponent, Lawrence Kohlberg who noted that "morality is neither the internalization of established cultural values nor the unfolding of spontaneous impulses and emotions; it is justice, the reciprocity between the individual and others in his social environment" (Kohlberg and Mayer 1972, 454-455).

For the structuralist, experience is the necessary condition for stage progression, although experience itself is not enough. Experience must be of a kind that presents genuine cognitive conflict, a discrepancy to some optimal extent between the individual's own cognitive structures and his or her present experience. An approach based upon cognitive-developmental theory stresses these principles:

1. Knowledge of the individual's stage of functioning.

2. Arousal among persons of genuine cognitive conflict and disagreement about problematic situations.

3. The presentation of modes of thought one stage above the person's own. (Kohlberg 1972, 9)

From a structural perspective, therefore, teacher education should be designed to stimulate candidates' functioning to higher stages of personal and professional development. Candidates would be selected on the basis of their level of cognitive and moral reasoning (or at least assessed upon admission using the variety of measures currently available [Bradley 1983]) and assigned to developmentally appropriate curricula intended to stimulate their movement to the next higher stage of development.

An Application

Recall the earlier conclusion that an effective program of moral education should provide opportunities for students to care for others, to make reasoned judgments about genuinely moral problems, and to act on the basis of their own careful deliberations. Multiplying these three dimensions of morality across three developmental perspectives gives us a comprehensive model for structuring educational interventions into the moral education of teacher education candidates. Although space is too limited here to give full exposition to such a model, some brief explanation seems in order. (The interested reader may wish to turn to Hersh, Miller, and Fielding 1980, 181-199, for a more detailed presentation applied to six different moral education models.)

Consider the caring dimension, for example. From a maturational perspective, students would be encouraged to discover and express their innate capacities for the nurture and protection of others–an inborn concern for the welfare of others. Opportunities might be provided for students to work as student aids, in daycare centers, or with the handicapped, the terminally ill, or the elderly (see, for examples, McPhail, Ungoed-Thomas, and Chapman 1975; Rogers 1983). Structurally, a curriculum would involve students in an examination of their relationships with and to others, of their connectedness to rather than their separateness from others, and of the problems of inclusion rather than of balancing claims (see, for example, Gilligan 1982; Kohlberg 1987). Finally, from a behavioral perspective, students might be presented with appropriate models of caring persons after which they might be rewarded for demonstrations of caring behavior consistent with those of the models (see, for example, Bandura 1986; Shaver and Strong 1976).

Curriculum Development in Moral Education

The discussion to this point has centered on the what rather than the how of moral education. In this section, the problems in developing curricula that are both morally educative and educatively moral will be introduced. For the teacher educator, the problem is not only how to select materials to introduce to students for their use in classrooms, but additionally how to select materials and design experiences for the candidates themselves.

In their work with classroom teachers, Reimer, Paolitto, and Hersh (1983) found a consistent pattern of activities that teachers used to incorporate moral development theory into their classrooms. Although not designed directly for use in teacher education or with all moral education approaches, their list of procedures provides a useful starting point for further study. Specifically, they suggest that educators planning a moral education curriculum begin by developing a rationale, which should be based upon a personal translation of the theory or theories to which one subscribes. A review of the principles outlined earlier and a thorough grounding in the readings available at the end of this chapter should prove sufficient to begin.

Second, educators should identify moral issues in the curriculum that can be used to illustrate and/or raise relevant moral concerns consistent with the proposed rationale. For example, behaviorally oriented interventions might assess the discrepancy between avowed institutional values related to hygiene and their practical demonstration in the lunchroom, faculty smoking practices, or student dress. Maturationally oriented interventions might be focused on the extent of student freedom in the development of the curriculum, while structurally oriented interventions might debate the rationale for justifying various programs or practices.

Third, educators should relate the moral issues to students' lives by identifying conflicts they are most likely to encounter in their teaching. The selection and use of controversial materials, handling racial, sexual, or religious issues in class, or maintaining student confidentiality in the face of administrative or parental demands all provide common experiences for assessing one's moral responsibility.

Fourth, educators should use material that promotes role-taking. Whatever the rationale, all moral education approaches recognize the importance of taking another's perspective in contributing to morality. Whether stimulating one's moral motivation to care for the other, or stretching students' cognitive abilities to imagine themselves from an external perspective, role-taking provides opportunities to act on another's behalf as if the other. Candidates who can appreciate the perspectives of parents, administrators, and colleagues as well as students with differing backgrounds, values, or developmental capabilities are more likely to succeed when confronted with these issues as teachers.

Fifth, students should be exposed to more adequate reasoning structures if they are to develop the level of sophistication necessary to understand and to articulate the moral issues they are likely to face. Research has shown that teachers at higher stages of development function more effectively in the classroom (Harvey, Hunt, and Schroder 1961).

Finally, because morality is little without action, strategies for increasing student involvement should include encouraging students to be curriculum developers and developing experiences in which students can act on their reasoning. Once students become familiar with what moral issues are, they will be quick to identify them in their personal as well as their professional lives. Student teachers should be encouraged not only to identify moral problems but to act on the basis of a reasoned analysis of the issues. Because morality is inherent in the enterprise of education, students should be helped to see that the moral education curriculum extends beyond the classroom into dimensions of their personal and professional lives.

Indeed, to be a professional is to recognize that the promotion of human welfare forms the basis for a code of ethical behavior from which there is no abdication of one's responsibility. This responsibility to act as well as to profess, raises important issues for the moral educator who intends to be morally educative as well as educatively moral.

Teacher Development and Moral Education

Perhaps more self-consciously than in any other part of the school curriculum, moral educators must be moral as educators. Programs of teacher education should be addressed, therefore, not only to the development of the requisite knowledge, skills, and attitudes for curriculum development and instruction in moral education, but also to the conscious moral development of teachers themselves.

Although much of what is known about the success of moral education programs was obtained through the study of children and adolescents, this limitation is due in part to the general failure until recently to recognize the possibilities for the moral education of adults. Nonetheless, some promising efforts have begun to yield results. Research into the intellectual and ethical development of college students (Loxley and Whiteley 1986; Stephenson and Hunt 1980; Whiteley 1982) and the construction of a college curriculum based on a valuing approach to education (Mentkowski, Moeser, and Strait 1983) demonstrate that deliberate programs of moral education can affect the moral development of young adults.

These studies suggest that teacher educators can incorporate what is known about the moral education of youth into their pre-professional development. In fact, studies begun under the direction of Norman Sprinthall at the University of Minnesota; and continued at North Carolina State University show the efficacy of moral developmental approaches with pre-service and inservice teachers (see Bernier 1976; Oja and Sprinthall 1978; Thies-Sprinthall 1984).

The most recent research in moral education, however, has moved beyond the confines of the classroom to involve entire institutions. In a series of studies, researchers have demonstrated consistently the efficacy of democratic approaches to stimulating moral development with elementary and secondary school students and teachers (see B. Hayes 1987; R. Hayes 1980; Kohlberg 1980; Lickona and Paradise 1980; Mosher 1979; Shaver and Strong 1976; Thompson 1982; Wasserman 1977). These studies demonstrate that classroom teachers can be involved self-consciously in enhancing their own moral development through direct involvement in programs of participatory democracy.

Implications for Further Development

Moral education, like moral development itself, is an organic process, which demands constant attention and re-invention. Because no one theory satisfactorily explains moral development nor moral education in its entirety, the teacher educator must be familiar with a variety of approaches, their methods, their underlying assumptions, and their limitations. How a single approach can incorporate an affective, cognitive, and behavioral approach to individual lifespan development within the context of a changing social pluralism remains to be seen. For the present, moral educators will have to be content with selecting from several approaches on the basis of what seems to work best.

Despite these differences, there is likely to be a search within the field for a unifying method or theory. As part of this effort, teacher educators should become involved in the continuous re-examination of curricula in moral education as part of their own, as well as their students', development. As a beginning, educators should be familiar with the assumptions that underlie existing approaches in their efforts to understand and promote their students' development through systematic programs of moral education.

References

Allport, G. 1962. Psychological models for guidance. *Harvard Educational Review* (34): 373-381.

Aronfreed, J. 1968. *Conduct and conscience.* New York: Academic Press.

Bandura, A. 1986. *Social foundations of thought and action.* Englewood Cliffs, N.J.: Prentice-Hall.

Bernier, J. 1976. A psychological education intervention for teacher development. Ph.D. dissertation, University of Minnesota.

Bradley, L. 1983. Developmental assessment. *Counseling and Human Development* 15: 1-16.

Chazan, B., and J. Soltis, eds. 1973. *Moral education.* New York: Teachers College Press.

Dewey, J. 1960. *Theory of the moral life.* New York: Holt & Co.

Dewey, J., and J. McLellan. 1964. The psychology of number. In *John Dewey on education: Selected writings,* ed. R. Archambault, 207-208. New York: Random House.

Dobson, R., J. Dobson, and J. Kessinger. 1980. *Staff development.* New York: University Press of America.

Gardner, H. 1978. *Developmental Psychology.* Boston: Little, Brown.

Gibbs, J. 1979. The meaning of ecologically oriented inquiry in contemporary psychology. *American Psychologist* 34: 127-140.

Gilligan, C. 1982. *In a different voice.* Cambridge, Mass.: Harvard University Press.

Hall, C. 1954. *A primer of Freudian psychology.* Cleveland, Ohio: World Publishing Company.

Hall, R., and J. Davis. 1975. *Moral education: In theory and practice.* Buffalo, N.Y.: Prometheus Books.

Harvey, O., D. Hunt, and H. Schroder. 1961. *Conceptual systems and personality organization.* New York: John Wiley and Sons.

Hayes, B. 1987. A human relations program to reduce teacher stress. Ph.D. dissertation, Boston University.

Hayes, R. 1986. Human growth and development. In *An introduction to the counseling profession*, ed. M. Lewis, R. Hayes, and J. Lewis, 39-95. Itasca, Ill.: F.E. Peacock.

Hayes, R. 1980. The democratic classroom: A program in moral education for adolescents. Ph.D. dissertation, Boston University.

Hempel, C. 1966. *Philosophy of natural science.* Englewood Cliffs, N.J.: Prentice-Hall.

Hersh, R., J. Miller, and G. Fielding. 1980. *Models of moral education.* New York: Longman.

Kohlberg, L. 1987. *Essays on moral development Vol. 3: Eduction and moral development.* New York: Harper and Row.

Kohlberg, L. 1984. *Essays on moral development Vol. 2: The psychology of moral development.* New York: Harper and Row.

Kohlberg, L. 1981. *Essays on moral development Vol. 1: The philosophy of moral development.* New York: Harper and Row.

Kohlberg, L. 1980. High school democracy and educating for a just society. In *Moral education*, ed. R. Mosher, 20-57. New York: Praeger.

Kohlberg, L. 1972. The concepts of developmental psychology as the central guide to education: Examples from cognitive, moral, and psychological education. In *Psychology and the process of schooling in the next decade: Alternative conceptions*, ed. M.C. Reynolds. Minneapolis: University of Minnesota Press.

Kohlberg, L. 1969. Stage and sequence: The cognitive-developmental approach to socialization. In *Handbook of socialization theory and research*, ed. D. Goslin, 347-480. New York: Rand McNally.

Kohlberg, L., and R. Mayer. 1972. Development as the aim of education. *Harvard Educational Review* 43: 449-496.

Kuhn, T.S. 1962. *The structure of scientific revolutions*. Chicago: University of Chicago Press.

Langer, J. 1969. *Theories of development*. New York: Holt, Rinehart & Winston.

Lickona, T., and M. Paradise. 1980. Democracy in the elementary school. In *Moral education*, ed. R. Mosher, 321-338. New York: Praeger.

Loxley, J., and J. Whiteley. 1986. *Character development in college students*, Vol. 2. Schenectady, N.Y.: Character Research Press.

Maslow, A. 1970. *Toward a psychology of being*. New York: Van Nostrand.

McPhail, P., Ungoed-Thomas, and H. Chapman, 1975. *Lifeline*. Niles, Ill.: Argus Communications.

Mentkowski, M., M. Moeser, and M. Strait. 1983. Using the Perry scheme of intellectual and ethical development as a college outcomes measure: A process and criteria for judging student performance, Vols. 1 and 2. Paper presented at the meeting of the American Educational Research Association, Montreal, April.

Mosher, R. 1979. A democratic high school: Damn it, your feet are always in the water. In *Adolescents' development and education: A Janus knot*, ed. R. Mosher, 497-516. Berkeley, Calif.: McCutchan.

Neill, A.S. 1960. *Summerhill*. New York: Hart.

Oja, S., and N. Sprinthall. 1978. Psychological and moral development for teachers: Can you teach old dogs? In *Value development as the aim of education*, eds. N.

Sprinthall and R. Mosher, 117-134. Schenectady, New York: Character Research Press.

Peters, R.S. 1967. *Ethics and education*. Chicago: Scott, Foresman and Company.

Piaget, J. 1968. *Six psychological studies*. New York: Random House.

Piaget, J. 1965. *The moral judgment of the child*. Glencoe, Ill.: The Free Press. (Original work published 1932.)

Reese, H.W., and W.F. Overton. 1970. Models of development and theories of development. In *Life-span developmental psychology: Research and theory*, ed. L.R. Goulet and P.B. Baltes, 115-145. New York: Academic Press.

Reimer, J., D. Paolitto, and R. Hersh. 1983. *Promoting moral growth*, 2nd Ed. New York: Longman.

Rogers, C. 1983. *Freedom to learn in the 80s*. Columbus, Ohio: Charles E. Merrill.

Schutes, R.E. 1975. Needed: A theory of teacher education. *Texas Tech Journal of Education* 2: 94-101.

Shaver, J., and W. Strong. 1976. *Facing value decisions: Rationale building for teachers*. Belmont, Calif.: Wadsworth.

Simon, S., L. Howe, and H. Kirschenbaum. 1985. *Values clarification: A handbook of practical strategies for teachers and students*. New York: Dodd, Mead, and Company.

Skinner, B.F. 1971. *Beyond freedom and dignity*. New York: Knopf.

Smith, B. 1980. Pedagogical education: How about reform? *Phi Delta Kappan* 62: 87-91.

Snarey, J., L. Kohlberg, and G. Noam. 1983. Ego development in perspective: Structural stage, functional phase, and cultural-age periods models. *Developmental Review* 3: 303-338.

Stafford-Clark, D. 1965. *What Freud really said.* Baltimore, Md.: Penguin.

Stephenson, B., and C. Hunt. 1980. Intellectual and ethical development: A dualistic curriculum intervention for college students. In *Developmental counseling and teaching,* ed. V.L. Erickson and J.M. Whiteley, 208. Monterey, Calif.: Brooks/Cole.

Thies-Sprinthall, L. 1984. Promoting the developmental growth of supervising teachers: Theory, research, programs, and implications. *Journal of Teacher Education* 35: 53-60.

Thompson, L. 1982. Training elementary school teachers to create a democratic classroom. Ph.D. dissertation, Boston University.

Tice, T. 1980. A psychoanalytic perspective. In *Moral Development and Socialization,* eds. W. Windmiller, N. Lambert, and E. Turiel, 161-199. Boston: Allyn and Bacon.

Wasserman, E. 1977. The development of an alternative high school based on Kohlberg's Just community approach to education. Ph.D. dissertation, Boston University.

Whiteley, J. 1982. *Character development in college students Vol.1.* Schenectady, New York: Character Research Press.

Wright, D. 1971. *The psychology of moral behavior.* Harmondsworth, Middlesex, England: Penguin.

Suggestions for Further Reading

The following list is intended not so much to be comprehensive as it is to be illustrative of the most available on moral education.

Books:

Bandura, A. 1986. *Social foundations of thought and action.* Englewood Cliffs, N.J.: Prentice-Hall.

This book presents a comprehensive theory of human motivation and action from the perspective of one of social-learning theory's leading scholars. It is the best current attempt to integrate the role played by cognitive, behavioral, and environmental factors in psychosocial functioning.

Berkowitz, M., and F. Oser, eds. 1985. *Moral education: Theory and application.* Hillside, N.J.: Lawrence Erlbaum Associates.

One of the most up-to-date collections of research, theory, and practice available in moral education. Its strength lies in the consideration of a variety of approaches under investigation in studies conducted around the world.

Carter, R. 1984. *Dimensions of moral education.* Toronto: University of Toronto Press.

Provides the reader with a basic grounding in the activities that characterize the Socratic approach to teaching and education. The author provides an excellent critique of the Values Clarification approach and an enlightened analysis of Kohlberg's moral reasoning approach.

Chazan, B. 1985. *Contemporary approaches to moral education: Analyzing alternative theories.* New York: Teachers College Press.

The author analyzes, categorizes, and compares several major twentieth century theories of moral education.

The analysis is philosophical, educational, and practical, pointing up the similarities and differences that arise among these various theories.

Gilligan, C. 1982. *In a different voice.* Cambridge, Mass.: Harvard University Press.

In this very important adjustment to Kohlberg's earlier work, the author calls for the recognition of different modes of thinking about relationships. Although the studies cited point to major differences between the empirical observation of the moral developmental experience of men and women, the book expands our understanding of the universal elements of the human condition.

Hersh, R., J. Miller, and G. Fielding. 1980. *Models of moral education.* New York: Longman.

Although now nearly ten years old, this book still stands as one of the clearest introductions to the field of moral education. Beyond an examination of the basic models of moral education currently being proposed and tested, the authors provide annotated bibliographies of the major writings from each of the perspectives presented.

Kohlberg, L. 1981, 1984, 1987. *Essays on moral development: Volumes I, II, and III.* New York: Harper and Row.

This three volume set presents a collection of the most important writings from the premier scholar in the field of moral education. The major topics considered include: the philosophy of moral development; the psychology of moral development, and the relationship of education to moral development.

Leming, J. 1983. *Foundations of moral education: An annotated bibliography.* Westport, Conn.: Greenwood.

Provides the most comprehensive collection of resources available for those interested in moral education. Although already becoming dated, this bibliography will provide newcomers and experts alike with a ready source for identifying the most important and useful works in the field.

Lickona, T. 1983. *Raising good children*. New York: Bantam Books.

Based on the work of Lawrence Kohlberg, the author has drawn upon his considerable experience as a teacher educator to present a comprehensive model of developmental moral education. Written for parents, the book contains a wealth of practical examples for dealing with children of all ages that teachers will find appealing. An extensive annotated bibliography of "books for kids that foster moral values" is included.

Loevinger, J. 1987. *Paradigms of personality*. New York: W.H. Freeman and Company.

This book presents a brief but comprehensive review of the major systems of personality theory. The emphasis is on the logic underlying the various approaches and provides a detailed bibliography of relevant works for the interested reader.

Reimer, J., D. Paolitto, and R. Hersh. 1983. *Promoting moral growth*, 2nd Ed. New York: Longman.

Kohlberg himself this book "the best introduction to the cognitive-developmental approach to moral education of Piaget or myself currently available (from the Foreword, ix). Provides a very readable presentation of the theory of cognitive moral development and its application to real classroom practice.

Rest, J. 1986. *Moral development: Advances in theory and research*. New York: Praeger.

A state of the art review of recent research into the theory and practice of assessment in moral development. Readers interested in understanding the complex issues raised by research into moral development or who want to become knowledgeable consumers of research results in this field will find this book must reading.

Rogers, C. 1983. *Freedom to learn in the 80s*. Columbus, Ohio: Charles E. Merrill.

An updated version of Rogers' 1969 classic, this book presents a humanistic approach to student-centered education. Specific means are presented to help teachers in developing an entire educational program of self-directed change.

Sapp, G. 1986. *Handbook of moral development.* Birmingham, Ala.: Religious Education Press.

A basic resource volume on the rapidly expanding field of moral development. The authors consistently emphasize the relationship between cognitive and affective factors on moral behavior.

Simon, S., L. Howe, and H. Kirschenbaum. 1985. *Values clarification: A handbook of practical strategies for teachers and students.* New York: Dodd, Mead, and Company.

Perhaps no other contemporary book in the field of moral education has caused as much excitement and controversy as this one. This latest edition contains a wide array of exercises designed to introduce a values clarification approach into the classroom and should be read by anyone who wants to know what the authors really advocated with this approach.

Windmiller, M., N. Lambert, and E. Turiel. 1980. *Moral development and socialization.* Boston: Allyn and Bacon.

This edited book examines three different perspectives on moral development and education: structural developmental, social learning, and psychoanalytic. Chapters provide detailed expositions of the major assumptions of each approach and include discussions of the limitations of other approaches as seen from each perspective.

Periodicals and Newsletters

Character II.

This newsletter is intended for educators interested in character, its definition and its development, and in the assessment and evaluation of educational programs designed to promote character development. Subscriptions are available for $10 by writing to Edward A.

Wynne, Editor, Character II, ARL, 14815 South McKinley, Posen, IL 60469

Ethics in Education.

A newsletter for teachers and educators covering topics in moral/values education. Published five times per year, it features reports on both theory and practice and provides information on materials and resources available for classroom use. Subscriptions are available for $18/yr by writing to Editor, *Ethics in Education*, OISE Press, 1074 Kensington Avenue, Suite 109, Buffalo, NY 14215.

Exchange for Philosophy and Moral Psychology.

This newsletter serves as an information exchange for scholars in the field of moral philosophy and psychology. Issues contain brief reviews of recently published works, ideas or research in progress, a list of subscribers' names and addresses, and recent bibliographies. Subscriptions are available for a small fee by writing to Thomas Wren, Editor, Exchange for Philosophy and Moral Psychology, Philosophy Department, Loyola University of Chicago, 820 N. Michigan Avenue, Chicago, IL 60611.

Journal of Moral Education.

The only international journal in the field of moral education, it is published three times per year. Its contributors and readers include educators at all levels and from a wide variety of disciplines including philosophy and psychology. Articles range from theoretical analyses and discussions to reports of empirical research, case studies, and descriptions of classroom practice. Subscriptions are available for $40/yr by writing to NFER-Nelson, Carfax Publishing Company, 85 Ash Street, Hopkinton, MA 01748.

Moral Education Forum.

This quarterly contains articles, interviews, an exhaustive annual bibliography of new research, and information about experimental programs and curricula that have a strong value dimension. Individual subscriptions are available for $20/yr; $35/2 yrs by writing to Editor, *Moral Education Forum*, University of Minnesota, Minneapolis, MN 55455.

Research in Humanistic Education: Implications for the Future of Teacher Education

Gary F. Render

Introduction

Teachers possess incredible power! They affect students' lives in profound and long-lasting ways. They have the power to nurture, develop, facilitate, support, humiliate, retard and discourage, among others. Teachers in public schools work with students who are compelled by law to be in their classrooms. They intervene, often uninvited, into young people's lives and attempt to change them from who they are to who they ought to be or could be. What an awesome responsibility! Unfortunately, not all teachers, parents, colleges of education or the general public take this responsibility as seriously as it should.

Schools are resistant to change. Generally schools change through external pressures and tend to be far more reactive than proactive. In the scramble to respond to the pressures from the society to improve educational opportunities for students, school administrators all too often seek quick and simple solutions to complex problems. Colleges of education are following a similar pattern. Unfortunately, most attempts at school reform do not focus on what is known from educational research as the basis for restructuring or reorganizing curricula and, until educators incorporate educational research into reform efforts, education will fall short of achieving the status of a true profession. A profession abandons tradition in light of evidence. Education has been woefully reluctant to do this: it clings to time-honored tradition despite insurmountable evidence that it should do things differently.

This chapter will focus on a major area of educational research which has been in process for more than 20 years and is largely ignored by administrators, teachers, and professors of education. The research focuses on the power of the teacher– mentioned previously–and indicates how teachers can affect virtually all educational outcomes without restructuring schools and curricula. The focus of the research is on the teacher and the teacher's behavior. I firmly believe that teachers *do* make a difference and the following information can insure that the effects of teachers are positive and productive rather than negative and retarding.

The research to which I have been alluding regards the work of David Aspy and Flora Roebuck in humanistic education. This research is an outgrowth of the work of Ned Flanders, Carl Rogers, and Robert Carkhuff. At this time, research in humanistic education has been conducted in 42 states and seven countries, and more than 200,000 hours of classroom interactions have been analyzed. The results of the research have been consistent cross-culturally, across content areas, and across grades (investigations have taken place from kindergarten through graduate school) (Rogers 1983). Unfortunately, this body of work has been largely ignored by teachers, administrators, curriculum developers, and professors of education. One cannot help but conclude that most professional educators are not doing their homework. The following excerpt is an example of the ignorance exhibited by some professional educators. It is a summary in a chapter of an educational psychology textbook–the chapter is titled "Humanistic Perspectives in Education."

> There are a few objective reviews of humanistic education, and they provide ambiguous support for humanistically oriented programs. As a rule, children in such programs perform academically as well as or slightly less well than do children in more traditional, teacher-centered programs, but their attitudes toward learning often seem to be more positive. . . . (Seifert 1983, 344)

Seifert credits only Gage and Peterson as providing data for this statement. *No* research studies or researchers in humanistic education are cited by Siefert. His statement, as will be seen, is inaccurate and misleading. The statement certainly does not reflect the true state of the art. I do not mean to suggest that Seifert is the only writer guilty of such inaccurate statements, but he is a clear example of those who are not only ignoring a major area of research but suggesting that humanistic education is at best a method that may affect student attitudes. Seifert unfortunately is not alone in his perceptions.

The lack of knowledge by writers would be more understandable if humanistic educational research were just beginning; however, this area of research has been conducted since the 1950's. There is no excuse for professional educators not to be well versed in the research findings in humanistic education. Hopefully this chapter will help alleviate this undesirable condition.

Review of the Literature

Several reviews of research in humanistic education are available (Aspy 1972, 1986; Aspy and Roebuck 1976, 1977; Render 1985; Rogers 1988). The following is an overview of findings. Please keep in mind that all findings are:

1. statistically significant (at least $p < .05$);
2. consistent across grade levels;
3. consistent across subject areas;
4. consistent across regions of the United States;
5. consistent across cultures; and
6. based on more analyses of classroom variables and on more subjects than virtually any other area of investigation in the field of education.

Aspy (1986) suggested that this data base is the largest in the world about what happens in U.S. classrooms! Keeping these points in mind, let's review the data.

Ned Flanders' work on classroom interaction analysis really set the stage for further research in humanistic education. I believe that Flanders deserves credit for greatly expanding understanding of the teaching/learning process. The results of Flanders' analyses of classroom interactions led to the categorization of teachers into two groups, direct and indirect.

Direct teachers were characterized by the following behaviors:

1. Teacher lectures.
2. Teacher gives clues.
3. Teacher criticizes.

Indirect teachers were characterized by other behaviors:

1. Teacher accepts student's feelings.
2. Teacher praises student.
3. Teacher accepts or uses student's ideas.

4. Teacher asks questions.

After determining these two types of teachers, the question arose regarding a possible relationship between the two teacher types and students' cognitive and affective outcomes.

In studies comparing student outcomes of indirect versus direct teachers, the indirect teachers' students consistently performed significantly better (Aspy 1972). This was true in such areas as:

1. Student attitude development in eighth grade social studies.

2. Student achievement in eighth grade mathematics, seventh grade social studies, and eighth grade biology.

3. Student achievement and attitude development in arithmetic in elementary classes.

4. First graders' compositions, both in measures of quantity and quality.

5 Achievement in culturally deprived kindergarteners.

6. Third, fourth, and fifth grade students' high achievement.

7. High levels of critical thinking in students in grades two to six.

8. Third and fourth graders' scores on a verbal creativity measure.

Remember that the preceding are only selected findings to provide a sample of what was found. Aspy stated:

It is apparent that the micro-elements involved in the indirect/direct relations (indirectness) do affect achievement and attitude development in almost every subject area at almost every grade level from K-9 (1972, 18).

Flanders and others found that teachers talk most of the time, as much as 80%, and therefore in many cases indirect teaching was not being used. Keep in mind that this was known more than 30 years ago!

With this information available, David Aspy and Flora Roebuck decided to establish a theoretical basis for research to provide more specific information on behaviors which could be associated with "indirect" teaching. The model developed was based on the work of Rogers, who suggested that learning would be facilitated when a helper, teacher, or counselor provided high levels of empathy or understanding, congruence, or genuineness and positive regard, or respect. Aspy and Roebuck then formulated testable hypotheses which stated that the higher levels of empathy, congruence, and positive regard given students by teachers, the more the students will learn (Aspy and Roebuck 1976).

Empathy is the ability to feel what someone else is feeling. It is critically important that educators not forget what it feels like to be a student. Congruence, also referred to as genuineness, realness or authenticity, is the ability to be who one truly is. That is, one behaves in accordance with what one is truly feeling. Educators need to avoid ritualistic teacher behavior. Teachers have feelings and it is appropriate to be reasonably open about those feelings. Positive regard, or respect, is a characteristic that indicates that all people are worthy of respect and should, at all times, be treated accordingly. Teachers have been given advice such as "don't smile until Christmas" or "don't let students call you by your first name" as ways to gain students' respect. One guaranteed way to gain students' respect is to treat them with respect.

Rogers believed that these three characteristics were essential for counseling or therapeutic effectiveness. The goal of therapy is to facilitate growth and change. This is also the goal of education: to facilitate growth and change. It is reasonable, therefore, to assume that empathy, congruence, and positive regard are characteristics essential to effective teaching. Robert Carkhuff (Carkhuff, Berenson and Pierce 1977) shared this assumption, and also felt that these characteristics could be both taught and measured. Therefore, he developed the Carkhuff Interpersonal Process Scales (CIPS) to measure one's levels of empathy, congruence, and positive regard for both therapists and teachers. These characteristics are referred to as interpersonal skills and have served as the focus of some of, if not the most revealing research regarding teaching effectiveness available. David Aspy and Flora Roebuck (Aspy 1972; Aspy and Roebuck 1974, 1976, 1977; Render 1988; Roebuck 1983; Rogers 1983) have investigated the impact of interpersonal skills on educational outcomes and are primarily responsible for 200,000 hours of classroom observations and analyses.

Aspy first found that teachers' levels of empathy, congruence, and positive regard were significantly and positively related to student achievement. After several pilot studies funding was sought and received from the National Institute of Mental Health to support the establishment of the National Consortium for Humanizing Education (NCHE) in 1971 (Aspy and Roebuck 1976). Since the founding of the NCHE the work has been progressing and the results have been strong and consistent.

Aspy and Roebuck, using Rogers' three dimensions of empathy, congruence and positive regard as their theoretical basis, employed the aforementioned CIPS for evaluating individual levels of teacher interpersonal functioning in relation to students. These scales assess interpersonal functioning in empathy, congruence, and positive regard using a five-point scale and have been shown to have very acceptable supporting data regarding reliability and validity (Aspy 1972). These scales also were used to train teachers to raise their levels of interpersonal functioning. The researchers added two variables to the three identified by Rogers: success promotion and student involvement. Aspy developed five process scales assessed at five levels: teachers' level of empathy, congruence, positive regard, student involvement, and success promotion. Strategies were also developed to train teachers to raise their facilitative levels of these five conditions as Carkhuff had used his scales in training psychotherapists (Render 1988).

Scales used for analyzing interpersonal skills are broken down to 5 levels as follows:

Level 1 - Very ineffective (crippling)
Level 2 - Ineffective (hurting)
Level 3 - Minimally effective
Level 4 - Very effective (adding significantly)
Level 5 - Extremely effective (adding, encouraging and exploring)

These scales developed for teachers were based on the CIPS but were rewritten for teachers rather than counselors. Empathy, congruence, and positive regard can all be measured on this 5 point scale. These scales can be used to analyze teachers' interactions with students and to assist teachers in raising their interpersonal skill levels and be facilitative rather than retarding (facilitative levels are approximately 3.2 on the scales and retarding levels are below 3.0, that is, lower than minimally effective).

The first area of investigation regarding interpersonal skills was to establish the average level of interpersonal skills among teachers. Over the years the following findings emerged:

1. The average level of empathy, congruence, and positive regard among teachers is about the same as the general population or the "person on the street."

2. The average level of interpersonal skills for teachers is below 3.0 (2.2-2.3).

3. The average level of interpersonal skills for principals and counselors is below 3.0.

4. The average level of interpersonal skills for professors of teacher education is below 3.0.

5. Discipline problems can be predicted if a teacher's interpersonal level is known.

6. There are 5 retarding teachers for every one facilitating teacher in a typical school.

All of these findings are important and the last is, of course, intolerable.

Using the interpersonal skills scales in classroom observations, the use of time in a typical classroom can be assessed and the following trends have been found (Aspy and Roebuck 1977; Render 1988; Rogers 1983):

1. Teachers talk about 80% of the time (note that this figure hasn't changed since the work of Flanders). Students talk about 10% of the time and there is silence and confusion about 10% of the time.

2. Approximately 80% of classroom activity is spent in memorization. About 10% of classroom activity is spent in thinking. (Unfortunately this is generally pseudo-thinking; that is, problems which don't exist in the real world. For example, train A leaves point X going east at 50 miles per hour and train B leaves point Y going west at 60 miles per hour. At what point will they crash into one another?) About 10% of classroom activity is non-cognitive. This non-

cognitive does not mean affective development is happening but is the same 10% previously mentioned as silence and confusion.

3.   There is generally no response to human feeling in classrooms.

Other findings indicate that:

1.   Students are going along with the teacher approximately 95% of the time, are distracted 4% of the time and are excited 1% of the time.

2.   In first grade 95% of questions in a classroom are asked by students. In third grade 95% of questions are asked by teachers.

3.   At all levels 75% of students sit in straight rows (good for listening to a central figure but not conducive to interaction).

John Goodlad (1984) stated that if teachers talking and students listening are what we want, we can be assured that we have it. But is this what we want?

Teachers and others can, in relatively short amounts of time, be taught to significantly raise their interpersonal skills to the 3.0+ level. Systematic training can be effective but teachers can also learn some of these skills through personal practice. For example, the 5 levels of interpersonal skills can be characterized as follows:

Level 1 - No expression or expression unrelated to learner ignoring learner's message.

Level 2 - Responding to content–usually some advice given–ignoring learner's feeling.

Level 3 - Responding to both feeling and meaning of learner's statements. This is done by employing the response "You feel ____because _____."

Level 4 - Personalizing understanding of learner's goal(s). The response to be used is "You feel because ____ and ____."

Level 5 - Developing a step-by-step program to achieve learner's goal(s).

Relating Research to Practice

I encourage everyone to practice at least the level 3 minimally effective response as often as possible, and with others in our lives besides students. Training and practice will allow this responding to become a natural part of our repertoire of interpersonal skills. Remember, respond to *feeling* and *meaning*. For example, a student says "I work very hard and can never get a high grade." A level 3 response could be "You feel frustrated because your efforts just don't seem to get the results you want." This is just one example of a response–as you can imagine there are many possible. This same response at a level 4 could be "You feel frustrated because your efforts just don't seem to be getting the results you want and you are working hard." Both of these responses follow the previously mentioned "fill in the blank" responses.

If teachers can operate at an average of 3.0+ the results can be startling. Teachers who operate at this facilitative level will have students who will be statistically significantly different from students whose teachers are not facilitative. Facilitative teachers' students (Render 1988; Rogers 1983):

1. Miss fewer days of school.
2. Score higher on self-concept measures.
3. Make greater gains on standardized achievement measures in math and reading.
4. Present fewer discipline problems.
5. Commit fewer acts of vandalism.
6. Have increased scores on intelligence measures.
7. Make gains in creativity scores.
8. Behave more spontaneously.
9. Exhibit higher levels of thinking (analysis, synthesis and evaluation on Bloom's taxonomy).
10. Exhibit more student talk.
11. Do more problem solving.
12. Exhibit more verbal initiation.
13. Ask more questions.
14. Are more involved in learning.
15. Have more eye contact with the teacher.
16. Exhibit more physical movement.
17. Exhibit fewer feelings of anxiety.

An impressive list to be sure! Remember all of these outcomes are statistically significant and are found to be true across grades levels, (kindergarten through graduate school), across subjects, across states and across cultures. Archimedes said "give me a place to stand and a lever long enough and I can move the world." One of Aspy and Roebuck's (1976) books is called *A lever long enough.* By incorporating interpersonal skills in our teaching, we have the lever to move the world and develop healthy, fully functioning people.

There are some simple ways to start this change. In one study teachers were required to respond after student talk using one of these words–happy, sad or angry. Their students' reading scores doubled. Another study focused on increasing teachers' eye contact with students for one year. This increased eye contact resulted in a statistically significant increase in school attendance.

The following are a few more findings worthy of note (Render1988; Rogers 1983):

1. Teacher empathy is the most frequently recurring predictor of students' growth in self-concept, student achievement, attendance, and disruptive behavior.

2. Low facilitative teachers' students suffer a decrease in self-concept scores.

3. Teachers' fatigue, poor nutrition, and lack of physical exercise are deterrents to positive interpersonal relationships.

4. It takes only one retarding teacher to neutralize the effects of one facilitative teacher and two facilitative teachers to eradicate the effects of one retarding teacher.

5. Facilitative teachers can produce the same positive outcomes with educationally handicapped students.

6. A principal's level of interpersonal functioning is related to teachers' level of interpersonal functioning which is related to students' cognitive and affective achievement.

7. There is a significant positive correlation between a teacher's self-concept and students' performance on the Stanford-Binet and standardized achievement tests.

We can all become facilitative teachers and that can affect virtually all educational outcomes. We need to practice

high level interpersonal skills whenever possible and in a variety of settings. Facilitative teachers provide:
1. More response to student feeling.
2. More use of student ideas in ongoing instructional interactions.
3. More discussion (dialogue) with students.
4. More praise of students.
5. More congruent (less ritualistic) talk.
6. Explanations which fit the immediate needs of learners.
7. More smiling with students.

Educators deal with students who are experiencing major changes. These students need to feel important. They feel important when they are heard. Facilitative teachers are needed at all levels to assist students in their growth and development. Arthur Combs (1988) has said that people develop feelings that they are liked, wanted, acceptable, and able from having been liked, wanted, accepted, and from having been successful. One learns that one is these things not from being told but only through the experience of being treated as though one were so. Here is the key to what must be done to produce more adequate people.

The power of a teacher to affect students' lives is awesome. Teachers can facilitate growth, teachers can facilitate regression. High levels of interpersonal skills *will* facilitate growth!

Tausch (1978) conducted several studies in Germany to investigate some of the same variables studied by Aspy and Roebuck. The following are some of the findings of this research:

- In 18 elementary teachers, seven subjects and students studied, a high level of warm respect in teachers plus a low level of directiveness was significantly related with (a) the quality of student contributions to a class, (b) students' independent thinking behavior, (c) students' independent productive thinking, (d) students' spontaneous behavior and (e) students' taking initiative and making their own decisions.

- In a study of 96 teachers in both secondary schools and elementary schools in the subjects of German, sociology, mathematics, and science, it was found that facilitative teachers' students showed significantly enhanced intellectual processes, were more spontaneous, were more interested in lessons, and said more of what they felt and thought.

- A study of 36 elementary teachers of German and over 1,000 students indicated that facilitative teachers' students exhibited significantly higher intellectual quality in contributions to the class, more independent thinking, greater spontaneity, and greater communication with each other about their lessons.

Tausch went on to report that, in his studies of teaching, empathic understanding, genuineness, warm respect, and non-directive facilitative activities significantly affected the quality of students' contributions to lessons, spontaneity, independence and initiative, positive feelings about lessons, and positive perceptions of teachers. Tausch's findings agree with the findings of Aspy and Roebuck as can be seen from the following:

Summary and Recommendations

Over 200,000 hours of classroom interactions have been recorded and analyzed at all educational levels (kindergarten through graduate school), in 42 states and seven countries. This is probably the largest existing data base regarding what happens in classrooms. Virtually all important educational outcomes have been investigated, and the results of these observations are consistent and statistically significant. The level of interpersonal skills of teachers is *critical* to positive educational outcomes.

At a time when so many elements of the society are calling for substantial educational reform and improvement one can only wonder why such an incredibly comprehensive body of research is ignored by many, in fact, most professional educators. Research in humanistic education has been available for more than 20 years.

Yet problems certainly exist regarding parents' and teachers' relationships with students. For instance, according to Holmes (1986):

1. Teenagers receive an average of 32 seconds of positive interaction with their parents per day.

2. Parents give an average of 8 criticisms for every compliment teenagers receive from them.

A Comparison of Research Findings in Humanistic Education

Research Question Asked	NCHE Answer (USA) (Aspy & Roebuck)	Tausch Answer (Germany)
1. Do students benefit when high levels of Rogers' facilitative conditions (empathy, congruence, positive regard) are offered by their teachers?	YES. Benefits include: more physical movement, more prob-lem solving, more academic achievement, more verbal initiation, more involvement in learning, more question asking by students, more verbal response to teacher, higher gains in creativity, higher scores on IQ tests, higher levels of cognition, higher self-concept scores, less absenteeism, fewer acts of vandalism, and fewer discipline problems.	YES. Benefits include: more independent spontaneous behavior, more independent productive thinking, more decision making, more initiative, more interest in learning, more candid expression of self, more motivation to work, more favorable emotional response to schools, higher intellectual processes, higher perceptions of having learned, favorable perceptions of teacher, better achievement, fewer feelings of anxiety.
2. How many teachers offer high levels of these conditions naturally (without special training)?	VERY FEW. The mean for all teachers is 2.3 (without training); slightly lower for secondary teachers and slightly higher for elementary teachers.	VERY FEW. About 12% of all teachers were rated high on all three dimensions (11% of secondary and 14% of elementary teachers).
3. Are these dimensions related to other teacher characteristics?	NO. Levels of facilitative conditions were not related to age, race, sex, years of teaching experience or geographic location.	NO. Levels of facilitative conditions were not related to years of teaching experience, class size, or didactic teaching skills.
4. Can teachers learn to offer high levels of these conditions?	YES; through systematic training in interpersonal skills.	YES; through university courses and encounter group experiences.
5. Do students benefit from "trained" high levels as well as from naturally occurring high levels of the facilitative conditions?	YES; same benefits as in #1 above.	YES; same benefits as in #1 above.
6. When text material is organized in a person-centered manner, do students benefit?	Not tested.	YES; benefits included better learning, better retention, shorter completion times, improved interest, more enjoyment, and texts were perceived as more intelligible and more practical.
7. Is physical fitness of the teacher related to the levels of facilitative conditions offered?	YES; as an enabling factor. Physically fit teachers can maintain high levels for a longer duration.	Not tested.
8. Do the facilitative conditions make a difference in non-classroom settings?	YES; in the home, and in health care settings.	YES; in the home, in sports, and in counseling disturbed children and adults.

3. Teachers provide an average of 18 criticisms for every compliment teenagers receive from them.

4. In teachers' lounges there is an average of 59 criticisms to every compliment teachers make about the teenagers in their school.

Should we be surprised that there is often alienation of youth in this society? Jonathan Winters has said that he was raised in a "house of correction" in which he was continually made aware of his errors and shortcomings. Obviously this "house of correction" mentality exists in homes and is even stronger in schools. Can such a climate facilitate free and open inquiry, growth, and learning?

The preceding review has provided direction for the much needed reform in teacher education. Colleges of education are attempting reform, but all too often the changes are superficial. For example, colleges of education are changing entry requirements such as grade point averages. There is no evidence that indicates that grade point averages are related to teaching effectiveness. Colleges of education are having students take various content examinations. There is no evidence that the scores on these measures are related to teaching effectiveness. Some colleges of education are attempting reform of the teacher education curriculum. The curriculum should change in light of knowledge about effective learning. Teacher education curriculum change has been difficult and seldom included the findings from research presented in this chapter.

Contrary to the comments by Siefert (1983) quoted at the beginning of this chapter, the preceding discussion suggests that the results of humanistic educational research are far from ambiguous. The work of Aspy, Roebuck, and others, however, has gone largely unnoticed in the educational community.

The implications for teacher preparation are clear. The following are only a few I consider to have high priority:

1. Professors of teacher education must do their homework and learn of the results of the 30 years of work in humanistic education. They then must practice raising their own levels of empathy, congruence, and positive regard as it is believed that teachers will teach as they were taught.

2. Teacher education students should receive training in high levels of empathy, congruence, and positive

regard and a teacher education curriculum should include specific training in these levels of required participation in sensitivity and/or encounter group experiences.

3. Teachers in training should receive experiences specifically designed to enhance and develop their positive self-concepts and high levels of self-esteem.

4. Professors of education must develop and assist their students in developing nondirective facilitative ways of teaching which include success promotion, student involvement, and dialogue rather than didactic behavior.

5. Teacher preparation programs which emphasize only cognitive growth and development will not produce truly effective teachers. The affective behaviors of teachers are *critical* to their ability to facilitate growth and learning in others.

These suggestions would significantly affect teacher effectiveness. To ignore educational research in a teacher education program is, I believe, malpractice and cannot be tolerated if education is to be viewed as a profession. Humanistic education is not a panacea, but it certainly can greatly improve the outcomes of education.

Aspy (1986) has titled a new book *This is school: Sit down and listen.* The chapter titles include the following:

Lesson 1: Don't Feel!
Lesson 2: Don't Think!
Lesson 3: Don't Talk!
Lesson 4: Line Up!
Lesson 5: Don't Get Involved!

He reviews the research that supports the idea that these are the lessons students are learning in school. This situation must change and can change. We have a lever long enough.

References

Aspy, D.N.   1986.   *This is school: Sit down and listen.*
Amherst, Mass.: Human Resource Development Press.

An update of all of the years of research in humanistic
education in a brief, cogent, and easily readable format.
An excellent overview of the research.

Aspy, D.N., and C.B. Aspy. 1985. Intensity: The core of thinking. *Education*105 (Summer): 414-416.

Aspy, D.N., and F.N. Roebuck. 1977. *Kids don't learn from
people they don't like.*   Amherst, Mass.:   Human
Resource Development Press.

Aspy, D.N., and F.N. Roebuck. 1976. *A lever long enough.*
Dallas, Tex.: National Consortium for Humanizing
Education.

This book describes the formation of the National
Consortium for Humanizing Education and updates the
continuing research.

An excellent book in which is presented 15 research
studies, findings, and implications.

Aspy, D.N., and F.N. Roebuck. 1974. From humane ideas to
humane technology and back again many times. *Education* 95 (Winter): 163-171.

Aspy, D.N. 1972. *Toward a technology for humanizing education.* Champaign, Ill.: Research Press.

This book describes the pilot research studies
conducted and reviews of the research of Flanders. The
development of Aspy's approach to research in
humanistic education is clearly presented.

Carkhuff, R.R.   1986.   Learning in the age of information.
Education Summer 106: 264-267.

Carkhuff, R.R., D.N. Berenson, and R.M. Pierce. 1977. *The
skills of teaching: Interpersonal skills.* Amherst, Mass.:
Human Resource Development Press.

An excellent activity book to help develop facilitative skills using the scales that are in use in skills training and research.

Combs, A.W. 1988. Developing self-esteem for maintaining your health. A keynote address presented at the annual meeting of the Association for Humanistic Education, April. Paducah, Kentucky.

Combs, A.W. 1979. Humanistic education: Need or nonsense? *Journal Humanistic Education* 3 (Spring): 1-5.

Combs, A.W. 1975. Humanistic goals of education. In *Humanistic Education Sourcebook*, ed. D.A. Read and S.B. Simon, 91-100. Englewood Cliffs, N.J.: Prentice-Hall.

Combs, A.W. 1973. The human side of learning. *The National Elementary Principal* (January): 38-42.

Combs, A.W. 1970. Sensitivity education: Problems and promise. *Educational Leadership* (December): 235-237.

Combs, A.W. 1964. The personal approach to good teaching. *Educational Leadership* (March): 369-377.

Farmer, R. 1984. Humanistic education and self-actualization theory. *Education* 105 (Winter): 162-172.

Goodlad, J.I. 1984. *A place called school.* New York: McGraw-Hill.

An excellent book on effective schools, teachers, and strategies.

Holmes, K. 1986. Using humanistic concepts with teenagers. *Infochange* 42: 13.

A brief summary of trends in interactions between adults and teenagers.

Maslow, A.H. 1968. Some educational implications of the humanistic psychologies. *Harvard Educational Review* 105 (Winter): 685-696.

Patterson, C. H. 1986. Carkhuff principles and skills of human relations serve as a model of excellence. *Education* 106 (Summer): 262-263.

Render, G. F. 1988. Humanistic education: What research offers middle school educators. *Dissemination Services on the Middle Grades* 19 (February): 5.

Render, G. F. 1985. Research in humanistic education: Implications for teacher preparation. *Teacher Education Quarterly* 12 (3): 68-74.

An article that provides a brief overview of research in humanistic education.

Richards, A.C. 1978. Evaluation in a humanistic classroom: Basic assumptions and expectations from my perspective. *Colorado Journal of Educational Research* 17 (Winter).

Roebuck, F.N., and C.B. Aspy. 1987. Changes in teachers' behaviors and perceptions of self and students after training in Carkhuff's program development. *Person-Centered Review* 2 (May): 217-232.

Roebuck, F.N. 1983. Strategies for person centered education. Presented at the American Educational Research Association annual meeting, April. Montreal.

Provided contemporary information about research in humanistic education and reviewed the continuing work of Tausch.

Rogers, C.R. 1983. *Freedom to learn for the 80's.* Columbus, Ohio: Charles E. Merrill.

Certainly one of the best books on education generally and humanistic education in particular. Ideas for teachers are included as well as descriptions of successful strategies employed by teachers. There is an entire chapter devoted to research in humanistic education.

Rossiter, C.M. 1976. Maxims for humanizing education. *Journal of Humanistic Psychology* 16 (Winter): 75-80.

Seifert, K. 1983. *Educational psychology.* Boston: Houghton
    Mifflin.

    A standard introductory educational psychology text.
    Typical in its cavalier treatment of humanistic education
    and related research.

Tausch, R.   1978.   Facilitative dimensions in interpersonal
    relations: Verifying the theoretical assumptions of Carl
    Rogers in school, family education, client-centered
    therapy, and encounter groups. *College Student Journal*
    12 (Spring): 2-11.

    An excellent overview of many studies (as the title
    suggests) which support the findings of Aspy and
    Roebuck.   The studies involve various samples of
    teachers, students, subjects, grade levels, and settings
    other than schools.

Measurement and Research in the Classroom: Directions for Preservice Education of Teachers

Kathy E. Green

This chapter summarizes position papers and empirical studies regarding the role of research and measurement in preservice teacher education. The current status of research and measurement training in teacher education programs, the use of reseach and measurement by inservice teachers, discrepancies between optimal and actual practice, and suggestions for change are described. The chapter concludes with recommendations for directions teacher education programs may take to provide students with greater expertise in research and measurement.

The areas of research and measurement, though intimately related, are generally conceptualized and taught separately and will be developed separately in this chapter. The concluding recommendations will encompass both areas.

Measurement

Measurement as an area of study examines the theory, construction, and use of tests and other evaluation instruments. Testing in American schools has been and continues to be a subject of controversy from the local to the national level. Testing at all levels has increased with the accountability demands placed on district, state, and national educational institutions and the informational demands of objective-based instructional systems and competency-based evaluation. The overwhelming majority of states have instituted some form of minimum competency testing—for high school graduation, for college matriculation, for teacher certification (Yeh 1980). Achievement testing is conducted as early as kindergarten and continues through high school. Teacher education students may need to pass a competency test to enter the program, a skills test to exit the program, and competency and performance tests to keep their jobs and advance in the profession. The modes and content of tests may be changing, but testing remains a fact of academic life. Given the frequent use of tests in American schools, there is general agreement among professionals (academic faculty, school administrators, AFT-NEA officials, legislators) that teachers need training in tests and measurement.

Measurement Preparation

Selection tests for civil servants were used in China as early as the 24th century B.C. Tests for selection became commonplace in the United States when the United States Civil Service Commission began in 1863. Examinations at universities were originally oral (e.g., at the University of Bologna in 1219) but with the widespread use of paper in the 1500's, written exams ensued. In 1836, the University of London was chartered as an examining organization with no instructional program of its own. By the mid-1800's, written examinations were recognized as the basis for decisions about entrance to professions and about the granting of degrees. But while testing in one form or another has been common practice for centuries, test theory (and training in test preparation and analysis) is relatively new. Traditional test theory originated in the early 1900's but item response theory or modern test theory did not develop until the mid-1900's.

Formal preparation in testing and evaluation began in the 1900's with the content of today's measurement courses influenced by work done in the 1960's (Conant 1963; Mayo 1964, 1967). Common elements of a basic course in tests and measurement are units on the relationship of testing and test item types to instructional objectives, item and test design, test administration, reliability and validity, basic statistics, item and test analysis, standardized testing, non-test evaluation techniques, and grading systems. Today courses may also provide information about testing for special needs students, legal issues in testing, the use of microcomputers in testing, test theory, etc.

While the content of a basic tests and measurement course is similar across many institutions, the perceived importance of the course varies. Measurement courses are not uniformly required as part of the preservice teacher education curriculum. Noll (1955) found that 83% of the institutions surveyed offered a measurement course but only 14% required it and only 10% of the state departments specified a measurement course for certification. Mayo (1964, 1967) found, as did Noll, that <u>most</u> institutions offered a course in measurement but that it was not required by either the institution or the state department. Roeder (1972, 1973) reported that 42% of 940 institutions surveyed required a measurement course. Schafer and Lissitz (1987) conducted an extensive survey of AACTE member institutions: most programs did <u>not</u> require measurement with the exception of special education and school counseling. Further, in most cases, measurement was not required by the state (not required for elementary/secondary teachers in 78% of the cases).

Though a tests and measurement course is not uniformly required, is it taken by most preservice teachers? When offered as an optional course, professors report that 25% or less of teacher education students take the course (Gullicksen & Hopkins 1987). Goslin (1967) found that 40% of the teachers surveyed had some formal measurement training. Several studies have been conducted more recently. Yeh, Herman, and Rudner (1981) and Newman and Stallings (1982) found 77% of the teachers surveyed to have one or more tests and measurement course. Newman and Stallings reported that of those taking this class, 78% did so because it was required. Other estimates of the percent of teachers with tests and measurement training are 73% and 84% (Green & Stager in press; Gullicksen 1982). Thus, it appears that the proportion of teachers who take a tests and measurement course as part of their preservice preparation has increased since Goslin's 1967 study, but that the course is not taken by most students unless it is required. (In contrast, a 1965 study showed measurement to be a requirement at the doctoral level in only 27% of the 76 institutions surveyed—Kratwohl, 1965.)

While the provision and requirement of introductory tests and measurement courses should increase the knowledge base, Newman and Stallings (1982) and Yeh(1980) suggest there has been little change in competency since Mayo's 1964 study. They conclude that the training provided at the preservice level is inadequate with little inservice provided to strengthen teachers' knowledge. Hills (1977) asked district coordinators to judge the measurement competency of their teachers: only

25% were judged to have thorough, effective training in tests and measurement. Leiter (1976) agrees in stating that the existing tests and measurement background of teachers leads to the development of unreliable, potentially invalid tests.

Thus, while most programs offer, and some require, a tests and measurement course, the course is not uniformly considered a necessary part of teacher education. And, when taken by preservice teachers, this course has not been shown to be effective in providing an adequate foundation in measurement. Tests are here in increasing numbers and apparently here to stay. Since so many decisions affecting children are made on the basis of test results–grades, placement, selection, curriculum revision, counseling into and out of occupations–understanding and using test results properly is not only desirable but necessary. The next section addresses inservice teachers' actual use of testing and measurement techniques.

Inservice Use of Tests and Measurement

Teachers have been found to use classroom tests extensively. The reported percentages of classroom tests which are teacher-constructed range from 0-100% (Gullickson 1982; McKee & Manning-Curtis 1982; Newman & Stallings 1982) with averages of from 50-93%. Teachers have reported spending from 10% to 15% of their time in test construction, administration, scoring, and return of tests (Carlberg 1981; Fennessey 1982; Gullickson 1982; Newman & Stallings 1982; Stager & Green 1984). The reported average percentage of students' course grades that are based on test scores is 40-50%, with a range of 0-100% (Gullickson 1982; McKee & Manning-Curtis 1982; Stager & Green 1984). In contrast, while often given annually, and at most grade levels, the results of standardized tests are reported to be used very little by classroom teachers (Beck & Stetz 1979; Fennessey 1982; Goslin 1967; Lazar-Morrison Polin Moy, & Burry 1980; Stager & Green 1984; Stetz & Beck 1978). Hall, Villeme, and Phillippy (1985) found teachers use their own tests and statewide competency tests more than district-mandated standardized tests for making decisions. Actual use of teacher-made tests and other assessments by teachers, then, is heavy with little use made of standardized test results.

Measurement experts have suggested that some aspects of test construction and analysis are systematically neglected by teachers. The results of several studies suggest that while teachers' use of testing practices varies with grade level and content area, teachers use classroom tests mainly as measures of achievement with other frequently mentioned purposes being to evaluate teaching and to determine grades. Short answer and matching items are reported to be used extensively (Gullicksen 1982; Stager & Green 1984). In contrast, item and test analysis, test reliability, and item files are used relatively little. Test items are predominantly written at the lower levels of Bloom's taxonomy (80% according to Flemming and Chambers 1984) and so the entire range of cognitive skills is not addressed by most tests.

Differences Between Prescription and Practice

Clearly, discrepancies exist between expert prescription and inservice practice. Prescribed measurement practices include: clear links between instruction and evaluation, assessment at all levels of the cognitive domain, and item/test analysis used to improve evaluation tools. The primary differences between prescription and practice appear in the lack of item and test analysis and predominance of evaluation at lower cognitive levels. Little evidence exists of the use of descriptive item statistics for item improvement or the use of item banks.

Inservice teachers appear to place more emphasis on nontest evaluation strategies than do professors of educational tests and measurement and also evidence more concern with the identification and evaluation of exceptional children (Gullicksen 1986).

Suggestions for Change

The existence of differences between expert opinion of adequate measurement practices and teachers' actual use of tests indicate several areas in need of attention. Since teachers do not generally use some of the measurement practices emphasized by their instructors, the benefits of these practices must be more clearly pointed out. For example, exactly how are descriptive statistics useful and how can they be readily obtained? Other practices such as nontest evaluation strategies are used by teachers but are not emphasized in coursework. Professors of educational tests and measurement may need to work more closely with inservice teachers to adapt instruction to teachers' actual needs. Several states have mandated that education professors demonstrate maintenance of contact with the field; e.g., returning to the classroom for limited periods of time (Wisniewski 1986). Closer contact with the classroom may provide information to realign measurement courses.

Fennessey (1982) suggests that tests and measurement training should be focused on the student's curricular area–English, physical education, mathematics–whenever possible, as well as being structured to respond to the different needs of prospective elementary, middle level, and high school teachers. Testing practices at different grade levels and in different subject areas are not uniform. To parallel classroom testing activities, courses would need to be tailored to the special needs of different grade levels and subject areas. The observed differences in the field may not, however, reflect "best practices." That is, the teachers at some grade levels and in some subject areas may be unnecessarily restricting their testing practices.

It has been found that teachers with more measurement coursework report more facility in testing (Newman & Stallings 1982; Green & Stager in press). A single introductory course may be insufficient to fully acquaint preservice teachers with item and test capabilities. Supplemental work may be needed to effect change in testing practices. If this initial coursework were adapted by grade level and subject area, the student might be able to gain more expertise in use of a limited number of testing principles and techniques. A follow-up course would then be used to expand the teacher's repertoire. If only one course were offered, however, it would seem desirable to acquaint the prospective teacher with the entire range of test and item types. Appropriate use of these item and test types must then be concretely demonstrated to students in all subject areas and grade levels. A choice is often made between providing education in the theory of tests and measurement and providing training in test construction, interpretation, and analysis, with most professors giving each topic equal weight (Gullicksen & Hopkins 1987). Instruction in the former topic provides a theoretical understanding of measurement and the latter provides survival skills. Both are necessary for optimal understanding and use of tests.

Measurement coursework is not consistently required and probably should be. But, even if it were uniformly required, one introductory course may be insufficient to provide a foundation in measurement. Ebel (1967) suggested that inservice workshops be offered regularly as a way of improving teachers' competency in measurement. Required inservice training may be preferable to added preservice courses. After one or more years of teaching, the teacher will have an experiential base and possibly more motivation to expand his/her testing repertoire, but may not yet be firmly ensconced in patterns of testing.

To summarize, change in measurement instruction could come via reorientation of the introductory course, the requirement of this and additional preservice coursework, or in additional inservice instruction. Since recent developments in measurement and technology bring with them greater flexibility and sophistication, it is desirable to incorporate these developments in teacher preparation programs. The use of microcomputers for testing and test analysis may promote the use of item and test analysis and revision that is currently lacking. Restructuring the introductory course to take advantage of test analysis software coupled with greater receptivity to classroom practice would provide needed survival skills while promoting effective test use.

As Ebel (1967) noted, further intruction in measurement would be appropriately provided through inservice workshops taken after a year or two of teaching. Both the preservice and inservice work should be required; the former for initial certification and the latter for fulfillment of continuing education requirements and continued certification. A primarily skills approach at the preservice level would be followed by a more theoretical approach at the inservice level. In many cases, this would impinge on other required preservice/inservice courses. Efforts to change, then, need the cooperation of the entire education faculty as well as the measurement instructors.

Research

Recent years have found much attention paid to the reform of teacher education. One suggested reform is to increase the research base of teacher education by promoting active research and scholarship on the part of teacher educators. Scholarship is held to be an essential element of good teaching; teacher educators without a commitment to scholarship "contribute to education's second class status" (Wisniewski 1986, 288). Just as scholarly activity is held by many to be essential at the university level, it is also argued that the practice of engaging in research and critical inquiry is essential to the classroom teacher's performance and sense of professionalism (e.g., J.D. Brown 1960; Griffin 1984). To this end, a number of programs have been implemented to help teachers become classroom researchers and to use research findings to change teaching practices (e.g., P. Brown 1976; Griffin & Barnes 1986; McConaghy 1987).

Those arguing for an increased knowledge and use of research by teachers state that teachers with an understanding of research can evaluate pieces of research and identify their applications and limitations--"consumer protection" (Lanier & Glassberg 1981). Conduct and knowledge of research allows for greater understanding of the school as a workplace, informs development of a technical core of teaching, promotes questioning and reflection, and helps articulate one's views of teaching by provision of counterpoint (Griffin 1984). Egbert (1984) notes that educational research is at this time insufficiently developed with primitive mechanisms for transformation into usable processes and products; there is no commitment to research, either in attitude, funding, or time. So, rather than viewing research methods and conclusions as fait accompli, they may be seen as points for discussion. Teachers can compare their own understanding and experiences with the "truth" of research. With more attention to critical thinking and research, the teacher ideally would be scholar as well as clinician.

It must be kept in mind that an integral part of providing appropriate preservice preparation in research methods is the identification of what basic knowledge and skills are needed to read and conduct research in the classroom. This requires identification of current and future directions taken in educational research. Should instruction in research methods emphasize quantitative techniques and experimental design or is classroom research better based in ethnographic methods? Can the stylized language of research reports be changed to allow comprehension by literate nonresearchers or will research reports become even more complex? The literature on teaching research methods to undergraduate education students is essentially nonexistent and so prescriptions based on empirical review are lacking. Recommendations regarding the place of research, then, are general and based on professional opinion.

Research Preparation

Research and teaching were conducted separately in French schools after the French revolution. The French authorities attempted to establish new schools with a practical utilitarian focus separate from specialized research institutions. But Ben-David (1972) suggests that the new system was detrimental to the development of science because research as an activity remained separate from teaching. The unity of teaching and research came to be of crucial importance for scientific research and was a cardinal principle in the development of the 18th century German universities (Redner 1987). In the United States and other Western countries, the nineteenth and twentieth centuries saw the development of universities and separate teacher education institutions (normal schools) that were devoted to practical, utilitarian causes but not to the development of science. The normal schools were on the bottom rung academically, overtaken by women and meant for vocational training. Mattingly (1975) argues that when teacher education programs were designed in the late 1800's, conceptual analysis and critical thinking skills were consciously excluded. While today's teacher education institutions in the U.S. are generally housed in universities, the research tradition found in other disciplines is still absent (Rudduck 1985).

Teacher educators are not, by and large, researchers. This fact is underscored by the provision of funds at the national level to train teacher education faculty in research methods. In education, there exists a traditional animosity between those who view themselves as researchers and those who view themselves as practitioners or trainers. Many teacher educators were not engaged as researchers; they were not expected to produce research. They themselves probably came from settings lacking a research tradition. Fattu (1960) reported that only 10 of the 94 doctorate-granting colleges and universities surveyed had adequate facilities and faculty time allotted to research. The remainder emphasized teaching skills and field service. Guba and Clark (1978) reported that less than 20% of 1,367 education units in higher education had faculty involved in educational research and development. Wisniewski (1986) argues that "unless the overwhelming majority of professors in a college engage in scholarship, the institution is not likely to be very effective" (290). Berliner (1984) describes teacher education as timid, ignorant, and lacking in vision with teacher educators who avoid "reading, critiquing or using the scientific literature about teaching" (1-2). Ineffective use of research by classroom teachers would seem to follow in the footsteps of the nonresearch or even anti-research tradition in many schools of education. No widespread appreciation for research is likely to develop among practicing teachers if their academic mentors show no such appreciation. This nonresearch orientation of schools of education is one explanation for the omission of research methods from teacher preparation programs.

Training in research methods is not a conventional course in initial teacher education at the undergraduate level although exceptions to this rule do exist. Some institutions offer teacher education as an upper level undergraduate or graduate level program. Postbaccalaureate programs exist in most cases at large institutions offering many different programs. These institutions are more likely to offer and to require students to complete research methods courses. But there is currently no indication of a wholesale shift in teacher education programs to the postbaccalaureate level (Guyton & Antonelli 1987). Research methods courses are more frequently offered as part of higher degree programs and are required by numerous graduate programs. The National Council for the Accreditation of Teacher Education (NCATE) has a standard requiring the study of research methods and findings in advanced programs. A 1965 survey of 76 institutions awarding the doctorate showed that a research methods course was required in all but 11 (Kratwohl 1965). A more recent survey found an introductory course in research required by master's programs in 21 of 31 universities in a 13-state region (Doak1982). As Kratwohl (1965) noted, if research methods were taught in all courses there would be less need for separate courses. Research skills, though generally taught to master's and doctoral level students, are occasionally taught through inservice programs (e.g., McConaghy 1987). And, a few undergraduate programs have trained prospective teachers in research skills. Preservice courses at the University of Southern California, California State University-Sacramento, the Ohio State University, and the Alabama Polytechnic Institute taught prospective teachers to interpret and conduct research (Bargar, Okorodudu, & Dworkin 1970; Beaumariage 1973; Frymier 1959; Marks 1972). But these programs are the exceptions. Eaker and Huffman (1981) reported that 75% of the teachers sampled agreed that research findings, if not methods, should receive greater emphasis at the undergraduate level; 64% believed graduate programs in education are the most appropriate place to learn about research methods.

The effectiveness of introductory research methods taught at any level has rarely been empirically assessed. Todd and Reece (1987) surveyed teachers, administrators, and other professionals who had taken an introductory research methods course at master's level between 1980 and 1985. The course was perceived as most helpful in providing familiarity with research terminology and developing the background needed to critically evaluate research reports. Just over half of the sample perceived the course as useful in their job.

The clear lack of preservice training in research methods indicates that currently teacher educators do not feel that teachers need or want research skills, that research skills are not an appropriate part of the agenda for initial teacher education, or that the issue has not yet been addressed. The dearth of evaluation studies of research methods courses provides little empirical evidence upon which to base recommendations.

Inservice Use and Perceptions of Research

The lack of research training leads to several results. Ammons (1970) described teachers' attitudes toward research as being ones of either complete trust or complete fear. Without a research language to use and without the statistics and design skills to do research, teachers are perceived to have negative attitudes towards its use and to fail to accept it (e.g., Brown 1976; Howey & Kearn 1970; Zahorik 1984). The perceived failure to use educational research is thought to stem from several sources. Research may be viewed as irrelevant to classroom reality, too general, overly simplistic, lacking in practicality, wrongly or improperly supported, and hard to understand and so threatening (Adams 1976; Asbury 1975; Brown, 1976; Huling & Johnson, 1983; Kaplan, 1976; Rudduck, 1985; Rumstein 1972; Shaver 1982). But these perceptions were not supported by a 1981 study by Eaker and Huffman. In their study, 105 teachers were asked about the usefulness of research in improving instruction and how effective various research dissemination systems are. Teachers viewed research findings as contradictory but reported valuing research that focuses on classroom teaching. They did agree (97%) that ideas for applying findings should be included in reports of research.

Classroom use of research methods or findings, then, is perceived to be minimal although, again, there is little empirical evidence to support this perception.

Suggestions for Change

The effective use of research would seem to require changes in attitude, direction, philosophy, policy, and perhaps the structure of teacher education institutions. As Rudduck (1985) states, the relationship between research, teaching, and teacher education must be redrawn. One suggested revision is the destruction of the monopoly on educational research held by academics and the subsequent development of the teacher-researcher. But, with negative attitudes and minimal training, the fledgling teacher-researcher faces an imposing challenge in surmounting decades of subordination to academics.

A number of possibilities have been suggested for improving teachers' knowledge and use of research. They include provision of some incentive (i.e., release time) to study research findings/methods, inservice workshops, research offices within the school district, collaboration with universities and with school faculty-university faculty projects, research "translators" who work for a school or for a district, trained teacher-researchers as exemplars in schools, research opportunities as part of student teaching or lab experiences, and undergraduate programs in education with research majors or minors (Adams 1976; Ala-kurikka, Mannisto, & Isohella 1973; Bargar et al. 1970; Cruickshank 1985; McConaghy 1987; Porter 1987; Rauth, Biles, Billups, & Veitch 1983). Research internships coupled with introductory research methods classes may provide for the development of functional skills.   Kratwohl (1965) states that the "doing of research is probably the most important means of learning its methods and of adopting proper attitudes" (81). Research skills are said to be "learned by doing and taught mainly by contagion" (American Psychological Association 1959). At a minimum, Ammons (1970) sees a need to familiarize students with the major kinds of research, the characteristics of each type, and the place of research as well as clinical experience in a teacher's work.

Other suggestions are to change the character of the institution: provide a favorable research climate with faculty and student opportunities for research and hire university faculty with strong research interests.

The need to incorporate research findings in teaching and teacher education has been given lip service for decades. The result has been stagnation in some areas and schools of education with faculty who not only fail to use research in their own work but who find it aversive. If classroom teachers are to be taught to use and to do research, university faculty must be exemplars. This will require a greater commitment to educational research on the part of colleges of education and the university as a whole. Education faculty who are caught up in heavy teaching loads and student supervision have less time to devote to research than some of their colleagues in other fields. Even if only faculty with strong research interests are hired in schools of education, there must be time and facilities available for them to develop their research programs.

Research methods courses can be made a part of the curriculum and perhaps should be, if not as research per se then as critical thinking or inquiry skills courses. An introductory course, as in measurement, could provide language and basic concepts. These would ideally be repeated across the curriculum with specific studies and results discussed in other courses. If research and measurement issues were addressed in the majority of preservice courses, there would be less need for separate instruction in these topics.

But, as has been suggested, doing research may be the best way of learning research. This could be accomplished via research internships that require students to engage in the research process if not to conduct their own studies. Research internships would require a considerable amount of research activity on the part of the faculty and also extensive supervision time. But, the opportunity could be made available to undergraduates in a structured form and required of postbaccalaureate students.

Directions for Teacher Education

Critics of the traditional university-based teacher education program have proposed reform schemes ranging from the elimination of the traditional program with certification of liberal arts graduates to placing teacher education programs in the public school system to forming strictly postbaccalaureate teacher education programs (McCaleb, Borko, Arends, Garner, & Mauro 1987). Directions taken in research and measurement training will obviously need to meld with overall changes in teacher education programs. The area of highest priority in teacher education reform is curriculum revision rather than movement of the program to another level or college (Guyton & Antonelli 1987). Lanier and Little (1986) summarize research on the evaluation of the teacher education curriculum: The overall coursework ". . . remains casual at best and affords a poorly conceived collage of courses across the spectrum of initial preparation" (549). To be most effective, research and measurement issues must be incorporated into a thoughtfully structured tapestry of preservice coursework. Introductory courses in research and measurement could provide language and basic ideas in these areas. Incorporation of research and measurement results, methods, and problems in other courses would then reinforce and add to this foundation. Continuing education or postbaccalaureate requirements could facilitate teachers' theoretical understanding of research and measurement concepts.

Some envision the classroom of the future as a place where teaching methods and the curriculum itself are continually shaped by the results of empirical research and the concomitant measurement techniques. An old adage suggests that he who controls the tests controls the curriculum. In a research-based educational system, he who controls the research process controls the curriculum. The teacher in this system with no understanding of research and measurement is necessarily subservient to the "expert" and has little real professional power. The teacher with the skills to evaluate research, conduct research, and assess the outcomes of instruction with measurement tools of his/her own choosing will have far greater control of the classroom, the instructional methods used, and the curriculum. If we as teacher educators preach about the importance of research and measurement in making decisions about curriculum and instruction, we need to practice these skills.

The provision of optimal instruction and evaluation using current research and measurement techniques requires the conversion of teacher training to teacher *education* and this conversion requires both the development and evaluation of theory in education and the development of skills necessary to understand theory and therefore research. The `trades' approach to teaching with application of psychological rules of thumb needs to give way to a more abstract theoretical approach that can inform a theory/practice debate. While teacher education must supply survival skills, it must also provide the inquiry, theoretical, philosophical, and critical thinking skills that allow teachers to progress as scientists and professionals.

References

Adams, R.D. 1976. Strategies for more effectively interpreting and utilizing education research findings: Implications for professional educators. Paper presented at the American Educational Research Association annual meeting, ERIC ED 124505.

A list of consumer research competencies was developed along with suggestions to increase educators knowledge of research.

Ala-Kurikka, R., Y. Mannisto, and V. Isohella. 1973. The utilization and communication of research results: Information bulletin. Finnish National Board of Education, Helsinki, April, ERIC ED 090089.

A project to translate and disseminate research to teachers in Finland is described.

American Psychological Association. 1959. Report of the seminar on "education for research in psychology." *American Psychologist* 14 (April): 167-179.

Ammons, M. 1970. The teacher as a producer of research and development products. In *Research development and the classroom teacher producer/consumer*, ed. M.V. DeVault. Washington, DC: Association for Childhood Educational International.

Asbury, C.A. 1975. Why educational research is of limited use to the community. Howard University, ERIC ED 103398.

Asbury outlines reasons for the failure of research application.

Bargar, R.R., C.P. Okorodudu, and E.P. Dworkin. 1970. Investigation of factors influencing the training of educational researchers. Washington, D.C.: Office of Education, Ohio State University Research Foundation, May, ERIC ED 045609.

Institutional variables conducive to the production of researchers were examined and suggestions made for improving training.

Beaumariage, G.N., Jr. 1973. Training of vocational education teachers in research methodology and research report writing. Sacramento: California State University, ERIC ED 087922.

The suggestion is made that vocational education students need technical report writing and research methods prior to matriculation.

Beck, M.D., and F.P. Stetz. 1979. Teachers' opinions of standardized test use and usefulness. Paper presented at the American Educational Research Association annual meeting, San Francisco, April.

Ben-David, J. 1972. *American higher education.* New York: McGraw-Hill.

Berliner, D. 1984. Contemporary teacher education: Timidity, lack of vision, and ignorance. Paper presented for the American Academy of Education, Washington, D.C.

Brown, J. D. 1960. Education for a learned profession. *American Scientist* 48: 210A-16A.

Brown, P. 1976. Educational research and practice: A literature review. *Journal of Teacher Education* 27: 77-79.

Reasons for the gap between research and practice are presented with a review of suggestions to remedy the situation.

Carlberg, C. 1981. *South Dakota study report.* Denver, Co.: Midcontinent Regional Educational Laboratory.

Conant, J. B. 1963. *The education of the American teacher.* New York: McGraw-Hill.

Cruickshank, D. R. 1985. Use and benefits of reflective teaching. *Phi Delta Kappan* 66: 704-706.

This paper describes how reflective teaching could be used in preservice, inservice, and graduate education of teachers and principals. These clinical experiences are currently missing from the teacher education curricula.

Darling-Hammond, L. 1987. The requirements of a profession. *The Holmes Group Forum* 1: 12-14.

Doak, J.L. 1982. A survey of the graduate introductory research class. Paper presented at the Mid-South Educational Research Association annual meeting, New Orleans, November.

Eaker, R.E., and J.O. Huffman. 1981. *Teacher perceptions of dissemination of research on teaching findings.* East Lansing, Mich.: Institute for Research on Teaching, Michigan State University, NIE Contract No. 400-76-0073 ERIC ED 205501.

   A sample of Michigan teachers was asked for their perceptions of educational research and its dissemination. Conclusions were that teachers do value research findings and do not perceive tha principals or undergraduate programs place sufficient emphasis on research.

Ebel, R. L. 1967. *Improving the competence of teachers in educational measurement. assessing behavior: Readings in educational and psychological measurement* , ed. J. Flynn & H. Garber, 171-182. Reading, Mass.: Addison-Wesley.

Egbert, R. L. 1984. The role of research in teacher education. In *Using research to improve teacher education: The Nebraska Consortium.* R.L. Egbert, ed. March, ERIC ED 246022.

Fattu, N.A. 1960. The role of research in education--present and future. *Review of Educational Research* 30: 409-421.

   This review paper discusses the present and desirable future role of research in education.

Fennessey, D. 1982. Primary teachers' assessment practices: Some implications for teacher education. Paper presented at the annual conference of the South Pacific Association for Teacher Education, Frankston, Victoria, Australia, July ,ERIC ED 229346.

   Responses to a mail survey of 129 teachers regarding test use are reported.

Flemming, M., and B. Chambers. 1984. *Windows on the classroom: A look at teachers' tests.* CAPTRENDS, Center for Performance Assessment, Northwest Regional Testing Laboratory, Portland, Oregon, September.

Frymier, J.R. 1959. Research for undergraduates in teacher education. *Journal of Teacher Education* 10: 413-416.
   A project incorporating reading and doing research in an undergraduate program is described.

Goslin, D.A. 1967. *Teachers and testing.* New York: Russell Sage Foundation.

   Goslin studied the use of standardized tests at the elementary and secondary levels. Teachers use standardized tests primarily in diagnosis and for feedback but make little use of standardized test results in general.

Green, K.E., and S.F. Stager. In press. Differences in teacher test and item use with subject, grade level taught, and measurement coursework. *Teacher Education and Practice.*

Green, K.E., and S.F. Stager. In press. Effects of training, grade level, and subject taught on the types of tests and test items used by teachers. *Educational Research Quarterly.*

   Significant effects were found in the types of tests and items used by Wyoming teachers at different grade levels in different content areas. The amount of coursework in tests and measurement also had significant effects on teacher facility in testing.

Griffin, G.A. 1984. Why use research in preservice teacher education? A proposal. *Journal of Teacher Education* 35: 36-40.

Griffin, G.A., and S. Barnes. 1986. Using research findings to change school and classroom practices: Results of an experimental study. *American Educational Research Journal* 23: 572-586.

In a quasi-experimental study of the effects of introducing new findings from effective teaching and school leadership into ongoing school settings, significant differences were found in teacher behaviors.

Guba, E.G., and D.L. Clark. 1978. Levels of R&D productivity in schools of education. *Educational Researcher* 7: 3-9.

Gullicksen, A.R. 1984. Teacher perspectives of their instructional use of tests. *Journal of Educational Research* 77: 244-248.

Teacher attitudes toward testing and the classroom use of tests were assessed. Results indicate that teachers use tests heavily but have limited testing expertise.

Gullicksen, A.R. 1986. Teacher education and teacher-perceived needs in educational measurement and evaluation. *Journal of Educational Measurement* 23: 347-354.

The views of professors and teachers about preservice educational measurement courses were compared. In five of eight content areas, the emphases given by professors differed from those recommended by teachers. Major differences and their implications are discussed.

Gullicksen, A.R. 1982. The practice of testing in elementary and secondary schools. Paper presented at the Rural Education Conference, Kansas State University, Manhattan, Kansas, ERIC ED 229391.

Responses to a survey of 336 South Dakota teachers regarding test use were analyzed by grade and curricular level.

Gullicksen, A.R., and M.C. Ellwein. 1985. Post hoc analysis of teacher-made tests: The goodness-of-fit between prescription and practice. *Educational Measurement: Issues and Practice* 4: 15-18.

Elementary and secondary teachers from South Dakota were surveyed regarding their measurement preparation and testing practices. The widest gap between reported practice and prescription came in the use of test and item statistics.

Gullicksen, A.R., and K.D. Hopkins. 1987. The context of educational measurement instruction for preservice teachers: Professor perspectives. *Educational Measurement: Issues and Practice* 6: 12-16.

Professors from 28 midwestern colleges expressed their views regarding measurement course activities, course content, and their own preparation.

Guyton, E., and G. Antonelli. 1987. Educational leaders' reports of priorities and activities in selected areas of teacher education reform. *Journal of Teacher Education* 38: 45-48.

A survey of AACTE institutions was conducted to determine what curricular and program changes were occurring.

Hall, B.W., M.G. Villeme, and S.W. Phillippy. 1985. How beginning teachers use test results in critical education decisions. *Educational Research Quarterly* 9: 12-18.

Weights were assigned to teacher-made, district, and statewide tests by first year teachers. Results suggest that greater weight is placed on statewide assessments for making educational decisions.

Hills, J.R. 1977. Coordinators of accountability view teachers' measurement competence. *Florida Journal of Education Research* 19: 34-44.

Howey, K.R., and J.M. Kean. 1970. The teacher as a consumer of research and developmental products. In *Research, development, and the classroom teacher producer/consumer*, ed. M.V. DeVault, S. Sunderlein, & V. Rapport. Washington, D.C.: Association for Childhood Education International.

Huling, L.L., and W.L. Johnson. 1983. A strategy for helping teachers integrate research into teaching. *The Teacher Educator* 19: 11-18.

A cooperative project between university and public school teachers is described. The project was designed to promote collaborative action research.

Kaplan, L. 1976. Survival talk for educators--the teacher as researcher. *Journal of Teacher Education* 27: 67.

The lack of faculty support for incorporating research competencies in a teacher education program is discussed.

Krahmer, E. 1967. Teachers' lack of familiarity with research techniques as a problem for effective research dissemination. Paper presented at the American Educational Research Association annual meeting, February.

Responses of samples of North Dakota teachers and AERA Division D members to questions assessing familiarity with research were compared. AERA Division D members were more certain of their answers and evidenced greater variability in response.

Kratwohl, D.R. 1965. Current formal patterns of educating empirically oriented researchers and methodologists. In *The training and nurture of educational researchers*, ed. E. Guba & S. Elam, 73-93. Bloomington, Ind.: Phi Delta Kappa.

A survey of 104 doctoral degree granting institutions was conducted to assess the preparation of teachers of research methods, measurement, and statistics.

Lanier, J.E., and S. Glassberg. 1981. Relating research in classroom teaching to inservice education. *Journal of Research and Development in Education* 14 : 22-23.

Lanier, J.E., and J.W. Little. 1986. Research on teacher education. In *Handbook of research on teaching,* 3rd Ed. ed. M.C. Wittrock, 527-569. New York: Macmillan.

Lazar-Morrison, C., L. Polin, R. Moy, and J. Burry. 1980. A review of the literature on test use. Los Angeles: Center for the Study of Evaluation, California State University, ERIC ED 204411.

Leiter, K.C.W. Teachers' use of background knowledge to interpret test scores. *Sociology of Education* 49: 59-65.

Marks, M.B. 1972. Research: The preservice missing link. *Journal of Teacher Education* 23: 453-456.

Mattingly, P.H. 1975. *The classless profession.* New York: New York University Press.

Mayo, S.T. 1967. Preservice preparation of teachers in educational measurement (Contract No. OE-4-10-011). Chicago: Loyola University, December.

        A large random sample of students in teacher education programs was asked about their training in tests and measurement and given a measurement competency test. A posttest given after graduation showed no evidence of increased knowledge.

Mayo, S.T. 1964. What experts think teachers ought to know about educational measurement. *Journal of Educational Measurement* 1: 79-86.

McCaleb, J.L., H. Borko, R.A. Arends, R. Garner, and L. Mauro. 1987. Innovation in teacher education: The evolution of a program. *Journal of Teacher Education* 38: 57-66.

        A postbaccalaureate certification program is described that is theory and research based.

McConaghy, T. 1987. Teachers as researchers: Learning through teaching. *Phi Delta Kappan* 68: 630-631.

        A teacher-as-researcher program used in the Edmonton, Alberta public schools is described.

McKee, B.G., and C. Manning-Curtis. 1982. Teacher-constructed classroom tests: The stepchild of measurement research. Paper presented at the National Council on Measurement in Education annual meeting, New York, March.

Newman, D.C., and W.M. Stallings. 1982. Teacher competency in classroom testing, measurement preparation, and classroom testing practices. Paper presented at the

American Educational Research Association annual meeting, New York, March, ERIC ED 220491.

Teachers in Alabama, Florida, and Georgia were surveyed to establish the extent of preparation and testing practices and knowledge. Results suggest no change in competency since that reported in 1967.

Noll, V.H. 1955. Requirements in educational measurement for prospective teachers. *School and Society* 82: 88-90.

Eighty educational institutions were surveyed regarding measurement requirements for graduation and certification in the state.

Porter, A.C. 1987. Teacher collaboration: New partnerships to attack old problems. *Phi Delta Kappan* 69: 147-152.

Rauth, M., B. Biles, L. Billups, and S. Veitch. 1983. AFT educational research and dissemination program. Washington, D.C.: National Institute of Education, NIE-G-81-0021, January, ERIC ED 234050.

A model was established for disseminating research to classroom teachers via trained teacher research "linkers" placed in schools.

Redner, H. 1987. The institutionalization of science: A critical synthesis. Social Epistemology 1: 37-59.

Roeder, H.H. 1972. Are today's teachers prepared to use tests? *Peabody Journal of Education* 59: 239-240.

Roeder, H.H. 1973. Teacher education curricula--your final grade is F. *Journal of Educational Measurement* 10: 141-143.

Rudduck, J. 1985. Teacher research and research-based teacher education. *Journal of Education for Teaching* 11: 281-289.

Obstacles to the inclusion of research training in initial teacher education courses are discussed as is the potential value of research to the teacher and to teacher education.

Rumstein, R. 1972. Teachers' evaluation of research findings in educational psychology. *California Journal of Educational Research* 13: 71-82.

Elementary school teachers and educational psychologists judged the validity and practical significance of a set of statements based on research findings. Implications for teacher education are discussed.

Schafer, W.D., and R.W. Lissitz. 1987. Measurement training for school personnel: recommendations and reality. *Journal of Teacher Education* 38: 57-63.

Results of a national study of teacher preparation in measurement are reported. The authors conclude that recommendations from professional groups are not being met and suggest that curricular changes be undertaken to ensure that teachers have adequate assessment skills.

Shaver, J.P. 1982. Making reseach useful to teachers. Paper presented at the National Council for the Social Studies annual meeting, Boston, November, ERIC ED 224754.

Reasons for the failure to use research are presented and avenues for future study suggested.

Stager, S.F., and K.E. Green. 1984. Wyoming teachers' use of tests and attitudes toward classroom and standardized tests. Report to the Wyoming State Department of Education, Dept. of Educational Foundations and Instructional Technology, University of Wyoming, Laramie, Wyoming.

Stetz, F.P., and M.D. Beck. 1978. Comments from the classroom: Teachers' and students' opinions of achievement tests. Paper presented at the American Educational Research Association annual meeting, San Francisco, March.

The results of a national study of teachers' opinions of the usefulness of standardized tests are reported.

Todd, R.F., and C.C. Reece. 1987. An Introductory educational research course: Attitudes of a selected group of graduate students toward its helpfulness. Paper presented at the American Educational Research Association annual meeting, Washington, D.C.

This paper reports the results of a survey of teachers and other professionals who had taken a graduate level introductory research course. Subjects responded to questions about the usefulness of the course in various areas.

Wisniewski, R. 1986. The ideal professor of education. *Phi Delta Kappan* 68: 288-291.

This paper discusses the place of scholarship in effective teaching.

Yeh, J.P. 1980. A re-analysis of test use data. Los Angeles: Center for the Study of Evaluation, California University, ERIC ED 205590.

Teacher education, knowledge, and test use are analyzed.

Yeh, J.P., J.L. Herman, and L. M. Rudner. 1981. Teachers and testing: A survey of test use. Los Angeles: Center for the Study of Evaluation, California University, ERIC ED 218336.

California elementary school teachers were surveyed regarding their use of tests and competency in contemporary measurement practices.

Zahorik, J.A. 1984. Can teachers adopt research findings? *Journal of Teacher Education* 35: 34-36.

The argument is presented that the conception and conduct of research may be a problem in the adoption of research by practitioners as well as obtuse presentation of results.

The Many Voices of Multicultural Education

Phyllis F. Maxey

A confused clamor rises on every side, and a
thousand voices are heard at once, each expressing
some social requirements. The people reign over the
American political world as God reigns over the
universe.

Alexis de Tocqueville, 1831

Pluralism and diverse viewpoints have been part of
American society from its beginnings. The constitutional
government that the founders created in 1787 was designed to
protect diverse views and to structure peaceful expression and
resolution of differences. Yet many voices were excluded from
that dialogue and the ideals have been far from the reality.
American history reflects a tension between a dominant
national culture and disenfranchised subcultures. The story of
"We the People" includes institutionalized racism and
discrimination as well as unique opportunities for freedom.
Cultural groups, drawn together by shared race, ethnicity, religion, age, sex, or sexual preference have protested the distribution of society's benefits and burdens, and protested the
dominant culture's intolerance of pluralism.

Multicultural education has many advocates, but also
many critics who disagree about the goals and even the definition of multicultural education.   A common element of most
approaches is the recognition and appreciation of cultural
diversity through the school curriculum as well as the climate
and organization of schools and classrooms. The preparation
of future teachers to teach students of many different subcultures–based on race, sex, religion, ethnicity–is a challenging
task.   How can teachers understand and nourish cultural
groups and yet still provide students with the skills and
knowledge to participate in the national culture?   Before
addressing the issue of what can be done to better prepare

teachers, we need to examine the diverse views of the substance of multicultural education.

Goals of Multicultural Education

Culture is a major human achievement. It provides a pattern of beliefs, social organization, goals for living. Parekh (1986) describes the breadth of perspective gained when a person understands culture as the expression of the efforts and aspirations of a group of intelligent fellow human beings Multicultural education is therefore an education in freedom–freedom _from_ inherited biases and narrow feelings and sentiments, as well as freedom _to_ explore other cultures and perspectives and make one's own choices in full awareness of available and practical alternatives (Parekh 1986, 26).

The function of school then, in both its curriculum and organizational setting, is to help children understand and appreciate their own experience and to extend that experience in broader contexts. In accord with this view of a pluralistic society, several professional organizations have developed policy statements advocating multicultural education. Three such statements will be examined: National Council for the Accreditation of Teacher Education (NCATE), the American Association for Colleges of Teacher Education (AACTE), and the National Council for the Social Studies (NCSS).

In 1973 AACTE prepared a statement, "No One Model American" (1973):

> To endorse cultural pluralism is to endorse the principle that there is no one model American . . . . Cultural pluralism rejects both assimilation and separatism as ultimate goals . . . . Education for cultural pluralism includes four major thrusts: (1) the teaching of values which support cultural diversity and individual uniqueness; (2) the encouragement of the qualitative expansion of existing ethnic cultures and their incorporation into the mainstream of American socio-economic and political life; (3) the support of explorations in alternative and emerging life styles; and (4) the encouragement of multiculturalism, multilingualism, and multidialectism.

The National Council for the Social Studies (NCSS) narrowed the focus to ethnic pluralism in an effort to more explicitly address the goal of ethnic literacy. The argument for such a focus was based on the need to study the problems resulting from discrimination in the United States. *Curriculum guidelines for multiethnic education* state that:

> The Guidelines should focus on ethnic pluralism and not on cultural pluralism . . . . Multiethnic education is concerned with modifying the total educational environment . . . . This includes not only the study of ethnic cultures and experiences but making institutional changes within the educational setting so that students from diverse ethnic groups have equal educational opportunities and the institution promotes and encourages the concept of ethnic diversity.

The National Council for the Accreditation of Teacher Education (NCATE) required college and university programs that prepare teachers for the elementary and secondary levels to have multicultural education as part of their teacher education programs by 1979:

> Multicultural education is preparation for the social, political, and economic realities that individuals experience in culturally diverse and complex human encounters. These realities have both national and international dimensions. This preparation provides a process by which an individual develops competencies for perceiving, believing, evaluating, and behaving in different cultural settings. Thus, multicultural education is viewed as an intervention and an on-going assessment process to help institutions and individuals become more responsive to the human condition, individual cultural integrity, and cultural pluralism.

Multicultural education can be viewed as an effort to reach beyond individual experience, beyond one point of reference, in order to benefit from contact with others. The NCATE statement includes both the national and international dimensions of a multicultural perspective. As individuals participate in the global arena as employers, workers, consumers, travelers, or advocates of a particular cause, they need an understanding that extends personal experience. As voters selecting people or policies that will bind all Americans, an educated person needs to think and act without hypocrisy and prejudice, taking into account the perspectives of many others. Without a multicultural perspective, individuals can erroneously assume that society will adjust to them, that there are no other legitimate points of view.

Deficient or Different?

There are several issues that are important to address in the field of multicultural education. One goal of multicultural education is to improve the performance of lower class and minority children in school so that they can effectively participate and benefit from the dominant culture. In this view members of certain subcultures are seen as deficient due to genetic differences (Jensen 1969) or due to cultural deprivation (Bereiter and Engelman 1966). Cultural deprivation has been attributed to language deficiencies, learning styles, and parental interaction. Whatever the cause, the goal is to help students overcome these handicaps and become effective participants in society.

In 1909 a British writer, Israel Zangwill, introduced the concept of the "melting pot" in a play by that name. Zangwill envisioned a society in which all cultures would fuse together to create a superior and new American culture, something better and beyond the Anglo-Saxon model (Bullivant 1981). From this view, those who are different are seen as threats to a unified American Anglo-Saxon society in which all immigrants to the United States abandon their former cultural ties. But the reality of American society belied the concept of the melting pot: certain groups did not "melt" and the dominant culture "rejected as unmeltable many ethnic groups, including native Americans, Afro-Americans, Spanish speakers, and Orientals" (Bullivant 1981).

Dissent and Dialogue

Imbedded in the concept of multicultural education is a view of what American society is and should be. Future teachers need to assess their own views of a pluralistic society and their own tolerance for diversity. Some may have a melting pot viewpoint and reject democratic pluralism. Others may fear that multicultural education is simply a grandiose scheme that may make a few superficial changes in curriculum, but essentially reinforces the exclusion of various subcultures from social participation. Some may argue that multicultural education draws attention away from real problems that threaten the future of ethnic minority youth. In discussing national reports advocating educational excellence, Harold Howe II reminds us that fundamental changes are desperately needed: " If I may be excused for some rhetoric, I would assert that our republic is in greater danger from the combined problems of school dropouts and youth unemployment than it is from academic deficiencies" (Howe 1985).

Banks (Banks and Lynch 1986) describes a cyclical process of ways in which excluded ethnic minorities respond to discrimination and racism. He refers to such dissent as "ethnic revitalization movements." The first phase is characterized as the precondition phase in which the conflict between the democratic ideas and institutionalized racism creates rising expectations and a perception that the conditions faced by the minorities is intolerable. The first phase is characterized by polarization, controversy, and protest. Banks sees the use of single-cause explanations of problems as a necessary part of this phase as ethnic groups try "to get racism legitimized as a primary explanation of their problems" (Banks and Lynch 1986, 7). In a later phase, racism is seen as only one of several causes of problems and Banks states that "emotions cool during this phase and individuals who disagree can engage in fruitful dialogue without accusations and epithets" (Banks and Lynch 1986, 8). Nations facilitate the movement from early to later phases of ethnic revitalization "by making symbolic concessions to ethnic groups, such as black studies programs, the hiring of ethnics in highly visible positions, the establishment of affirmative action policies, and the creation of a middle class ethnic elite that serves as visible proof that ethnics can make it" (Banks and Lynch 1986, 8). In the final phase, reforms are institutionalized, and may be extended to other subcultural groups such as handicapped people and women. The ethnic and racial groups are included structurally within the nation state, although Banks does not describe what such structural inclusion might look like.

The goal of cultural pluralism could produce two very different societies. In Pacheco's conception of democratic pluralism, "there is a balance of power between competing and overlapping religious, ethnic, economic, and geographical groupings" (Bullivant 1981, 116). Each of these interest groups strives to protect its own concerns and participates in making decisions that are binding on all groups in society. Each of these groups shares a belief in values and procedures that allows differences to exist and allows for resolution of conflicts.

But there are other pictures of a pluralistic society. Perhaps each group preserves its own language, religion, and customs, living separately except in the area of economic trade.

The individual develops a commitment to his/her ethnic group stronger than any national commitment. The nation state provides political structures which allow ethnic groups to maintain their differences and represent their interests. Ethnicity and separateness become important features of such a society.

Neither of these views of American society describe the present reality. The first model of democratic pluralism hides the realities of power and social class and could produce programs which as MacDonald states, "affirm the rights of individuals in the context of structures which predispose the competitive success of certain subcultural groups " (MacDonald 1977, 13). The second model is perhaps more descriptive of a country such as Canada than the United States, but could reflect a future direction for the United States and other pluralistic societies. Each of these views has important implications for education as we struggle to answer the question, "What are schools for?"

Diversity in the Schools

If we are to respect and acknowledge diverse viewpoints, the schools will have to provide different curriculum and instruction to build students' skills, knowledge and attitudes toward diversity and conflict. To exclude different views from the classroom is to impose one view, and deny students opportunities to learn of democratic procedures for conflict resolution, compromise, winning and losing. Horace Mann advocated schools without controversy:

> But when the teacher, in the course of his lessons or lectures on the fundamental law, arrives at a contro-verted text, he is either to read it without comment or remark; or, at most, he is only to say that the passage is the subject of disputation, and that the schoolroom is neither the tribunal to adjudicate, nor the forum to discuss it. (Cremin 1957, 97)

Mann was concerned about the support for public education from the majority of citizens, and he concluded that is was better to have public schools that were neutral, rather than to have none at all. But how are we to make the concerns of various cultural groups legitimate if we do not allow diverse opinions and perspectives to be recognized and understood? Teaching the ideals embodied in the American national culture is vitally important. If the ideals are applied to the present, and past failures and successes acknowledged, students can internalize these ideals. If constitutional principles such as consent of the governed are only taught as abstractions, they will have little impact on students' thinking or on the conduct of school life.

I have found in working with credential students throughout the California State University's nineteen campuses both ignorance and fear about conflict and controversy in the classroom (Maxey 1987). One of the approaches suggested in preservice classes was the use of case studies that show a conflict of interests and values between two or more parties. As an example we used a legal case in which Fred Korematsu, a Japanese American, violated the order in which Japanese Americans were evacuated from the West coast during World War II, and relocated in internment camps. Many students did not know of the case or the outcome in which the U.S. Supreme Court supported the relocation of all Japanese-Americans because of military necessity (Korematsu v. United States 1944).

In each class students became engaged in a lively discussion of the legal and moral arguments in the case, the historical setting, and parallels in recent years. But there was both hesitation and resistance to using such a case study in a secondary school classroom. The future teachers expressed several concerns:

1. It would embarrass Japanese American students.
2. The case showed the American justice system at its worst.
3. This case or others that arouse controversy will bring parent complaints.
4. Discussions of racism and discrimination can cause classroom disruptions.

Teacher education programs need to help teachers learn to constructively use conflict and dissent in the classroom and provide models both in the university as well as the public schools. The future teachers raised important concerns regarding classroom climate, teaching values, and the vulnerability of teachers to complaints from parents and community interest groups. Each of these issues must be addressed if multicultural education is to be more than rhetoric. Future teachers need to consider their answers to the question, "What are schools for?" They need to encounter examples of school programs that allow expression of many voices representing the student body, and give students experiences in solving problems in the school related to justice, equal treatment, and minority rights.

The Community in the Curriculum

Within classrooms as well as within the total school environment, teachers have succeeded in incorporating multicultural education into the curriculum. Future teachers need to see many examples of these programs, discuss them in university classes and observe them in action in local schools. Noreen Austin's fifth-grade classroom was described in a recent issue of *Educational Leadership* (Vasconcellos and Murphy 1987). She built an entire curriculum around the immigrant experiences of her students. She began by using colored threads to represent blocks of time (pre-1800, 1800-1840, post 1975), tracing each family's travel to the United States.

> Three things happened as each child's "thread" was traced across the wall. First, the commonalty of the immigrant experience emerged through the telling of vastly different stories. Second, the identity of being an "American" shifted from abstract notions to concrete histories of struggling families. Further, the "first Americans" were no longer the Pilgrims, but rather the families of Tina, and Terri and Daniel, whose roots were Native American. The next oldest Americans were black classmates, whose ancestors had been forcibly brought here well before most of the other families had migrated. (Vasconcellos and Murphy 1987, 71)

The teacher did not stop with a book of family histories, but extended the study into the ways personal histories were linked to the history of others, and the interdependence of people within and among communities. This teacher's curriculum was changed by the diverse group of students in her class; she shared with the students the responsibility of deciding what knowledge is most worthy of time and study.

Diaz, Moll, and Mehan (1986) report a project in which data collected from an ethnic community was used to inform classroom practice. Most of the families of the 27 students in the study were from Mexico; few parents had more than five years of schooling. The families were poor and the predominant language spoken at home was Spanish. Based on ethnographic data collected in the homes of these students there was little writing in the home other than shopping lists and phone messages. The most frequent writing was the students' homework assignments. The parents were concerned with their children's education and valued writing, but the researchers found that "virtually every conversation that began as a discussion of writing eventually turned to the problems of youth gangs, unemployment, immigration, and the need to learn English " (Diaz, Moll, and Mehan 1986, 21).

This ethnographic data was incorporated in a curriculum plan for a high school class. The students in an English as a Second Language class (ESL) developed with their teacher a survey of community attitudes toward language and bilingual abilities. The teachers received training in approaches to writing developed by Graves (1983). The combination of students writing about an issue of great concern to themselves and their parents and of collecting the information themselves was successful in that it capitalized on students strengths. Their weaknesses in vocabulary and written English were addressed as needed in relation to the project. They did not do workbook exercises unrelated to the writing activity. Diaz reports that "students who would otherwise do little or no classroom writing were writing essays in their second language that incorporated information collected from the community" (Diaz, Moll, and Mehan 1986, 29). If the university can provide such opportunities for future teachers to connect the content and skills of formal education with the strengths and concerns of the communities in which their students live, we may have a powerful impact on students.

Curriculum Organization

The curriculum can be changed in a variety of ways to incorporate the goals of multicultural education. A teacher might create separate units on ethnic groups represented in the school, region, or nation. The advantage of separate units is the in-depth study provided. We are reminded by the anthropologist Francis Hsu, that to truly understand another culture takes a great deal of study:

> Understanding the events and behavior patterns of another society may be compared, to be trite, with assessing an iceberg on the high seas. We can easily see what is on the surface . . . . But unless the observers know something about the submerged portion of the iceberg, consisting of the psychocultural patterns deeply rooted in what went on before, they are likely to be superficial in what they see or,

much worse, to misunderstand what they see. (Hsu 1974, 11)

The disadvantages of separate units are that they can be fragmentary and contrary to certain goals for multicultural education. Geneva Gay states that such a curriculum should be broadly conceptualized "to include both minority and majority ethnic groups, comprehensive treatment of all ethnic group life experiences, and permeate all learning experiences of all children" (Gay 1977, 99).

Banks suggests an approach in which a historical or social event is studied using a multiethnic or multinational model (Banks 1987). Teachers provide the perspectives of several ethnic groups or other nations on any given topic. One perspective is not seen as superior or inferior to another. There are several problems with this approach to multicultural education. The danger of stereotyping is very real, since all members of an ethnic group do not share similar views. The difficulty of finding materials to represent each group's perspective places a great burden on the teacher.

As teachers select curriculum materials and design their own curriculum, they may prefer to use thematic or conceptual approaches to multicultural education. The thematic approach is found frequently in literature texts with stories and poetry selected to speak to universal human concerns: the search for identity, the struggle for survival, for justice, or for a good life. Authors from many different cultural groups can be selected to explore these issues.

In teaching skills in any subject area, a teacher can be sensitive to the variety of learning styles in the classroom and include visual materials and experiential activities as well as the written word. Many of the cooperative learning strategies (Johnson and Johnson 1982) seem to work better with children from particular subcultures (Ramirez and Casteneda 1974, 1979; Witkin & Berry 1975). There are several checklists available to assess curriculum materials for representation of diverse groups, bias, dated content, stereotyping (Rodriguez 1983). Student teachers can use these criteria to review selected curriculum resources. A curriculum that emphasizes basic skills can be enhanced to include those needed for living in a pluralistic, democratic society. Such skills might include stating a point of view, small group work in problem solving, decision making, compromise, and listening to others' views.

Teacher preservice education can include experiences in which future teachers work directly with students from a variety of subcultures. In California teacher candidates are required to student teach in a school which has students who are ethnically different from the student teacher. Many teacher preparation programs require observation in the schools in conjunction with their education coursework. Perhaps one of these observation periods could include developing a unit for an ethnically diverse class and then teaching that unit. This would help university students, who have not yet taught a class, to move beyond the easy criticism that comes as they watch others teach. There is also the insight (and humility) that results from writing a curriculum plan, implementing it, and evaluating the results. The direct interaction of the teacher with the learners that this preprofessional activity produces is also helpful in another way. Teacher preparation programs can become very skills-oriented, giving future teachers a technical set of competencies, but failing to apply those skills to the complexities of the classroom. As Ada states, "Teachers are trained to conform to a mechanistic definition of their role rather than to recognize it as involving a relationship between human beings, with a possibility of growth for both teachers and students" (Ada 1986, 388).

In addition to studying the school curriculum (hidden and explicitly planned curriculum), teacher education programs can provide future teachers with experiences working and living with a cultural group substantially different from their own. At Indiana University cultural immersion was included as part of teacher preparation experiences. After on-campus seminars and workshops, 291 teachers (over a nine year period) each served 17 weeks in schools in isolated Navajo and Hopi Indian communities. Anglo female education majors were minorities in these communities and were taught pedagogy, adaptation skills, and ethnic understanding by Native Americans. The outcomes of such an intensive learning and teaching experience were very positive. They learned to adjust their teaching styles and strategies as needed in working with the Native American children. Student teachers reported coming with uncertainty, leaving with several close Native American friendships, and feeling highly pleased with the experience (Mahan 1981).

Many Voices, Many Views

Diverse people and perspectives bring a complexity to education that may at times be threatening, overwhelming, and/or enriching. Delpit (1986), in a very personal description of the dilemmas of being a black teacher and then a teacher of teachers, describes two different reactions to a new writing project. The philosophy of the writing project is that skills and correctness can stifle a student's writing so there is a major emphasis on fluency in writing. However, Delpit found a major disagreement about process writing:

> Progressive white teachers seem to say to their black students, "Let me help you find your voice. I promise not to criticize one note as you search for your own song." But the black teachers say, "I've heard your song loud and clear. Now, I want to teach you to harmonize with the rest of the world." Their insistence on skills is not a negation of their students' intellect, as is often suggested by progressive forces, but an acknowledgement of it: "You know a lot; you can learn more. Do It Now!" (Delpit 1986, 384)

Delpit makes the argument that not all reforms will effect all students in the same ways. Her own experience with the open classroom in a Philadelphia school reinforced her belief in children's differences. The white students in her classroom worked hard in the open environment and their achievement scores reflected their progress. Some of her black students made progress in reading, but not as rapidly as the white students. Other black children used the open classroom to play rather than work, and responded better to a more traditional environment. Delpit makes the plea that we examine the impact of new programs on all children, and that we listen to the voices and the concerns of all teachers.

It is critical that we recognize that, in Maxine Greene's phrase, "a plurality of American voices must be attended to, that a plurality of life stories must be heeded" (Greene 1986, 440). From these many voices can come a richness for our schools and society as the complexities of living together are no longer hidden from view. Tension between subcultures and the dominant culture will persist, but we can provide experiences with diversity for future teachers that will give them the insight and skills to teach all of the children in our society.

References

AACTE. 1973. No one model American, *Journal of Teacher Education* 24 (Winter): 4.

Ada, A.F. 1986. Creative education for bilingual teachers. *Harvard Educational Review* 56 : 386-394.

Banks, J.A. 1987. *Teaching strategies for ethnic studies.* Newton, Mass.: Allyn and Bacon.

Banks, J.A., and J. Lynch. 1986. *Multicultural education in western societies.* New York: Praeger Publishers.

Bereiter, C., and S. Engelman. 1966. *Teaching disadvantaged children in the preschool.* Englewood Cliffs, N.J.: Prentice-Hall.

Bullivant, B.M. 1981. *The pluralist dilemma in education.* Sydney, Australia: George Allen and Unwin.

Cremin, L.A. 1957. *The republic and the school; Horace Mann on the education of free men.* New York: Bureau of Publications, Teachers College, Columbia University.

Delpit, L.D. 1986. Skills and other dilemmas of a progressive black educator. *Harvard Educational Review* 56: 379-385.

Diaz, S., L. Moll, H. Mehan. 1986. Sociocultural resources in institution : A context-specific approach. In *Beyond Language.* Bilingual Education Office, California State Department of Education.

Gay, G. 1977. Curriculum design for multicultural education. In *Multicultural education: Commitments, issues, and applications,* ed. C.A. Grant. Washington, D.C.: ASCD.

Graves, D. 1983. Writing: Teachers and students at work. Exeter, New Hampshire: Heinemann.

Greene, M. 1986. In search of a critical pedagogy. *Harvard Educational Review* 56: 427-441.

Howe, H., II. 1985. Giving equity a chance in the excellence game. In *The great school debate: Which way for*

American education? , eds. B. Gross and R. Gross, New York: Touchstone.

Hsu, F. 1974. Intercultural understanding: Genuine and spurious. (Occasional Paper Five.) Evanston, Ill.: Center for the Teaching Professions, Northwestern University.

Korematsu v. United States. (1944). 323 U.S. 214, 65 S. Ct. 208, 89 L. Ed. 243.

Jensen, A.R. 1969. How much can we boost IQ and scholastic achievement? *Harvard Educational Review.* 39: 1-123.

Johnson, D.W., and R.E. Johnson. 1982. Effects of cooperative, competitive, and individualistic learning experiences on cross-ethnic interactions and friendship. *Journal of Social Psychology* 118: 47-58.

Mahan, J.M. 1982. Community involvement in culturally-oriented teacher preparation. Paper presented at the Annual Meeting of the Association of Teacher Educators, Phoenix, Arizona, ERIC document.

MacDonald, J.B. 1977. In *Multicultural education: Commitments, issues, and applications,* ed. C. A. Grant, Washington, D.C.: ASCD.

Maxey, P.F. 1987. Civic education for future teachers. Paper presented at the National Meeting of the Social Science Association, San Jose, California.

National Council for the Social Studies. 1976 *Curriculum Guidelines for Multiethnic Education Position Statement.* Washington, D.C.: NCSS.

Parekh, B. 1986. The concept of multi-cultural education. In *Multicultural education,* ed. S. Modgil, et al. 19-32. London: Falmer Press.

Ramirez, M.A., and Casteneda. 1974. *Cultural democracy, bicognitive development, and education.* New York: Academic Press.

Vasconcellos, J., and B. Murphy. 1987. Education in the experience of being citizens. *Educational Leadership* 45: 70-73.

Witkin, H.A., and J. Berry. 1975. Psychological differentiation in cross-cultural perspective. *Journal of Cross-Cultural Psychology* 6: 4-87.

Global Education: The Future Is Now

Fred Baker

"What, Me International?"

My first class at the university was at 8 o'clock in the morning. My alarm clock from Hong Kong went off at 6 a.m. After my shower I put on my shirt from Taiwan, my pants from the People's Republic of China, my tie from England, shoes from Italy and a sports coat from Poland. At breakfast I sat in a teak chair from Honduras, drank tea from Bangladesh and ate pineapple from the Philippines. The tuna sandwich I made for lunch was made of fish from Thailand. As I drove to work in my American car it occured to me that it was assembled in Canada with parts supplied from all over the world. There was no way to get around it. Before I even entered my classroom I had all the trappings of a global person. As I entered the Dean's office for a meeting after my class I noticed him settling back for a pre-conference smoke. It reminded me of an article I had read in an undergraduate history class. In 1936 Ralph Linton had written:

> an American Indian habit, consuming a plant domes-
> ticated in Brazil in either a pipe, derived from the
> Indians of Virginia, or a cigarette, derived from
> Mexico. If he is hardy enough he may even attempt a
> cigar, transmitted to us from the Antilles by way of
> Spain. While smoking he reads the news of the day,
> imprinted in characters invented by the ancient
> Semites upon a material invented in China by a
> process invented in Germany. As he absorbs the
> accounts of foreign troubles he will, if he is a good
> conservative citizen, thank a Hebrew deity in an Indo-
> European language that he is 100 percent American.

Even the most sheltered of our university collegues and students now realize we live in an increasingly international world. Events from around the globe are seen in our living rooms in glorious color on the nightly news. Products from foreign lands fill our markets. American goods as well can be purchased in all corners of the world. It is a two edged sword. While we are the world's largest supplier of food we are also dependent on others for vital commodities, such as oil and copper. Rapidity of change has imposed special burdens on our institutions of higher education which must somehow equip our young to live successfully in a world that is, paradoxically, much larger and much smaller than it once was.

What Is Global Education?

Global Education is the awareness of the interdependence and inter-relationship of the world's population and the ability to take effective action through cultural and/or technological components to ensure our present and future survival. It is a life-long study of world communities and the interworkings of its people and systems—ecological, social, economic, and technological. It requires an understanding of the values and priorities of the many cultures of the world's communities. It leads to implementation and application of global perspectives in striving for just and peaceful solutions to world problems. It is education which provides insight into conditions in other countries, the interdependence among countries and peoples, their common problems and the relativity of the values of one's own country with respect to other cultures. It should aim at creating understanding of other people and a feeling of responsibility in the face of world problems. As Harold Taylor (1974) once said: "In the modern world, there are no foreign problems, only human problems, shared by all societies, in the family of humankind."

There is an obvious need in teacher education programs to provide students with information focusing on new analytical, evaluative, and participatory skills, as well as content information. Essential to the use of these skills is a set of multidisciplinary educational goals that provide a basis for international perspective. These goals may have been best stated by the University of Southern California's Director of the Center for Public Education in International Affairs, Steven Lamy (1983, 43)

1. To develop within students a recognition of the complexity of transnational affairs and the interdependent and dependent relations that link the vari-

ous actors (e.g., nation-states, international organizations and multinational corporations)within the
world's political, economic and socio-cultural
systems.

2. To reach an understanding and appreciation of basic
human commonalities and differences. Students are
encouraged to explore things as the quest for basic
human needs: food, clothing, shelter, health, and
education (as access to culture) from a comparative
perspective.

3. To develop an awareness of how perceptions, values,
and priorities differ among various individuals,
groups, and cultures. In particular, students are
introduced to the importance of "perspectives or
world views" in our decision-making process and in
determining how we interact with others.

4. To introduce students to a variety of analytical and
evaluative skills that will enable them to respond
creatively to local, national, and international events
and participate effectively at those various levels.
These would include an understanding of how
power in a system is organized, decision- making
skills in cross-cultural situations, foreign language
and cross-cultural communication skills, conflict
resolution, mediation and bargaining skills.

These goals are necessary to provide a domino effect in
internationalizing our curriculum. In order for the students in
our public schools to gain competence in these areas the
would-be teachers now studying in our universities must first
come to grips with the realities of our ever-changing world.
The goals of teacher education with a global perspective–to
improve the likelihood of effective and responsible participation in the world system–can be described as working toward
competency in perceiving one's involvement in the world 's
system, in making decisions, judgments, and exercising influence.

Global Education in the perspective of a curriculum for
teacher education, is concerned with scientific, ecological, and
economic issues which affect everyone. These include
questions of war and peace, interdependency of natural
resources and their use, climate control, the use of the sea bed,

the population issue, and other concerns where national positions are not necessarily controlled by inherited, prescientific, political positions. This outlook is characterized by heightened awareness and understanding of the global arena and the global system. It is marked by relatively high levels of attention to conditions, happenings, and developments planetwide and by sensitivity to interactions and consequences. Since it involves increased consciousness of the intimate relationships of self, humankind, and biosphere, it may lead to a somewhat amplified sense of personal identity and to somewhat more responsible decision-making.

Global education is an attempt to heighten awareness and understanding of the global arena, its history, and its systems. It is based on an understanding of the earth and its inhabitants as part of a historic and interrelated network, an awareness of the choices facing individuals and nations at any moment in time, and the far and future consequences of these decisions. These are coupled with an increased sensitivity to the perceptions, cultures, and choices of other peoples who may have different values from us. These issues are concerned with a mastery of basic skills and content necessary to the understanding of the cultural, ecological, scientific and economic issues which affect everyone. It includes a broad interpretation of "survival" skills necessary for the teacher facing a classroom in the year 2000.

In broad terms this chapter will seek to provide a framework for internationalizing our teacher education curriculum by speaking to the following issues: (1) Recognition of Global Interdependence, (2) Multicultural Education, (3) Setting the Historical Context, (4) Conflict Resolution, and (5) Critical Thinking.

Recognition of Global Interdependence

> I've often thought there ought to be a manual to hand to little kids, telling them what kind of planet they're on, why they don't fall off it, how much time they've probably got here, how to avoid poison ivy, and so on. I tried to write one once. It was called "Welcome to Earth." But I got stuck on explaining why we don't fall off the planet. Gravity is just a word. It doesn't explain anything. If I could get past gravity, I'd tell them how we reproduce, how long we've been here, apparently, and a little bit about evolution. And one thing I would really like to tell them about is cultural relativity. I didn't learn until I

was in college about all the other cultures, and I should have learned that in first grade. A first grader should understand that his or her culture isn't a rational invention; that there are thousands of other cultures and they all work pretty well; that all cultures function on faith rather than truth; that there are lots of alternatives to our own society. Cultural relativity is defensible and attractive. It's also a source of hope. It means we don't have to continue this way if we don't like it.

Kurt Vonnegut, Jr. (Kenworthy 1978, 35)

I doubt very much that "interdependence" meant much of anything, to most of us before the energy crisis of the early 1970's. Our daily newspaper reminds us how closely we are now tied to the rest of the world. As the 1981 Bay Area Global Education Program (BAGEP) Summer Institute members so clearly stated:

The various world systems—economic, geo-political, technological, argicultural—have been becoming increasingly interdependent/interconnected over the past four decades. This process has affected the quality of life both positively and negatively for millions of people throughout the world but has also helped create major worldwide problems which have affected groups of people differently. Problems, such as environmental pollution, inequitable distribution and managment of resources, definitions of standards of human rights, economic competition and political conflict, have had disproportionate impact on the poor, especially women and children. These problems cannot be solved by any single nation. Students need to understand interdependence/interconnectedness, both its benefits and costs.

Global systems have been evolving for thousands of years. During the past few decades, however, that rate of change has reached staggering proportions. In our own society, for example, one-third of the shelf items in local supermarkets were not there ten years ago. There are a quarter of a million words in our present English language which Shakespeare did not know. Nearly a thousand new books are published each day. In addition, 50% of today's factual knowledge is expected to be obsolete in ten years. An obvious reason for this accelerated rate of change has been an improvement in technology. This technological advancement has affected agriculture and industry along with increasing the rate of communication, trade and transportation among the world's peoples.

In an interesting list of facts, Gary Marx and Tomas Collins have put together the following current facts:

- The United States is either completely or almost totally dependent on imports for such key minerals as platinum, diamonds, manganese, tin, bauxite, nickel, chromium, and cobalt.

- One American in six owes his or her employment to foreign trade.

- Fortune 500 lists show that at least half of our leading corporations are foreign based and owned.

- One out of every three acres producing in this country is devoted solely to export. More than half of our wheat, soybeans, and rice is sold abroad.

- When a fire alarm sounds in Malmo, Sweden, a fireman puts the address of the fire into a computer terminal and a minute later gets back a description of potential hazards at the scene. The computer that stores that data is in Cleveland, Ohio.

This mutual dependence and interaction involving the various geophysical and social systems of our globe is a fact that our universities must accept and understand if they are to produce teachers for a global age. Our education students must be helped to analyze the interdependent systems that affect the quality of their lives. This will help them understand its importance as they take responsibility for preparing future citizens.

Multicultural Education

Again, from BAGEP:

All students bring unique and multiple perspectives to their viewing of the world. These perspectives, which are neither static nor necessarily conscious, are conditioned by our membership in various groups.

For example, an important part of one's identity is the fact that some people are female and others are male, and this reality cannot be separated from who people are, how they live in the world, and what perspectives of the world they adopt. Students need to recognize the sources and importance of their own perspectives and to gain an understanding of the process by which societies and individuals come to have a particular perspective on the world. Such perspective-taking ability will enable them to appreciate the multiplicity of views on any issue and to function better in an increasingly interdependent/interconnected and diverse world.

Our universities are swamped with cries for cultural diversity. Teacher education is by no means insensitive to this issue. The National Council for the Accreditation of Teacher Education (NCATE), the American Association of Colleges of Teacher Education (AACTE) the Association of Teacher Educators (ATE) and others all issue multicultural standards by which we are evaluated.

In the state of California, for example, all student teachers must receive an experience in a multicultural classroom. It is hoped that this type of experience will increase the empathy level and sensitize our students to those of differing cultures. The questions are, "Is this too little too late?" Is multicultural education an add-on or something to be integrated into our entire teacher education curriculum? How much work would it take for us as teacher educators to ensure that all courses and field experiences we are responsible for include multicultural dimensions? This may seem a tall task for rural America where multicultural communities may not exist, but all of our conditions are changing rapidly. New models of sharing are needed. Consortiums need to be expanded between institutions to build alternatives for all.

An exciting example of this movement can be seen in a joint statement issued in 1983 by the International Council on Education for Teaching and The American Association of Colleges for Teacher Education (1983, 4). This statement transcends national and cultural differences. Their slogan, One World or None, supports the notion that all of humanity is of a single species, on a single planet that shares a common future. Molding this future is the educational imperative of today. It is their feeling that global perspectives should be found within all aspects of a teacher education program. According to the statement these perspectives require:

1. a responsive and informed administration capable of instituting programs for global education;

2. the inclusion of issues of interdependence, competition, cooperation, and the interrelatedness of world problems in the general, special and professional studies components;

3. students to develop intercultural communication skills including learning other languages, learning to assess cultural, political, economic and educational issues from a global perspective; students to clarify conflicting or differing values inherent in international affairs and to formulate plans for teaching a global perspective with a multidisciplinary and multilinguistic approach;

4. faculty development and evaluation policies that assess the ability of faculty to teach from a global perspective and allows research and sabbatical opportunities for enhancing this ability;

5. a continual review system of progress in achieving global education goals.

Perhaps being visionaries in their own right, in 1980 a small group of teacher educators petitioned the ATE to create a Council for Intercultural Teacher Education. The Association adopted the following resolution (1980, 2):

> BE IT RESOLVED . . . that the Association of Teacher Educators create the Council For Intercultural Teacher Education to serve as a clearinghouse of information on intercultural professional field experiences and to promote the study, development, dimensions and researching of programs through interinstitutional cooperation.

A survey by this council determined that over 100 institutions have sponsored 1,000 student teachers in some 55 foreign countries (1980, 4) Implementation models for delivering these programs varied from informal placements, to consortiums, to institutionally identified programs. These international experiences are seen as a means to further the development and growth of our students' personal philosophy. Through encounters with those who have developed under different conditions and backgrounds, one should be able to see oneself, one's own values, and one's society in a new light. The student should develop both understanding of other cultures and increased ability to make comparative decisions and judgments. These experiences are preparation for intelligent participation in the student's own society and the furthering of international understanding. This implies that our students, through immersion in another society, can better understand all human societies and in the future work more effectively as a national and international citizen. Overseas student teaching is a stimulus to the student's growth in academic competence. This includes knowledge and understanding of international affairs—economic, political, social, and cultural—and of the geography and physical nature of the world.

> Educational theory is one thing, because you can continue to go to class. But you don't have the experience. When you get into another country, it's a different story. You're interacting with the kids in a different culture; you learn first hand, and that's the most valuable thing.
>
> Former Overseas Student Teacher, 1983

These international experiences are but one way of providing more of a multicultural dimension to our curriculum. Domestic alternatives must also be sought so as to provide for as many options as possible for our teachers-to-be.

Setting The Historical Context

The 1987 Ad Hoc Group on Gender Issues meeting in Las Palomas de Taos stated (Kobus 1987, 3):

> Every event or situation has a context which illuminates it and gives it meaning. Learning to search for and understand that context is crucial to the process of analysis and decision-making relative to that issue. Interpretations of history, geography, economics and culture studies all provide invaluable background data for would-be teachers. They provide the context which can give insight to contemporary issues through which students develop awareness of how

their own perspectives have been shaped by their backgrounds.

Within the curriculum of teacher education each situation has a context which affects its future direction or outcome. Our students must understand that context before trying to analyze it. Only in this way will they be able to make decisions for their future teaching. In our society news is communicated and sometimes shaped by electronic media. There is little or no context for the events that make the headlines. We have 30 to 60 seconds on the 6 o'clock news to form our opinions. There is little history given let alone alternative perspectives. With this type of information we are to make educated decisions within our society. Our students need to ask the question "Why"? of each of these issues confronting them. The refining of Postman and Weingartners' (1969, 10) "crap detector" will be a necessary condition to enable our students to evolve historical context. A "crap detector" becomes a filtering mechanism that allows students to sift those elements that have little or no logical relationship to those concepts they are studying. In defining historical context, each event can be better focused, expanded or clarified by more study of geography, history, economics, politics, society, and culture. This model can also be adapted to our studies in curriculum, methods, educational psychology, evaluation, sociology, and philosophy of education. This historical approach must enable our students to understand that the very context surrounding each educational issue in their classroom must be understood to a significant degree, in order to understand the event itself. Our programs must help our students look beyond the superficial facts of an event to find out why it occurred. They must view events with healthy skepticism while understanding that most issues they confront are likely culturally biased.

The challenges are obvious, whether they consider women and global issues, geographic patterns in our daily lives or the world population. Will our students teach differently by the year 2025 when over 80% of the world will live in Africa, Asia, and Latin America? There is one outstanding fact to remember in our historical context setting: There is no instruction book accompanying our Spaceship Earth.

Conflict Resolution

Although we realize that conflict is an on-going part of the human experience we do little to prepare our teachers for this eventuality. Wherever power relationships exist, whether in society or in the classroom, differences of opinion will occur. Working towards resolution is a much needed skill both in or out of the classroom. Unfortunately, for many societies, including our own, this conflict is not considered as a normal part of life. By denying it exists, tension is created that usually explodes before we can do anything about it. Ruth Sivard (1985, 5) states that 53 of the 113 third world countries have military dominated governments. It is the awareness of this inherent conflict between denial and tension that is of great importance to our teachers. Those that learn to deal with this conflict effectively have a good chance of leading more productive, less stressful lives. A multiplier effect leading from teachers to students, to the community, and public institutions must be the order of the day. Through this process it is hoped that international institutions needed to deal with global conflict may eventually emerge.

Most of our conflicts are resolved without violence. Certainly most of those occurring in the classroom end peacefully. The participants, however, usually have little understanding of the process they have gone through in dealing with their conflict. Educators use other terms like "classroom management," "disciplinary procedures," and "classroom climate." Many teachers have been involved in professional development workshops called "conflict resolution". Whatever we call it we are still dealing with basic human relationships, and healthy relationships are desperately needed in our classroom.

An excellent list of objectives that might start us on our way could include having our teacher education students:

1. demonstrate a growing capacity to accept conflict as an inevitable and natural part of the human experience

2. demonstrate a growing capacity to analyze the origins, dynamics and effects of conflicts ranging from the personal to the international level

3. evidence a growing capacity to perceive conflict as potentially manageable and to generate and use alternative methods for managing conflicts

4. evidence the capacity to understand that change and ambiguity are often sources of conflict and that like conflict, both change and ambiguity are part of the human condition

5. demonstrate the ability to compare the advantages and disadvantages of common conflict resolution strategies and to evaluate their effectiveness in given conflict situations

6. evidence the understanding that, while violence may have served certain functions throughout history, modern weaponry and global interdependence make resorting to violence increasingly dysfunctional.

These areas have been summarized by Palomares and Logan (1975, 13) in a listing of some seventeen conflict management strategies ranging from negotiating and compromising to postponing and sharing. It is practical methods like these that can help us explore creative alternatives in dealing with conflict.

The need for conflict resolution skills among our teachers will not pass. As a recent report from *Ground Zero* has stated (1983, 3):

> We are writing our future now–and it is possible that our present course is leading toward ever higher levels of confrontation. If we want to write a more cooperative future, we will have to act quickly . . . . Our work is cut out for us. Which of these fantastic scenarios is in the realm of possibility–none of them? all of them?–and how might we go about making them a reality? We owe it to our grandchildren to find out.

Critical Thinking

In an adaptation from BAGEP (1985, 5):

> Application of critical thinking and creative abilities enables a person to reach informed conclusions on issues, and to defend those conclusions. Problem solving, differentiating fact from opinion, understanding the biases and assumptions inherent in all sources of information, weighing consequences, understanding the nature of selective perception, testing hypotheses and inferences, incorporating intuitive thinking processes and other creative strategies, are all crucial elements in this thinking

process. Students can apply these skills and processes in examining a variety of value positions, and in so doing, strengthen their understanding of the world.

Once teacher education programs begin to implement a curriculum that recognizes global interdependence, multicultural education, historical context setting, and conflict resolution our students will be forced to think critically, and in that process begin to make moral judgements. Few educators would disagree that critical thinking and making moral value judgements are related and central to the act of effective teaching. There is much controversy surrounding the moral education field. Value clarification and moral development models have been criticized as being culturally biased. These and others must be continually assessed to provide our students with sound criteria for critical thinking. Concept formation and dialectical reasoning as described by Walter Parker (1987, 50) are excellent beginnings to infuse this element into our curriculum.

A great deal of research has been done on the skills of classifying, inferring, comparing, conceptualizing, imagining, hypothesizing, and evaluating. The point at which our students begin to make value decisions regarding the teaching act varies as to the individual. Research does, however, emphasize the importance of higher level thinking skills as absolutely necessary to that process. Specific thinking skills necessary in our global curriculum for the future include: comparing similarities and differences; identification of central issues and problems; distinguishing fact from opinion; recognizing stereotypes and clichés; recognizing bias, emotional factors, propaganda and semantic slanting; recognizing different value orientations; determining which information is relevant; recognizing the adequacy of data; checking consistency; formulating appropriate questions; predicting probable consequences; and identifying unstated assumptions.

This is obviously a tall order, but one necessary to allow the teachers needed for tomorrow to begin testing the systems of today.

Where Do We Go from Here?

People in the world have long been concerned about life around them. The first global poll of public opinion was conducted by the Gallup International Research Instutute in 1977. More than 9,000 persons in 70 countries on six continents

were surveyed. War worried them far less than illness or
financial pinches. The high cost of living was a top concern
the world over. Women's roles were seen changing, giving
them greater opportunities in most lands. All in all, most
people on every continent except Asia said they were either
very happy or fairly happy. More people (except in the U.S.
and Far East) believed living conditions were improving than
thought they were getting worse.

In the last few years much has changed. Starvation in
Ethiopia, war between Iran and Iraq, the Contra scandal in our
government, and the U.S. Navy protecting oil tankers in the
Middle East all speak to the turmoil of the world today. It is
these issues that confront the teachers of today. The obsession
of our educational system with teaching facts will not
overcome the problems of our world. The institution of new
priorites such as helping people adapt to a changing world,
develop skills of critical intellectual inquiry, and fostering the
development of positive self concepts are in order.

The future for global education in our teacher education
programs must certainly begin now. One state, Michigan,
became a leader in this movement when it stated (Guidelines
for Global Education1978, 1):

> It is imperative to involve our students in a lifelong
> process of understanding, through study and partici-
> pation, of the world community and the interdepen-
> dence of its people and systems. It will require an
> understanding of the values and priorities of the
> many cultures within our society and the larger
> world, as well as the acquisition of basic concepts and
> principles related to the world community.

A marriage of global education with teacher education
should lead to implementation and application of global
perspectives in striving for just and peaceful solutions to world
problems.

A viable rationale for including global perspectives in
our teaching curriculum should place an emphasis on the
personal behavior of all world-minded persons. This behavior
should reflect a concern for the person's immediate environment, as well as a more distant environment. Our students,
therefore, will be concerned with vital isssues and understand
that our earth is a fragile, finite planet whose resources are
limited. They will respect people throughout the world that
have numerous and diversed lifestyles. They will realize that
by respecting those who are different we enrich rather than

diminish each of us. It will become useful and enlightening to view life comparatively. What happens anywhere in the world determines how all of us live. They will understand that the armament race, if continued unabated, could lead to the destruction of humankind.

Our global student/teachers will then begin to act intelligently to promote a humane domestic and foreign policy. They will compassionately contribute to the solution of common problems. They will work realistically to eradicate hunger, poverty, pollution, and problems of a similar nature so that there can be a significant improvement in the quality of life for all people. They will act responsibly to curb wasteful consumption of the world's resources. They will vigorously promote justice as presently outlined in such documents as the Universal Declaration of Human Rights and the Declarations of the Rights of the Child. They will conscientiously become involved in the peaceful resolution of conflict and the ultimate outlawing of war.

Idealistic? Impossible? A dream? I think not. We have all we need inside us now. It is up to the teacher educators of this country to set in motion a process of global education. We have too long responded to crises in our society. The time now has come to lead. The decisions we make today will mold our future tomorrow. We may decide to sit and wait or stand up and move forward. Our global future has truly begun today.

References

Allen, Rodney F. 1975. *Deciding how to live on spaceship earth.* Evanston, Ill.: McDougal, Littell and Co.

Students confront open-ended problems involving human-land and human-nature relationships.

Association of Teacher Educators. 1980a. *Global issues 87/88: Annual editions series. Survey of International Student Teaching Programs.* East Lansing, Mich.: Michigan State University.

A collection of 52 up-to-date articles and essays examining major global issues, trends and prospects. Reprinted from prominent journals and periodicals, the articles address such topics as the current population explosion in Egypt, the long term health effects of the Chernobyl nuclear power disaster, poverty, and poliltics in Mexico, and humanity's agenda for the 21st century.

Association of Teacher Educators. 1980b. Minutes of the Executive Board Meeting. East Lansing, Mich.: Michigan State University, October 22.

Copy of the entire resolution is available from ATE, Robert Stevenson, Executive Director, Suite A, 1900 Association Drive, Reston, Va. 22091.

Backler, Alan, and Robert Hanvey. 1986. *Global geography.* New York: Teachers College Press.

Helps one appreciate the interconnection of worldwide events by alternating chapters on various regions of the world with chapters that teach basic geography concepts.

Baker, Frederick J. 1985. Alternative student teaching: Boon or boondoggle? *The Clearing House* 58: 285-86.

This article gives a rationale for building alternative, international student teaching programs overseas. It also explains how to counteract critics of international programs as well as providing a "how to do it" model for institutionalization.

Banks, James A. 1977. Multi-ethnic education: Practices and promises. Bloomington, Ind.: Phi Delta Kappa Educational Foundation.

A succinct pamphlet detailing aspects of multi-ethnic education including goals, practices, promises, and the characteristics of multi-ethnic schools.

Bay Area Global Education Program. 1985. Conflict analysis, management, recognition. Mimeographed. Stanford, California: Mills College Station, January 21.

Bay Area Global Education Program. 1985. Critical Thinking. Mimeographed. Stanford, Calif.: Mills College Station, revised January 21.

Bay Area Global Education Program. 1981. Summer Institute Theme Guides. Mimeographed. Stanford, Calif.: Stanford University.

Branson, Margaret Stimman, ed. 1982. *International human rights, society and the schools.* Washington, D.C.: National Council for the Social Studies, Bulletin No. 68.

Presents important issues, concepts and research related to international human rights. Includes instructional guidelines and teaching strategies.

Brown, Lester R. 1987. State of the world 1987. New York: Norton.

Drawing on sources such as government and private reports from the U.S. and abroad, this progress report monitors trends in the world's natural resource base, indicates whether nations wordwide are adjusting to changes in the base and provides guidelines for achieving a sustainable society.

Cornish, Edward, ed. 1984. *Global solutions: Innovative approaches to world problems.* World Future Society.

A collection of thought-provoking articles taken from *The Futurist* magazine which outline alternative futures, stressing that responsible planning can help to create a better, more rational, and humane tomorrow. Rejecting both a fatalistic resignation to the future, and the lure of works-while-you-sleep solutions, this book offers practical solutions to such problems as overpopulation, pollution, energy shortages, and international conflict.

Croddy, Marshall. 1982. *International law in global age.* Los Angeles: Constitutional Rights Foundation.

Teacher and student materials offer a framework for teaching about international law in a global age from five perspectives: global links,cultural contracts, actors and relationships, world order, and conflict. Topics include family law, human rights, and international conflict resolution.

Elder, Pamela, and Mary Ann Carr. 1987. *Worldways: Bringing the world into the classroom.* New York: Addison-Wesley.

A comprehensive sourcebook for integrating a global perspective into the curriculum of almost any subject area. Also included are resources for teachers and students, a broad-based rationale for global education, a list of embassies, and several appendixes.

Feinberg, Richard E., and Valeriana Kallab. 1985. *U.S.-Third World policy perspectives.* Washington, D.C.: Overseas Development Council.

Three volumes offer a variety of perspectives on U.S.-Third World policy, including trade policy, future development, and future U.S. policy options.

Fuller, Buckminster. 1981. *Critical path.* New York: St. Martin's Press.

Gallup, George. 1984. *Forecast 2000.* New York: Morrow.

Based upon an extensive series of polls, surveys, and interviews concerning the future, this look at the coming decades represents the opinions of leading educators, scientists, economists, and politicians from around the world. The book includes detailed looks at issues such as overpopulation, the environment, family life, politics, the economy, and nuclear terrorism. Concludes with recommendations and suggestions for

those who wish to be prepared to face and help shape the ⁄
future.

Global Education Center. 1986. *Global Education Center
Newsletter*. Minneapolis, Minn.: Global Education
Center, Spring.

A theme issue contains background articles and activities to introduce students to the problems and issues
facing developing regions. Each issue of the quarterly
newsletter focuses on a different global education theme.

Gross, Susan, and Marjorie Bingham. 1983. *Toward achieving
historical symmetry: A manual for teaching women's
history*. Santa Rosa, Calif.: National Women's History
Project.

This manual presents three models for teaching about
women cross-culturally, a framework for teaching
women's history in a global setting and lessons to introduce students to researching women's history.

Ground Zero. 1983. Knowing the adversary: What we don't
know can hurt us. 3.

Harf, James E., and Thomas B. Trout. 1985. *Essentials of
national security: A content handbook for teachers*.
Columbus, Oh.: Citizenship Development Program.

This source book outlines concepts and content basic to
classroom coverage of national security issues in a
nuclear age.

Hoopers, David. 1984. *Global guide to international education*.
New York: International Education Sourcebooks.

A specialized reference book containing an annotated
listing of about 2,500 resources for teachers or students of
international affairs. This cross-referenced source-book
lists the following types of resources on global affairs:
books, periodicals, publishers, film distributors,
academic programs, educational, and cultural exchanges,
private and governmental agencies, language schools,
and area and peace studies centers.

Hursh, Heidi. 1985. *Activities using the new state of the world atlas.* CITR.

A selection of teaching activities designed to be used with *The new state of the world atlas.* Students are encouraged to compare, analyze, and ask questions that add to further study in other sources. It uses an area studies approach focusing on geopolitical and cultural grouping of nations and explores stereotypes, similarities, differences, and interrelationships among nations. It also explores issues such as human rights, conflict and power.

Intercom 108. 1986. Introduction to international trade. (February).

A special theme issue contains 11 lessons on international development by the Stanford Program on International and Cross-Cultural Education. Lessons focus on jobs and trade, balance of payments, comparative and absolute advantage, protectionism, currency exchange, global products and global production systems.

International Council on Education for Teaching and American Association of Colleges for Teacher Education. 1983. A global perspective for teacher education. Washington, D.C.: ICET/AACTE.

Kenworthy, Leonard. 1978. *Helping boys and girls discover the world.* New York: Teachers College Press.

Kidron, Michael, and Ronald Segal. 1983. *The new state of the world atlas.* New York: Simon and Schuster.

A series of 66 colorful maps depict global pressures and interrelationships such as militarism, natural resources, world economy, business and labor, weapons exports and imports, and changes in government.

Kobus, D. 1987. Historical/geographical context setting. Las Palmas de Taos: Ad Hoc Group on Gender Issues, BAGEP, April.

Lamy, Steven. 1983. Resources for global perspectives education: A practitioner's view. *Social Studies Review* 22: 43-44.

Leinwand, Gerald. 1978. *Teaching of world history.* Washington, D.C.: National Council for the Social Studies, Bulletin No. 54.

Offers practical materials, approaches, guidance, specific examples and suggestions for teaching world history.

Linton, Ralph. 1936. *The study of man.* New York: Appleton-Century-Crofts.

Lisler, Ian. 1984. *Teaching and learning about human rights.* Strasbourg, France: Council of Europe.

Examines the role that teaching and learning about human rights plays in the social studies curriculum and considers what people should know and be able to do about human rights issues.

Mans, Lori. 1982. Thinking globally and acting locally: Environmental education teaching activities. Columbus, Oh.: ERIC Clearinghouse for Science Education.

Activities on food production and distribution, energy, solid waste in the environment, resource management, pollution, and endangered species help learners better understand the relationahips between their actions and the world environment. Focus is on cultural linkages and the interdependencies among the nations of the world and between people and systems.

Marx, Gary, and T.H. Collins. Undated. *It's a big, wide, interdependent world.* Arlington, Va.: American Association of School Administrators,

Masoner, Paul H., and David J. 1983. Guidelines for the redesign of teacher education. In *The redesign of teacher education for the twenty-first century: International perspectives on the preparation of educational personnel.* Washington, D.C.: International Council on Education for Teaching.

Presents a set of comprehensive guidelines that are
essential in redesigning programs for preparing professional educators. Especially emphasizes global priorities.

Myers, Norman, ed. 1984. *Gaia: An atlas of planet management.* New York: Anchor Press.

Gaia, Greek goddess of the earth, is a metaphor for the
self-sustaining biosphere that makes our world a living
planet, according to this sobering look at the interaction
of humanity with the environment. The book stresses
the vital importance of careful husbandry of the earth's
resources and addresses the need for more equitable
economic ties among first and third world nations.

Palomares, Uvaldo, and Ben Logan. 1975. *A curriculum on
conflict management.* San Diego: Human Development Training Institute.

Parisi, Lynn, ed. 1985. Creative role-playing exercises in
science and technology. Alexandria, Va.: ERIC.

Included in this publication of five science and society
simulations are two modules focusing on global
environmental issues. Also included are international
political, economic, and environmental issues in
mining the ocean floors.

Parker, Walter. 1987. Teaching thinking: The pervasive
approach. *Journal of Teacher Education* (May-June): 50.

Postman, N., and C. Weingartner. 1969. *Teaching as a subver-
sive activity.* New York: Delta.

Richardson, John M., ed. 1982. *Making it happen: A positive
guide to the future.* USACOR.

A thought-provoking analysis of what the future may
hold in store for America and the rest of the world.
Written as a project for the U.S. Association for the Club
of Rome, this comprehensive study urges readers to
actively shape the kind of future they want. A wide
variety of topics and perspectives are presented. While a
number of scenarios are considered, the book emphasizes that aggressive planning and education can fend off
potential disasters.

Salmolz and Katz. 1986. The forgotten subject. *Newsweek* (September 1): 60.

Sanborn, Michelle, Rachael Roe, and Heide Hursh. 1986. *Teaching about world cultures: Focus on developing regions.* Denver: Center for Teaching International Relations.

More than 30 learning activities help one examine the relationship between culture and modernization. The unit emphasizes the impact of development on people's lives.

Seelye, H. Ned. 1984. *Teaching culture: Strategies for intercultural communication.* New York: National Textbook.

Practical strategies for combining language and culture study. This basic handbook outlines seven goals for cultural instruction and helps create specific learning activities for reaching the goals. The author shows how language and culture influence the development of human relationships and emphasizes the importance of cultural understanding.

Sivard, Ruth. 1985. *World military and social expenditures.* Wellesley, Mass.: World Priorities.

Smith, Gary R. 1979. *Cultural sight and insight: Dealing with diverse viewpoints and values.* New York: Global Perspectives in Education.

Dozens of activities help students deal directly with factors that influence our perceptions. Forms of ethnocentrism and their harmful effects are explored.

Smith, Gary R. 1978.*Guidelines for global education.* Lansing, Mich.: State of Michigan Department of Education.

Taylor, Harold. 1974. *The world as teacher.* Carbondale, Ill.: Southern Illinois University Press.

United Nations. 1984. On the front lines: The United Nations' role in preventing and containing conflict.

New York: United Nations Association, Publications
Dept.

This booklet examines the United Nations' role as
peacekeeping forum along with attempting to provide
balanced information needed to analyze policy choices
facing U.N. member states.

What people around the world say about hopes, fears, life
today. 1977. *U.S. News and World Report.* January 24.

West, B. Bradley. 1985. The state of the profession: International field/student teaching experiences in undergraduate teacher preparation. Paper prepared for the Guidelines For International Teacher Education Project of
AACTE, East Lansing: Michigan State University,
College of Education.

West, B. Bradley. 1980. *A directory of overseas student teaching programs.* East Lansing, Mich.:   ATE Council for
Intercultural Teacher Education.

This directory is the result of a nationwide survey of
teacher preparation institutions to determine who
conducts or participates in intercultural programs. The
survey also provides data on program calendar, years in
operation, placements made and some of the conditions
and structure of each experience.

Wheatcroft, Andrew.   1983.   *The world atlas of revolutions.*
New York: Simon and Schuster.

Examining revolutionary movements-their causes,
successes, and failures-this graphic sourcebook uses
maps, photographs, and text to illustrate over 35 case
studies in violent change.   Spans time from the
American Revolution to the ongoing revolutionary
struggles in the world of the 1980s.

Wheatcroft, Andrew.   1984.   *Focus on human rights and
democracy.*   Wellesley, Mass.: World Eagle.

A theme issue offers statements from Europe on
several human rights issues;   a map showing the
relative freedom of people in the countries of the world;
a general classificatioin of human rights; a chronology of

key international human rights conventions, declarations and codes; and other primary source data.

Woyach, Robert B. 1983. *Bringing a global perspective to economics.* Columbus, Oh.: Mershon Center, Ohio State University.

This volume contains lessons designed to add a global dimension to topics usually dealt with in economics. Included are perspectives on global food production, foreign investment, multinational corporations, international cartels and international petroleum production, trade and dependence.

Woyach, Robert B. 1983. *Bringing a global perspective to world history.* Columbus, Oh.: Mershon Center, Social Studies School Services.

This publication adds a global dimension to topics covered in world history courses. Included are lessons using a global perspective to explore such topics as national heroes, the impact of industrializing and urbanization, foreign policies for peace, and interaction between different cultures.

Zola, John, and Jaye Jola. 1985. *Teaching about peace and nuclear war: A balanced approach.* Boulder, Colo.: Social Science Education Consortium.

This teacher-developed source book contains rationale, resources, and activities for considering the issues surrounding and the perspectives on peace and nuclear war. Guidelines for balanced consideration of controversial issues are included.

Challenge Education: A Model for Individualizing Teacher Education Courses

Devon J. Metzger

One of the more practical and enduring tasks confronting teacher education is determining what courses, assignments or activities will accompany the student teaching experience. If confronting this task is forgotten, students are quick to complain, describing the various assignments as less than a challenge and more as an unnecessary hindrance to their daily student teaching experience. As any faculty member who has worked with student teachers can attest, once students become involved in student teaching, it is difficult to take "other work" seriously.

A solution utilized by some teacher education programs is to simply not plan formal courses, systematic assignments, or sequential activities designed to enhance the student teaching experience. It is a tempting solution and an understandable reaction to the often weary and reluctant student teacher. However, it is not an appropriate answer both because it ignores a very realistic need of the student teacher and abdicates the responsibility of the teacher education program.

Teacher educators who recognize the importance of a useful and complementing experience to student teaching, create and revise programs that can be effective in helping the student teacher to learn and to grow professionally. This chapter will propose and explain a program that is unique and compatible with the student teaching experience. Challenge Education applies the "learning by doing" approach to education, fully involving students in managing their own learning experience.

Currently, and for many years, we, as teacher educators, have generally agreed that students learn better when they have some measure of influence over their own learning. It is thought that when students have the chance to play a role in what or how they learn, they learn better and retain longer what they learn (Gibbons and Phillips 1978). Closely aligned to student self-influenced learning is the equally accepted and important idea of student participation. In a society based upon a participatory democracy, it is critical that students learn how to learn, learn the skills of decision making, and understand the value of responsibility for their own decisions and actions (Kohler 1981). Teacher educators have also embraced the concept of individual differences (Guild and Garger 1985). It is considered important to be aware of individual differences and demonstrate instructional strategies that take into account the uniqueness of each student.

Helping students to assume more influence over their own learning, teaching students to become participating citizens, and recognizing the importance of individual differences are all generally accepted ideas that are passed on to students as potential teachers. However, when teacher educators promote these ideas, it is rarely through practice. The actual experiencing of these educational ideas is not usually incorporated into teacher education programs (Conrad and Hedin 1981). In other words, we believe in these ideas, we pass on these ideas, but we are often remiss in using the ideas ourselves. Challenge Education is a program that attempts to redress the "preach but not practice" oversight, and is premised upon the acceptance and practice of the above ideas. Students, as teacher candidates, are able to determine their own unique needs and chart a path for their own learning.

Brief History

Challenge Education is based upon the Walkabout concept first introduced to North American educators by Maurice Gibbons (Gibbons 1974). The Walkabout concept is a unique educational analogy to the Australian aborigine Walkabout, a rite of passage which tests an adolescent's readiness to become a full and contributing member of the tribe. (Interestingly, while there is a very good Australian film entitled *Walkabout* that inspired Maurice Gibbons, it is a current American film, *Crocodile Dundee*, that has introduced the term "Walkabout" to wider North American audiences.)

The Walkabout has been practiced for centuries by the aborigines. At age sixteen, youths are sent alone into the wilderness to experience an endurance test lasting six months. During the six months, the emerging adult must confront a hostile environment relying on the skills and knowledge learned during childhood. The test is not just a physical test but also a psychological challenge. The six month ordeal requires patience, courage, confidence, and the understanding that the youth alone is responsible for surviving or not surviving. A successful Walkabout demonstrates to the youth and the tribe that the time has arrived for assuming adult responsibilities. The adults are now confident they can rely on the youth who represents their hope for the future. A joyous celebration follows the youth's return because an event has occurred that is beneficial to all.

Gibbons was first attracted to the Walkabout concept because no such rite of passage seemed to exist for youth in North American contemporary society. At one time the rite of passage was met by high school graduation, an event now thought hollow in comparison. Furthermore, there seems to be a de-emphasis on demonstrating what the emerging citizen/adult has learned, especially in a way that can announce to the community that the adolescent is ready to make the passage to adulthood in a meaningful and productive manner.

While the Walkabout concept emerged as a specific response to secondary education, the substance remains intact and retains its legitimacy within the context of teacher education. "Challenge Education" challenges potential teachers in their passage from students to professional teacher. The student is also experiencing a journey, a rite of passage that, if successful, allows the student and the profession to know a new and responsible member has joined the group, a colleague that represents hope for the future. Challenge Education, like the Walkabout, requires students to develop and expand their knowledge, skills, and attitudes in a way that will stretch the potential of each individual.

Rationale

Teacher education is a professional and personal passage. An individual decides that he or she wants to become a teacher, enters a teacher education program, and pursues the requirements to become a professional educator. Requirements are certainly necessary, but too often the requirements are viewed as restrictive and judged as meaningless hurdles, lacking substance and realistic utility. Rarely does a program of learning invite a student to exceed the minimum and grow to one's unlimited potential. This does not suggest structure is unimportant. Structure need not serve as an inflexible parameter that limits student growth, but instead, can offer supporting guidance that will facilitate learning potential.

Challenge Education circumvents the traditional limits of learning by involving the learner in designing his or her own rite of passage. "What I can do" becomes the focus of planning rather than "what I cannot do." Eisner calls this intellectual independence and explains that students are ". . . encouraged to find and use resources for dealing with tasks and problems that they had some hand in conceptualizing" (Eisner 1983, 51). Eisner's proposal closely matches the theme of Challenge Education. He calls for students to be given the opportunity to ". . . formulate problems and projects that require the use of resources beyond those found in textbooks and workbooks" (Eisner 1983, 51). Challenge Education provides a structure from which an individual can creatively make planning decisions based on his or her own needs and interests. Furthermore, while students are playing a significant role in planning their own learning, they are also simultaneously developing a greater sense of confidence and becoming more self-reliant (Thayer 1978; Gardner 1977). Students who are free to do their own planning are also more likely to reflect on who they are, contemplate personal and professional needs, and begin to discover and clarify the kind of teacher they want to become. Learning to initiate, plan and evaluate one's own course of study can prove to be one of the most difficult approaches to learning. But the journey and a successful project completion can also prove to be one of the most rewarding learning experiences.

Challenge Education also serves as an important instructional model (Beeler 1978). To experience self-directed learning is to know self-directed learning. Encountering Challenge Education is an influential and impressive experience. Consequently, Challenge Education offers a valuable instructional option that participants can share and eventually use in one's own classroom (Skinner 1978). Although it seems safe to assume that most students, at the teacher education level, have experienced self-directed learning, the assumption is too often unwarranted (McCarthy 1978). Collegiate and precollegiate instruction does not require or offer ample opportunities for independent and self-directed learning. Ernest Boyer, Chair of the Carnegie Foundation for the Advancement of Teaching, describes colleges and universities as developing ". . . competence in getting and giving back information . . . students are caught up in the ritual of cramming and forgetting and preparing for credentials (Boyer 1986, 14). So while it might be tempting to discount the importance of self-directed learning at the teacher education level, the Challenge Education Program may be the first, or first authentic opportunity for students to explore and experience the self-directed path for learning.

Complementing the importance of managing one's own learning program is the overarching and learned skill of participation. Constructive participation builds confidence, and confidence creates a positive self-image (Conrad and Hedin 1981). Both attributes are vitally important to citizens living in a democratic society. Too often, students learn how to avoid participation. They become passive, in part, due to a formal education that gives them little or no opportunity to express themselves openly, freely, and safely. Students who are persistently "told" and "directed" do not acquire confidence, do not experience the satisfaction of making a difference, and, in contrast, develop the comfortable habit of not participating. Self-directed learning gives students the opportunity to understand their own abilities unfettered by restrictions that frequently result in judging or labeling.

It is not being suggested that self-directed learning is the only avenue for learning. However, self-directed learning does incorporate knowledge, skills, and attitudes favorable to a democratic society. Learning what one can achieve with a large measure of individual responsibility for planning and decision making can strongly influence a student's self-concept and give the student, as citizen, the experience to know he or she can make a difference.

Another advantage of Challenge Education is its potential ability to relieve stress. As Braun and Brown (1984) explain:

> From our own experience and those of our student teachers we learned that the sense of renewal and accomplishment that comes from completing a Challenge Education project can go a long way toward managing stress. Most of the literature on stress and teaching is aimed at alleviating distress, but little has been said about using difficult situations to build a sense of achievement, thus fostering what Hans Selye (1974) calls eustress. Such a sense of accomplishment can offset a great deal of distress. (602)

Challenge Education also offers a sense of control and can reduce the stress many student teachers and certified teachers feel from "other control" (Wangberg 1987). It is important to recognize, however, that if the project becomes only another assignment, or is viewed by the student as a means to a perfunctory end, stress may be increased. If the Challenge Education project is clearly understood, carefully planned, and sincerely pursued, the advantage of alleviating stress is surprisingly felt by the participating student.

Description

Each participant in Challenge Education must select, plan, and accomplish tasks in five areas: adventure, creative expression, practical skills, logical inquiry, and volunteer service. Adventure requires that a student demonstrate courage and endurance in an unfamiliar environment. Creative expression calls for the student to explore, cultivate, and express his or her imagination. Practical skill asks a student to learn a new skill. Logical inquiry requires that through an independent study, a student must show evidence of the ability to identify, use, and evaluate a variety of resources to acquire information systematically. Volunteer service requires that a student show evidence of responsibility to the community through volunteer work. Woven throughout these five task areas is the expectation that students will select tasks that challenge and stretch their abilities.

Challenge Education task opportunities are intentionally wide open. It is not being suggested that this important characteristic be changed. However, because the Challenge Education project, as proposed in this chapter, is interrelated with teacher education, task selections that utilize the school culture can be encouraged. One of the obvious intents of the student teaching experience is to immerse the student in the school culture. Frequently, a student teacher will spend most of his or her time with the students and faculty in their specific subject area. Encouraging school related Challenge Education tasks, offers the additional advantage of students learning to better understand the wider school culture. Again, it is important to note that encouraging school related tasks should not be viewed as restrictive, but rather as an appropriate option.

It is difficult to overemphasize the importance of correctly presenting the Challenge Education project. Because of previous school and university assignments, students may have difficulty in freely comprehending the unique opportunity of the Challenge Education project. The concern, because of such contrasting schooling experiences, is that students may struggle to break the traditional perception of limits and restrictions and not grasp the freedom of divergent decision making and creative learning. Consequently, Challenge Education must be offered with a clear and enthusiastic rationale. Realistic and diverse task examples should be presented to quickly alert students to the flexibility and openness inherent in Challenge Education. (One suggestion is that the 1974 and 1984 articles by Gibbons be assigned prior to the initial discussion of Challenge Education.)

As students immediately begin to brainstorm possible task areas, which they will do, the primary criteria for selecting tasks is that the tasks (1) are original and, (2) extend the student's abilities. This criteria may need to be repeated numerous times as students seek approval. To reiterate, students tend to perceive the assignment under the old rules, thinking about what they can or can't do, rather than freely imagining all the possibilities.

Challenge Education usually takes place during the student teaching semester. However, if, as in some teacher education programs, the curriculum includes several semesters, Challenge Education can parallel the same schedule. If the Challenge Education project coincides with the student teaching semester, it is better to introduce the project either several weeks before student teaching begins or several weeks after student teaching begins. The timing helps to avert anxieties raised by students who feel overwhelmed. Ideally, Challenge Education continues over two semesters allowing more time and more opportunity for project development and completion.

Each student, after a thorough discussion of the program, initiates and selects the experiences that fit into the five task areas. After the structure of the program is explained, there are no other instructor-mandated assignments. Students, relying on their own experience, self-awareness, professional needs and talents, and understanding of the environment where they live and student teach, propose a plan of action to the instructor. The instructor and the student discuss the proposal, working together to insure the five task areas are clearly identified and are original and challenging to the student. If the proposed plan is mutually acceptable, the student proceeds as planned.

During the semester, progress is periodically checked with a required midsemester or midyear report. The interim report summarizes the progress of the project and allows the student and the instructor to mutually agree on modifications and to carefully check the progress of the proposed time line.

The final project can assume many different forms appropriate
to the achieved tasks. However, a written summary report is
always included. Individual tasks, as completed, can be
presented and evaluated at different times throughout the
semester or year. Students conclude their project by evaluating
their experience and the program, including a personal
reaction to the Challenge Education concept.

Task Examples

Logical inquiry. Examples of logical inquiry are as
diverse as student's needs and interests. Students can research,
investigate, inquire, interview, survey and/or evaluate.
Students have investigated attitudes toward physical
education, learned how to write a grant, conducted polls on
various school issues, learned about teenage problems,
discovered additional information about school discipline and
mainstreaming, and pursued independent research topics
concerning the history of education. It is also possible to assign
a broad topic and "process" becomes the content. For example,
mainstreaming is the given topic. Students then develop
different approaches to investigating and finding out all they
can discover about mainstreaming. This approach allows the
instructor to be accountable for required topics of study while
continuing to give students divergent investigative
opportunities.
    Creativity. Students have developed a new floor plan
for an art room, corresponded with textbook authors to offer
suggestions for improvement, prepared resumes, written short
stories, composed poems about student teaching, kept a daily
diary, learned to draw, paint, play a musical instrument, learn
photography, and calligraphy.
    Volunteer service. Students have assisted a coach or
coached a sports team, worked at a local science museum,
organized academic and sports tournaments to be held during
the school lunch period or after school, started a club for young
women, officiated at sporting events, tutored students,
chaperoned school dances, club activities and field trips,
worked at jogging events, helped in nursing homes and
hospitals, and provided help in libraries.
    Adventure. Students have assisted in directing a school
play, participated in a professional conference for the first time,
conducted and played in school bands during a school
performance, led a group of students on a weekend field trip,
become involved in a physical fitness training program,
rappelled a cliff, learned to bowl, took an extended bike and/or

cross country solo ski trip, gave a presentation on watercolor painting, developed a personal diet plan to reach a weight loss goal, chaired a meeting using correct parliamentary procedure, conducted a nature hike, spent a week in a school environment very different from one's own school environment, traveled with a police officer for several nights, attended juvenile court for a week, camped for a weekend in the mountains, learned to ride a horse, and served as a guest on a local radio talk show representing education.

Practical skills. Students learned to use a computer, developed an outdoor education program, studied parliamentary procedure, earned a lifeguard certificate, crochet a sweater, skillfully operated all the school audio-visual equipment, took an auto maintenance course, made jewelry, learned to read music, received a CPR certificate, created pottery, painted wildlife pictures, learned to type, assumed responsibility for the family accounting records, planted a garden, learned Chinese cooking, took a stress management class, learned photography, completed a woodworking course, learned calligraphy and learned to play and teach the use of the recorder.

Summary

Challenge Education can be an exciting and innovative component of the teacher education program, providing change which is both needed and called for. Yet Challenge Education, for all its innovate qualities, is not necessarily new. The ideas which support Challenge Education have been widely understood as ideas equally supporting effective schooling. Students become actively involved in managing their own learning, learn the skills and satisfaction of participating to make a difference, and discover the importance of being an individual–all ideas with long histories and a contemporary educational allegiance.

Challenge Education is different because it "applies" these ideas. The result is students who experience, perhaps for the first time in their formal education, the joy of initiating, planning, pursuing, and completing their own learning programs. Along with gaining intellectual independence, students also develop personal satisfaction and confidence by extending their abilities. Challenge Education is not a panacea for improving teacher education. However, when properly and enthusiastically included as part of a teacher education program, the impact of Challenge Education can benefit the individual and the profession. The passage from student teacher to professional educator becomes a more worthwhile and satisfying educational journey.

References

Beeler, Kent D. 1978. Student teachers design walkabout challenges. *Walkabout* 3 (March): 4-5.

Explains the adaption of the Walkabout and real-life experiences to a teacher education and guidance and counseling program.

Boyer, Ernest L. 1986. Academia seeks the right formula. Interviewed by John Lynn Smith. *The Sacramento Bee* (October 14): A7

Reports on the rash of national reports critically evaluating instruction in higher education.

Braun, Joseph A., Jr., and Max Brown. 1984. Challenging student teachers. *Phi Delta Kappan* 65 (May): 601-602.

Although brief, this article offers a concise and practical description of a successful Challenge Education program. The real value of the article is due to authors who are actually using the Challenge Education program.

Conrad, Dan, and Diane Hedin. 1981. National assessment of experiential education: Summary and implications. *Journal of Experiential Education* (Fall): 6-20.

Assesses the impact of experiential education programs on the psychological, social, and institutional development of secondary students.

Eisner, Elliot W. 1983. The kind of schools we need. *Educational Leadership* 41 (October): 48-55.

An important article critiquing school reform proposals. The author's view of what schools need matches the basic rationale supporting Challenge Education. The focus is on developing independent and self-confident learners.

Gardner, Louis. 1977. Environmental education challenges Georgia teachers. *Walkabout* 2 (May): 1-3.

Summarizes the Environmental Education program at Georgia State University, a program based on the experienced-based Walkabout concept.

Gibbons, Maurice. 1984. Walkabout ten years later: Searching for a renewed vision of education. *Phi Delta Kappan* 65 (May): 591-600.

Perhaps the most valuable source for understanding the Walkabout concept and, therefore, Challenge Education. The author has had over ten years to experience and reflect on the Walkabout concept and the wisdom is evident. A very clear and convincing rationale and explanation of the Walkabout program.

Gibbons, Maurice. 1976. *The new secondary education.* Bloomington, Ind.: Phi Delta Kappa.

Although the book concentrates on secondary education, the discussion and examples explaining the author's view of the individual and education, make this a worthwhile reference for further understanding Challenge Education.

Gibbons, Maurice. 1974. Walkabout: Searching for the right passage from childhood and school. *Phi Delta Kappan* 55 (May): 596-602.

This is the seminal article introducing and explaining the Walkabout concept. It is an inspiring article by an author who enthusiastically discovers an educational analogy that works.

Gibbons, Maurice, and Gary Phillips. 1978. Self-directed learning challenges students to excel. *Walkabout* 3 (November): 1-8.

An excellent and thorough rationale and evaluation of self-directed learning at the secondary school level that can appropriately translate to students of all ages.

Guild, Pat Burke, and Stephen Garger. 1985. *Marching to different drummers.* Reston, Va.: Association of Curriculum and Supervision Development.

Reviews a wide variety of learning styles with the purpose of helping teachers to open educational opportunities to students who most need assistance.

Kohler, Mary Conway. 1981. Developing responsible youth through youth participation. *Phi Delta Kappan* 62 (February): 426-428.

Stresses the importance of teaching responsibility to young citizens, thereby helping the difficult transition to adulthood.

McCarthy, Henry. 1978. Teaching social responsibility. *North Carolina Education* 9 (November): 6, 17, 24.

Emphasizes, through examples and procedures, the need for teaching the "expectations" of student social responsibility.

Selye, Hans. 1974. *Stress without distress.* Philadelphia: J.B. Lippincott.

The pioneer publication of stress that defines positive and negative stress and offers solutions that continue to deserve consideration.

Skinner, Ray. 1978. New roles for teachers: Walkabout guides. *Walkabout* 3 (4): 1, 4-5.

A description of how a walkabout experience can be utilized in the university classroom, specifically its use in a teacher preparation program.

Thayer, Lou. 1978. Experience modules complement courses. *Walkabout* 3 (March): 5, 8.

Presents and discusses the utilization of the walkabout concept in an undergraduate student teaching program.

Wangberg, Elaine G. 1987. The missing link in reform: Listening to teachers. *The Clearinghouse* 60 (October): 76-80.

Looks at teacher stress and job dissatisfaction. Suggestions for change to diminish teacher stress point to the need for teachers to have more control over their own school environment.

Developing Preservice Teachers' Self-Awareness: An Examination of the Professional Dynametric Program

Bonnie Johnson

Teacher education has come a long way since the early teacher education program established by Emma Willard in Troy, New York. More than 12,000 women attended Troy between 1821-1871 (Scott 1979). Originally, Mrs. Willard sought state funding for her school to promote the training of female teachers. The state praised her ideas but refused her request. Undaunted, Mrs. Willard created her own private school. She selected a curriculum which consisted of mathematics, sciences, modern languages, Latin, history, philosophy, geography and literature. It was one of the first schools to include modern languages and sciences for teachers. In the science classes, students were required to set up their own experiments. Female students were expected to think for themselves. Mrs. Willard and her sister, Almira Lincoln, are credited with being the first teachers in the country to allow such freedom in the classroom.

Today we must ask if we are providing our preservice teachers enough opportunities to think for themselves, to discover who they are, or as Socrates would say, to "know thyself." Have we followed in the footsteps of Emma Willard and encouraged intellectual development and self-education for our preservice teachers? This chapter will briefly discuss the components of most teacher preparation programs, and then assess the importance of the human development aspect of teaching training. The remainder of the chapter will introduce the Professional Dynametric Program (PDP) and discuss its potential for teacher education and human development.

Teacher Preparation

There seems to be no precise way to discover what characterizes course work for teacher education students. The most common program components are educational foundation courses, courses on methods of teaching, field experiences, prestudent teaching, and student teaching (Mitzel 1982). However, what happens in those courses is as varied as the professors who teach them. Course work provided for teachers is "casual at best . . . a poorly conceived collage of courses . . . offerings lack curricular articulation within . . . and depth of study is noticeably and consistently absent" (Lanier & Little 1986, 549).

Teacher education programs include a myriad of ideas, devices, and techniques that are supposed to produce effective teachers in a given amount of time. Microteaching, simulation, protocol materials, and reflective teaching are some of the more recent innovations in instruction (Mitzel 1982). These innovations have helped preservice teachers improve the technical side of their teaching. As Lanier and Little (1986) report, the competency-based movement, accrediting bodies, and state agencies have resulted in teacher education programs focusing on classroom skills in the last decade. As a result teacher education has become more vocational and technical in nature. Course descriptions in college catalogs, (i.e., "Methods for Teaching English," "Classroom Management," "Computers in the Classroom," "Teaching of Reading") plus current articles in educational journals on teacher effectiveness (Rosenshine 1987, Berliner and Brandt 1986, Brophy 1986), and textbooks that focus on strategies and methods in teaching (Orlich et al. 1985, Cooper 1986, Callahan 1982, Kim and Kellough 1987) constantly remind us that we must attend to curricular materials, instructional procedures, and prescribed techniques in order to produce a well-trained teacher. Thus, teacher education programs use peer teaching, field experiments, videotaping, computer-assisted instruction, classroom management strategies, mastery teaching, etc. The emphasis on teacher techniques is very evident in today's teacher education curriculum.

Of course, it should be understood that the emphasis on methodology in teacher preparation programs has historical roots. In the early 1900's, when teachers were in great demand, coursework had to be flexible, entry accessible for the re-entry women who had previously done only domestic work, and the teacher preparation time had to be inexpensive because salaries were low. As a result, courses were valued for their immediate use on the job and for their efficacy in finding new jobs (Lanier

& Little 1986). Today, teachers of the '80's still demand courses with more practical, hands-on experiences. Teaching seems to be a profession ruled by pragmatism. "Too often teachers judge the success of education courses by the weight of the materials they can cart away" (Ohanian 1985, 697).

Fortunately, there are a growing number of teachers who are demanding ideas to grow on and not just ideas with immediate applicability. Unlike most of their predecessors, teachers "of today will likely be educated for lifelong careers in teaching" (Lanier & Little 1986, 556). Thus, teacher educators are being asked to provide novice teachers with a respect for the teaching profession that instills a lifelong commitment. Principals are questioning teacher applicants about professional commitment and demanding that schools of education make a concerted effort to develop professional pride within the ranks. "Teaching cannot survive as a pseudo-profession, and teacher education programs that foster the notion of teaching as a psuedo-profession will share its doom" (Marczely 1985, 703).

It is refreshing to also discover that teachers are seeking more than "how to's" for the present. One third grade teacher writes:

> The world does not come to us in neat packages. Even if we could identify just what a skill is, does more definitely denote better? What profiteth a child whose teacher has gathered up an immense pile of pishposh? We must take care, lest the examiners who claim they can dissect and label the educational process leave us holding a bag of gizzards. (Ohanian 1985, 700)

Human Development Education for Teachers

Change in education does not happen overnight. But teacher educators have begun to recognize that the education needs of previous generations will not fit a generation of teachers who are seeking lifelong careers. It is hoped that the 1990's will see a resurgence in curriculum development for teacher education to meet the need for lifelong learning. A vital component that seems to have been lost in the pragmatic orientation of the technical and practical work of the teacher education curriculum is human development. In his seminal study of teachers, Lortie (1975) noted that teaching is "people work." Yet, in teacher education there is little attention given to the personal uncertainties that teachers experience.

> Social workers, clinical psychologists, and psychotherapists are routinely educated to consider their own personalities and to take them into account in their work with people. Their stance is supposed to be analytic and open; one concedes and works with one's own limitations–it is hoped–in a context of self-acceptance. The tone of teacher interviews and their rhetoric reveals no such orientation; I would characterize it as moralistic rather than analytic and self-accusing rather than self-accepting. It does not appear that their work culture has come to grips with the inevitabilities of interpersonal clash and considerations of how one copes with them. Teachers seem lonely; they fight battles alone with their consciences, and it seems, frequently lose. (159)

Others have expressed their concern over the lack of attention given to the personal development of teachers in teacher education programs. B.O. Smith (1969) stated that reducing teaching to a craft leaves out an understanding of personality and teaching behavior. It is important for teachers in training to become aware of the fact that others are sharing similar feelings and attitudes and that there are differences in style of performance among teachers even though they employ the same techniques. "Teaching preparation should be designed to help the prospective teacher use his own style of behavior to best advantage" (89).

According to Iannone and Carline (1971) "teacher-training institutions have failed to recognize that teaching is primarily concerned with human beings interacting with each other in a very human process" (429). A teacher education program was proposed that included four principles:

1. opportunity for prospective teachers to progress at their own speed;

2. provision for the learning experience in accordance with human potential;

3. self-evaluation throughout the teacher preparation program;

4. self-examination with regard to teacher influence on professors, youngsters, and peers. (431)

Combs (1972) has asserted that teacher education is more than just dealing with the process of teaching, but as "a process of becoming, of personal discovery, of helping a person to become a teacher beginning from where he or she is" (287). Teacher educators should assist in helping prospective teachers to reach awareness of themselves. According to Wendt (1983), "The development of a human service educator may be the key to the direction of professional preparation" (183). How can teacher educators provide students with the skills of teaching without forfeiting the human dimensions?

Professional Dynametric Program

Darrol Lyons, a classroom teacher in Chico, California, who used a personality profile to assist businesses in matching employers with employees offered a possible solution for a way to improve the human development aspect of teacher training.

Student Teacher, S–commented:

> I have just had a psuedoreligious revelation . . . for the past week I've found it somewhat hard to fit myself into the mainstream of Jim's class. Each day I get the feeling that my message is not quite getting across to the class. I think I've been pretty hard on myself because I assumed it was fully my fault that I was not adapting to the classroom environment. At times I thought this line of work may not be my cup o'tea but, wallah, something clicked while writing my lesson plan–I wasn't really writing my plan, I was writing one just like Jim would! My personality profile is obviously not the same as Jim's. So, it's not a fault, it's just the way I happen to operate and the whole system in the class is set up for the way Jim operates. I am not a teller–I find it hard to stand up in front of the class and just lecture for three or four periods in a row just to get through the facts quickly. I am a seller. And what's more, I need the time to do what I gotta do, you know? I feel so much better now because I was really questioning my abilities and not trusting my feelings. I think the kids are somehow aware of this situation on a subconscious level, because I feel that we have good

> rapport and can interact on various levels and enjoy each other's company, yet I'm also sure my lectures are not as effective as they can be. What a dilemma, I feel like I'm half way to the finish line and now my shoestrings have come untied. (Journal Entry, 1987)

The student teacher who wrote this journal entry had just discovered important truths about himself.   After completing 12 weeks of observing other teachers, working with a cooperating teacher and finally teaching in that cooperating teacher's classroom for two weeks, the student teacher had discovered what he could and could not do because of who he was. However, his revelation was not just a psuedoreligious one, rather it was the result of his having acquired knowledge about himself. During his preservice training, this student teacher had developed a clearer image of self through the use of the Professional Dynametric Program (PDP). This program was developed by Professional Dynametric Program, Inc., of Woodland Park, Colorado.

An attempt to unite the practical world of teaching with the theoretical, and to add the affective component of self-awareness, was the reason the PDP was incorporated into the teacher education program at California State University at Chico. The PDP was seen to be a valuable tool to help student teachers analyze themselves in the context of the classroom. During student teaching, students should find a positive, reinforcing, and constructively critical environment.   "To know one's personality trait preferences and the probable role they can contribute to the student teaching experience is as much a part of teacher preparation as any professional competency (Pfeifer 1983, 17).

Checklists, rankings, peer evaluations, etc., are usually used as self-assessment devices. However, student teachers are seldom given an opportunity to have a concrete understanding of their personalities. Thus, they find it difficult to understand why they react to people, situations, or circumstances as they do.

Teacher candidates working with the author were initially asked to keep journals of their experiences in the public schools. As they observed in classrooms, they were to record their reactions, emotions, and feelings about what they saw. They were encouraged to "let it all hang out," and not be afraid to reveal what they felt as they witnessed various activities that occurred in the public school classroom. Jersild (1955) discovered in his survey of over a thousand students and teachers (mostly graduate education students) that two major concerns stood out for teachers. The first concern was the problem of meaning--who and what am I? Secondly, the pervasive concern was anxiety. "From one half to two-thirds indicated that the idea of self-understanding was or might be 'most significant' in their own professional education" (15).

The following entries from student teachers' journals support Jersild's findings (1955) and reflect some of the confusion and anxiety prospective teachers encounter as they begin their teaching career.

(K--)

_____is the art teacher here. Or is it baby-sitter? I think this job is about patience, not art. But wait, patience is an art--perhaps this could replace that experience of monastic life I've always thought about.

(Kr--)

I felt a sense of gloom come over me as soon as I entered this room. Right away I noticed that the teacher doesn't look very happy. She doesn't seem to be enjoying her job at all! and I think the kids pick up on that . . . Sometimes I wonder if the way a teacher conducts his/her class is not a direct result of his/her personality. Will a more energetic personality automatically capture the student's attention more easily? I am sure the two go hand-in-hand.

(M--)

I think they (students) are all real people looking for the things most people look for--attention, affection, feelings about belonging. I like that Tomorrow they will probably chew me up and spit me out.

(S--)

Again it has been reinforced to me that students definitely respond differently to male or female teachers. Actually, I feel that I have an advantage being male, but it makes me wonder what "relating" is not occurring because of gender. Are men and women geared specifically to types of classes? Is this good? bad?

(B–)
Good lecture on the Progressive Era. Probably my least favorite time period . . . very boring . . . . . He is having fun talking about it though. More than I can do! It points out something to me though. As a teacher, I must know even the "boring stuff" as the kids depend on it. So much for my career of selective attention to historical detail. I guess I must learn the garbage too.

The importance of effective decision making is crucial for a teacher's success. "While best judgments can be made in certain situations, very often the better or the best depends on the perspective of the decision maker" (Guild 1987). Therefore, to assist the beginning teacher in understanding where they are, why they react as they do, and what they can do to to make better decisions and thus reduce anxiety, it was decided to incorporate the Professional Dynametric Program into the teacher education program. The PDP is based on the belief that who people are and what they think is expected of them in a particular situation contributes significantly to the way they perform their jobs. Using a computer-based survey, a sophisticated and accurate analysis of a person's behavioral traits serve as predictors of performance in a given job.

At present the PDP has been used successfully in the business world only. Employers have used it to enhance employer-employee relations, create effective team building (PDP, 1978-84), and to recruit appropriate personnel (Mancuso 1987). The educational world has yet to see the value of the PDP.

Originally called Personal Dynamics Profiles, PDP measures the major aspects of self-perception. "It reveals the individual's basic personality, reaction to the environment, and predictable behavioral patterns" (PDP 1978-84, Introduction). Designed by Dr. Samuel R. Houston and Dr. Dudley Solomon, the system is based on research stating "that people respond from the perspective of what they think or believe themselves to be" (PDP 1978-84, Introduction).

The four cornerstone behavioral traits are measured in the PDP system: Dominance, Extroversion, Pace/Patience, Conformity. Dominance is defined as the "control" trait, Extroversion is defined as the "social and fluency" trait; Pace/Patience is defined as the "rate of motion" trait; and Conformity is defined as the "structure and detail" trait (PDP 1978-84).

A license is recommended to use the PDP software. This software produces a detailed readout. Three descriptions of a person are provided by the PDP, Pro Scan Comprehensive Report: (1) the BASIC/NATURAL type of person is how you feel you really are, (2) the PRIORITY ENVIRONMENT reflects your effort to adjust to circumstances, people and/or matters of importance, (3) the PREDICTOR/OUTWARD SELF describes how you will predictably come across in your interactions with others. One's energy level, energy loss due to stress, preferred styles for decision making, communication, management, leadership and back-up style (when you run out of energy and patience) and what motivates you, and your preferred environment, all can be determined using data from the these categories (PDP 1978-84).

With the assistance of Darrol Lyon, a classroom teacher who had received training in the use of the PDP, the author administered the short five-to ten-minute PDP survey. Respondents reacted to 60 adjectives on a five-point Likert scale. The split-half reliability of all adjectives has been found to exceed .804. The Test-Retest reliability has exceeded .704 (PDP 1978-84, Introduction). A more detailed description of the PDP (Hubby 1986) includes theoretical assumptions, development of item pool, reliability and validity. On the first side of the survey card, the student teacher was asked to mark the response which best describes "how you feel you really are." Words on that side of the card include Efficient, Enthusiastic, Patient, Flexible. On the second side of the card, the student teacher was asked to mark the response that best describes "how you feel others expect you to be or act." Words on this list include Demanding, Agreeable, Dedicated, Dependent.

After results had been compiled, Mr. Lyon talked with each student teacher. All the student teachers received individual printouts that identified areas of strength and predicted self-perception, how they were viewed by others, and how they might react to the environment. Student teachers were asked to continue writing in their journals about their reactions to events, incidents, and people as they continued their work in the public school classroom.

Time was spent during seminars to understand the implications of the PDP. Using scenarios, student teachers were asked to role play what they would do as the teacher. (For example: "The following has happened to you. The master teacher has given you hasty instructions to lead a group. You don't thoroughly understand and 'wing it.' This has happened at least three times in the past week. You are now in conversation with the master teacher over this issue." Or "You are having a parent conference with a parent whose child is a discipline problem. The parent believes the child is never wrong.")

After role playing, all observers were asked to comment on the strengths of the personality of the teacher portrayed. Through such activities, student teachers soon became adept at assessing another's personality and decision-making style.

Journal entries revealed new insights developing as student teachers applied their personality profiles to their student teaching situation.

(Ca–)
My impatience surfaces as I wait for another opportunity to teach. My dominance comes out because _____is also very dominant, and our personalities clash a bit at times.

(Kr–)
I can see how I am high in conformity. I always want to be sure of myself before I act and like things to be systematic, to fall in place, and not to have any disruptions. Then this is where the patience comes in. Although I don't like disruptions, I have the patience to deal with them when they do occur. I need time to make decisions to be sure I'm making the right ones. I also realized that I can be pushed up to a certain point but then will begin to be dominant and demand respect. But I would never (or rarely) use dominance as my initial reaction to a situation.

(Co–)
I need to take a deep breath during class more, not expect total attention at all times . . . My PDP said I was very dominant, but I never really thought I was that much. I finally had to put my foot down on the behaviors of two kids, after warning them many times. They pleaded with me, but I felt like I had to ask them to go sit down. It seemed to help my "presence" by not letting them get away with things. _____ said it's what I should have done. Guess, my PDP was right.

(B–)
A _____told the class to shut up and do their reading. Some kept talking so he gave each a half-hour detention. I have a strong amount of dominance and found this quite appealing at first. But even I work within a

system more than this! I tended to conform with fairness more than this. I immediately thought of the PDP when I saw this and saw how my dominance contrasted with his dominance and no patience. I am more patient and made a mental note to be so.

Conversations with student teachers during seminars and in the public school setting demonstrated that an awareness of self was easing the decision-making process. One student teacher reported, "I found I didn't handle kids right, according to my profile. This bothered me, so next time I did it my way." Another said, "I tried to play different roles, and this caused me problems. Kids didn't know what to expect."

(J–)

In the middle of my observations—mid semester—I was impressed with the subtle, effective way my cooperating teacher taught. He doesn't get hysterical or lose his temper or react to inattentiveness . . . . He would weave these students' names into his stories and create new stories about the students . . . captured many of the students' attention. I see my strong desire for harmony and more harmony at work here. I really like things to run smoothly.

A final assessment of the influence of PDP on their teaching experience revealed overwhelming support.

(D–)

It gave me good insights on my personality so that I could recognize my own unique way of handling a variety of situations. So I feel it was valuable in getting a more concrete picture of me and being able to feel comfortable with that. We are all so different, and it's good to feel secure with those differences instead of afraid that we aren't handling situations in the 'proper,' 'acceptable,' 'prescribed' method.

(Ke–)

I cannot honestly say that PDP, per se has consciously been in my mind, but certainly related tendencies I need to work on have been in the front of my mind, and I do think I'm improving. Explicit awareness of strengths . . . was a potential plus with the PDP.

(P–)

Knowing my profile, I tried to really minimize verbal attacks when I was pushed into a corner. I succeeded, and it has made situation which could have been negative, into a positive one.

(B–)

I felt the PDP was very beneficial and valuable. It should be used in the future. It helps one to realize one's personality rather than merely guessing. It helps me to know when I am about to steamroll, or go for the throat–two things which are OK in a coaching situation, but not so good for teaching.

(J–)

I was shocked when I saw how many of my traits and idiosyncrasies were so obvious . . . I guess I thought that if I didn't pay any attention to my weaknesses then others wouldn't. I don't see the PDP as gospel, but I do see it as valid enough to a very helpful tool. I have been helped by it.

(C–)

Knowing I am a high dominant person helped to tone me down a bit. It is good to be dominant but not to an extreme. Knowing I don't have much patience helped me to work on being more patient with my students.

(S–)

With the PDP for a sounding board, I felt that I not only had a point of reference for my actions and feelings, but also realized the best ways to use my energy. I felt much more settled because it allowed me to view my personality as an asset rather than as a liability.

These brief excerpts from student teachers would seem to indicate that they have discovered more about who they are and what kind of teachers they hope to become. They have developed a stronger sense of self-awareness. "Self-awareness helps people articulate their strengths and use them for effective action" (Guild 1987). The PDP is a tool, or a guide, that student teachers can refer to when they are assaulted by the many decisions that are inherent in the public school classroom. Combs (1978) asserted that a teacher education program should develop "a personal system of perceptions or beliefs to provide the young teacher with long-term goals and short-term guidelines for moment-to-moment decisions of classroom interaction" (559).

For the field of teaching, the PDP can assist in determining one's decision-making style. What you are is what your teaching style will become. Knowing one's personality in the areas of dominance, extroversion, patience, and conformity will provide better insights into the way decisions are made.

If we as teacher educators value the human dimension of teaching training, then the Professional Dynametrics Program offers a way prospective teachers can reach enhanced self-awareness. It is one way to promote the development of a human service educator.

For more information about Professional Dynametrics Program address correspondence:

Bass PDP Affiliated
Transamerica Pyramid
600 Montgomery Street, 4th Floor
San Francisco, CA 94111

References

Berliner, David, and Ronald Brandt. 1986. On the expert teacher: A conversation with David Berliner. *Educational Leadership* 44 (October): 4-9.

Brophy, J. 1986. Teacher influences on student achievement. *American Psychologist* 41: 1069-1078.

Callahan, Joseph, and Leonard H. Clark. 1982. *Teaching in the middle and secondary schools.* 2nd ed. New York and London: Macmillan Publishing Co. and Collier Macmillan Publishers.

Combs, Arthur W. 1978. Teacher education: The person in the process. *Educational Leadership* 36 (April): 558-561.

Combs, Arthur W. 1972. Some basic concepts for teacher education. *Journal of Teacher Education* 23 (Fall): 286-290.

Cooper, James M. 1986. *Classroom teaching skills.* Lexington, Massachusetts: D. C. Heath and Company.

Guild, Pat Burke. 1987. How leaders' minds work. Chapter 6 in *Leadership: Examining the elusive.* ed Linda T. Sheive and Marian B. Schoenheit, 81-92. Association for Supervision and Curriculum Development.

Hubby, Bruce M., and M.S. Williamson. 1986. Personal dynamics profiles occupational survey. June (Monograph No. 7). Woodland Park, Colo.: PDP Research Department 1-10.

Iannone, Ronald, and John L. Carline. 1971. A humanistic approach to teacher education. *Journal of Teacher Education* 22 (Winter): 429-431.

Jersild, Arthur T. 1955. *When teachers face themselves.* New York: Teachers College Press.

Kim, Eugene C., and Richard D. Kellough. 1987. *A resource guide for secondary teaching* 4th ed. New York and London: Macmillan Publishing Company and Collier Macmillan Publishers.

Lanier, Judith, and Judith Little. 1986. Research on teacher education. Chapter 19 in *Handbook of research on teaching*, ed. M.C. Wittrock, 527-569. New York: Macmillan.

Lortie, Dan C. 1975. *Schoolteacher*. Chicago: The University of Chicago Press.

Mancuso, Joseph. 1987. Hiring number two. *Success* (March): 8.

Marczely, Bernadette. 1985. Teacher education: A view from the front lines. *Phi Delta Kappan*. 66 (June): 702-703.

Mitzel, Harold E. 1982. *Encyclopedia of educational research*. New York: Free Press.

Ohanian, Susan. 1985. On stir-and-serve recipes for teaching. *Phi Delta Kappan* 66 (June): 696-701.

Orlich, Donald D., Robert J. Harder, Richard C. Callagan, Constance H. Kravas, Donald P. Kauchak, R.A. Pendergrass, and Andrew J. Keogh, eds. 1985. *Teaching strategies: A guide to better instruction*. Lexington, Mass. and Toronto: D.C. Heath and Company.

Pfeifer, Jeri. 1983. The effects of personality on success in student teaching. Paper presented at the National Field Directors Forum of the Annual Meeting of the Association of Teacher Educators. Orlando, Florida, January, ED 228199.

Professional Dynametric Program. 1978-84. Personal dynamics profiles manual. Woodland Park, Colo.: PDP, Inc.

Rosenshine, Barak. 1987. Explicit teaching and teaching training. *Journal of Teacher Education* (May-June): 34-36.

Scott, Anne Firor. 1979. The ever-widening circle: The diffusion of feminist values from the Troy Female Seminary 1822-1872. *History of Education Quarterly* 19 (Spring): 3-25.

Smith, B. Othanel. 1969. *Teachers for the real world.* Washington, D.C.: American Association of Colleges for Teacher Education.

Wendt, Janice. 1983. Professional preparation: A process of discovery. *Quest* 35: 182-189.

Author-Title Index

A lever long enough 242
A nation at risk 5, 50, 72, 188
A nation prepared:A report of the Holmes Group 12
American Association of Colleges for Teacher Education (AACTE) 20, 255, 280, 291, 301, 350
AACTE Task Force on Technology 112
Abrell, Ron 77, 79, 86, 88
Ada, A.F. 291, 289
Adams, Dennis M. 112
Adams, R.D. 263, 264, 267
Ahment, Robert 139
Ala-Kurikka, R. 264, 267
Alabama Polytechnic Institute 262
Allen, Rodney F. 310
Allen, Tom 52, 53, 63
Allport, G. 213, 222
American Association of Teachers Colleges 70
American Federation of Teachers 50
American Psychological Association 264, 267
Ammons, M. 263, 264, 267

Antonelli, G. 262, 265, 272
Appel, Marcia 118, 137
Apple, M.W. 172, 179
Applegate, Jane 25, 30, 44
Archimedes 241
Arends, R.A. 207, 265, 274
Aronfreed, J. 214, 222
Aronowitz, S. 174, 179
Asbury, C.A. 263, 267
Ashburn, Elizabeth A. 30, 88
Ashton, Patricia 11, 20
Aspy, C. 234, 235, 236, 237, 238, 239, 242, 243, 244, 246, 247, 248, 250
Aspy, D.N. 248
Association for Student Teaching 70
Association of Teacher Educators (ATE) 301, 302, 310
ATE Blue Ribbon Task Force 72
Backler, Alan 310
Baker, Frederick J. 310
Bandura, A. 214, 218, 222, 227

351

Banks, James A.162, 179,
    283, 291, 288, 311
Bargar, R.R. 262, 264, 267
Barnes, Susan 30, 259,
    270
Baron, J.B. 165, 179
Bay Area Global
Education Program
(BAGEP) 299, 300,
    306, 311
Beaumariage, G.N., Jr. 262,
    268
Beck, M.D. 256, 268, 276
Beeler, Kent D. 324, 331
Bell, Terrel H. 5, 20, 49,
    59,   63
Ben-David, J. 260, 268
Bennie, William A. 73, 88
Benson, Gregory M. 112
Bents, Richard 36
Bereiter, C. 282, 291
Berenson, D.N. 237, 248
Berkowitz, M. 227
Berliner, David 199, 204,
    261, 268, 336, 348
Bernier, J. 220, 222
Berry, J. 288, 293
Best, F. 129, 134, 136
Beyer, L.E. 172,179
Biles, B. 264, 275
Billups, L. 264, 275
Bingham, Marjorie 313
Blatt, B. 188
Bloom, B.S. 168, 170,
    175, 179, 204, 257
Blum, Robert 193, 197,
    203
Bok, Derek 11, 20
Borko, H. 207, 265, 274
Botkin, James W. 144,
    153
Bowman, Jim 146,153
Boyer, Ernest L. 324, 331

Bradley, L. 217, 222
Brameld, Theodore
    145, 153
Brandt, Ronald 336, 348
Branson, Margaret
    Stimman 311
Braun, Joseph A., Jr. 325,
    331
Brookover, Wilbur 197,
    204
Brooks, Douglas M. 25, 26,
    30, 88
Brophy, J.E. 168, 179,
    336, 348
Brown, J. D. 259, 263, 268
Brown, Lester R. 311
Brown, Max 325, 331
Brown, P. 268
Brown, William 140
Bullivant, B.M. 282, 283,
    291
Bunke, C.R. 127, 133,
    139, 142
Burdin, J.125, 127, 134,
    136
Bureau of the Census 121,
    122, 123, 136
Burgliavello, George 136
Burke, Peter J. 26, 31, 39,
    63
Burry, J. 256, 273
Buscaglia, Leo 120, 137
Bush, Robert N 112
Butler, C. 188, 205
California Mentor Teacher
    Program 59
California State
    University 285, 262
Callagan, Richard C. 349
Callahan, Joseph 336,
    348
*Cardinal Principles of
    Secondary Education* 7

Carkhuff Interpersonal Process Scales 237
Carkhuff, R.R. 234, 237, 238, 248
Carlberg, C. 256, 268
Carline, John L. 338, 348
Carnegie Corporation's Task Force on Teaching as a Profession 11, 13
Carnegie Forum on Education and the Economy 13, 20, 58, 63, 72, 73, 88, 130, 137
Carr, May Ann 312
Carter, Kathy 26, 31
Carter, R. 227
Case, Robert 194, 203
Casteneda 288, 292
Center for Excellence in Teacher Education 137
Center for Public Education in International Affairs 296
Cetron, Marvin 118, 124, 128, 137, 138
Cetron, Michael 204
Chambers, B. 257, 270
Chapman, H. 218, 224
Character II 230
Chazan, B. 211, 222, 227
Cheney, L.V. 72, 88, 163, 167, 180
Cherryholmes, Cleo H. 177, 180
Chi, M.T.H. 195, 204
Christensen, Judith C. 55, 63
Clark, Leonard H. 348
Clark, David L 148, 150, 153, 261, 271
Clark, R.E. 112

Clarke, Arthur C 138
Colbert, J. 79
Coleman, J 197, 204
Collegial Research Consortium 55, 56, 57, 64
Collins, Keith 116
Collins, T. H. 300, 315
Combs, Arthur W. 243, 249, 339, 346, 348
Commission on Population Growth and the American Future 138
Conant Report 71
Conant, James B. 88, 254, 268
Conrad, Dan 322, 325, 331
Cooper, James M. 336, 348
Cooperman, Saul 79, 89, 131, 138
Copeland, Willis D. 85, 89
Cornbleth, Catherine 150, 154
Cornett, Lynn 50, 54, 64
Cornish, Edward 124, 138, 311
Corrigan, Dean C.113, 148, 154
Council for Intercultural Teacher Education 302
Counts, George S 145, 146, 154
Cremin, L.A. 284, 291
Crocker, Linda 11, 20
Croddy, Marshall 312
Cross, K. Patricia 89
Cruickshank, D. R. 264, 268
Cubberley 171
Cummins, J. 167, 180

Darling-Hammond, Linda
 11, 190, 204, 269
Davidson 188
Davis, J. 223
De Brigard, Paul 138
Deal, Terrence E. 148,
 149, 154
Dede, Christopher J. 138,
 153, 15
Delpit, L.D. 290, 291
Dembo, Myron 195, 205
Dewey, John 70, 89, 145,
 154, 164, 171, 180,
 212, 216, 222
Diaz, S. 287, 291
Doak, J.L. 262, 269
Dobson, J. 213, 222
Dobson, R. 222
Dudley, Richard 26, 35
Dworkin, E.P. 262, 267
Eaker, R.E. 262, 263, 269
Ebel, R. L. 258, 259, 269
Eddy, Elizabeth M 31
Edmonds, Ronald 197,
 205
Egbert, R. L. 192, 205,
 260, 269
Eisner, Elliot W. 324, 331
Elias, Pat 42
Elder, Pamela 312
Ellwein, M. C. 271
Elmandjra, Mahdi 153
Engelman, S. 282, 291
English, Fenwick W. 52,
 54, 64
Enzer, Selweyn 138
*Equality of Educational
 Opportunity* 197
Ethics in Education 231
Evangelauf, Jean 113
*Exchange for Philosophy
 and Moral Psychology*
 231

Farmer, R. 249
Fattu, N.A. 261, 269
Feinberg, Richard E. 312
Feistritzer, Charles 205
Feistritzer, Emily 9, 20,
 78, 8 9
Fennessey, D. 256, 258,
 269
Fenstermacher, Gary 192,
 205, 240
Ferguson, Marilyn 144,
 146, 154
Fessler, Ralph 23, 32, 39,
 55, 63, 64
Fielding 210, 212, 218,
 223, 228
Finn, C.E., Jr. 163, 182
Fitch, Robert M. 139
Flanders 234, 235, 236
Flemming, M. 257, 270
Flexner Report 71
Flexner, Abraham 90
Flood 197
Flora, V. R. 25, 30, 44
Flowers Report 70
Flowers, John C. 90
*Focus on human rights
 and democracy.* 318
Freiberg, H. Jerome 51,
 54, 64
Frew, Thomas, W. 47
Froebel, F. 69
Frymier, Jack R.79. 90,
 262, 270
Fuller, Buckminster 312
Furtwengler, Carol 51, 64
Gage 234
*Gallup International
 Research Instutute*
 307
Gallup, George 312
Gardner, H. 213, 222
Gardner, Louis 324, 331

Garger, Stephen 322, 32
Garner, R. 207, 265, 274
Gay, G. 288, 291
Geertz, C. 161,180
Gehrke, Nathalie J. 32
Gibbons, Maurice 322,
    327, 332
Gibbs, J. 213, 222
Gilligan, C. 218, 222, 228
Gips 125, 127, 134
Giroux, H.A.172, 173, 174,
    175, 179, 180
Glassberg, S. 260, 273
Glasser, William 187, 191,
    195, 204, 205
Glickman, C. 82
Global Education Center
    313
Goldberg, Jack 114
Goldberg, Milton 90
Gollnick, Donna M. 16, 21
Good, Thomas 194, 195,
    205
Goodall, Robert 127, 133,
    139
Goodlad, John I. 86, 167,
    175, 181, 190, 206,
    240, 249
Goodman, K. 170,181
Gordon, Theodore 139
Goslin, D.A. 255, 256, 270
Gosman, Erica 8, 21
Gould, S.J. 166,181
*The governors' 1991
    report on education* 15
Graham, Patricia A. 10, 21
Gramsci 173
Graves, D. 287, 291
Gray, Marilynne M. 90
Gray, William A. 90
Green, Joslyn 21
Green, K.E. 255, 256, 257,
    258, 270, 276

Greene, M. 290, 291
Gregoric, A. 192
Griffin, Gary A 25, 26, 27,
    33, 34, 53, 65, 81, 90,
    91, 259, 260
Grissmer, David W. 81, 91
Grosenick, Judith K. 44,
    93
Gross, Lynne S 113
Gross, Susan 313
Ground Zero 306, 313
Grouws, David 194, 195,
    205
Gruesemer, L. J. 188, 206
Guba, E.G. 261, 271
*Guidelines for Global
    Education* 308, 317
Guild, Pat Burke 322, 332,
    342, 346, 348
Gullicksen, A.R. 255, 256,
    257, 258, 271, 272
Guyton, E. 262, 265, 272
Haberman, Martin 139
Haddon, P.C. 124, 139
Halberstam, David 6, 21
Hall, B.W. 256, 272
Hall, C. 215, 222
Hall, Gene 34
Hall, R. 223
Hamm, Mary 112
Hanvey, Robert 310
Harder, Robert J. 349
Harf, James E. 313
Harman, Willis W. 144,
    155
Harris, Louis 56, 65, 78,
    91
Hart, Leslie 187, 192, 206
Harvey, James 90
Harvey, O. 219, 223
Hawk, Parmalee 27, 35
Hayes, B. 223
Hayes, R. 214, 221, 223

Hedin, Diane 322, 325,
   331
Hegler, Kay 26, 35
Heideman, Robert G. 39
Heinich, R. 113
Hempel, C. 213, 223
Henry, Marvin A. 82, 91
Herbart 69
Herman, J.L. 255, 277
Hersh, R. 210, 212, 218,
   223, 225, 228, 229
Hills, J.R. 255, 272
Hirsch, E.D., Jr. 165, 166,
   167, 181
Hirschen, William 112
Hitz, Randy 36
Hodgkinson, Harold 206
Hoffer, William 139
Holmes Group 11, 21, 59,
   65, 73, 72, 77, 92, 148,
   188, 206, 244
Holmes, K. 244, 249
Holmstrom, E. 21
Holubec, E. 170, 181
Hoopers, David 313
Hopkins, D.K. 255, 258,
   272
Howe, L. 225, 230
Howe, H., II. 283, 291
Howey, Kenneth R. 26,
   27, 36, 37, 263, 272,
Hoyle, John R. 127, 139
Hsu, F. 287, 292
Hubby, Bruce M. 348
Huffman, J.O. 262, 263,
   269
Huling-Austin, Leslie 25,
   37, 38, 263, 272
Hunt, C. 219, 220, 226
Hunt, D. 219, 223
Hunter, M. 167, 169,
   181, 193
Hursh, Heidi 314, 317

Iannone, Ronald 348
*Illinois State Board of
   Education* 34
Intercom 314
*International Commission
   on the Development of
   Education* 139
*International Council on
   Education for Teaching*
   301, 314
*International Resource
   Development, Inc.* 139
Ishler, Peggy 26, 39, 92
Ishler, Richard 133, 140
Isohella, V. 264, 267
Jackson, P. 198, 206, 207
Jensen, A.R. 282, 292
Jersild, Arthur T. 340,
   348
Johnson, D.W. 181, 292
Johnson, Glenn R. 127,
   139
Johnson, Jim 69, 70, 92
Johnston, John M. 23, 24,
   25, 26, 30, 39, 40, 44
Johnson, R.E. 263, 288,
   292
Johnson, R.T. 170, 181
Johnson, W.L. 272
Jola, Jaye 319
Jordell, Karl 40
*Journal of Moral
   Education* 231
Joyce, Bruce 206
Judge, H. 166, 181
Kahn, Herman 140
Kallab, Valeriana 312
Kaplan, L. 263, 273
Kauchak, Donald P. 344,
   349
Kauffmann, Draper L., Jr.
   144, 155
Kay, Richard 26, 40

Kearn 263, 272
Keller, George 114
Kellough, Richard D. 336,348
Kenworthy, Leonard 299, 314
Keogh, Andrew J. 349
Kerr, D.H. 163,181
Kessinger, J. 213, 222
Kester, Ralph 26, 40
Kidron, Michael 314
Kim, Eugene C. 336, 348
Kirby 81,91
Kirman, Joseph M. 114
Kirschenbaum, H. 225, 230
Klagholz, Leo 79, 89,131,138
Klein, M. Frances 65
Kliebard, H.M. 171, 182
Kluender, M. 192, 204
Kobus, D. 303, 314
Koehler 26,31
Kohlberg, L. 170, 182, 213, 214, 215, 216, 217, 218, 221, 223, 224, 225, 228
Kohler, Mary Conway 322, 333
Kohut, Sylvester 65
Korematsu v. United States 285, 292
Krahmer, E. 273
Kratwohl, D.R. 255, 262, 264, 273
Kravas, Constance, H. 349
Kuhn, T.S. 213, 224
Kunkel, R. 16
Lamola, A.P. 124, 139
Lambert, N. 230
Lamy, Steven 296, 314
Langer, J. 213, 224

Lanier, Judith E.162,182, 188, 205, 265, 273, 349, 336, 337
Lasley, Thomas 25, 30, 41,44, 92
Lazar, Frederic, D. 138
Lazar-Morrison, C. 256, 273
Leinwand, Gerald 315
Leiter, K.C.W. 256, 274
Leming, J. 228
Levy, Jerre 191, 206
Lezotte, Lawrence 197, 206
Lickona, T. 221, 224, 229
Linton, Ralph 295, 315
Lisler, Ian 315
Lissitz, R.W. 255, 276
Little, Judith W. 162, 182, 205, 265, 273, 336, 337, 349
Loevinger, J. 229
Logan, Ben 306, 316
Lortie, Dan C. 28, 42, 55, 65, 337, 349
Los Angeles Unified School District 79
Loxley, J. 220, 224
Lynch, J. 283, 291
MacDonald, J.B. 284, 292
Mager, G. 25, 30, 44
Mahan, J.M. 289, 292
Manning-Curtis, C. 256, 274
Mannisto, V. 264, 267
Mans, Lori 315
Mancuso, Joseph 342, 349
Marczely, Bernadette 337, 349
Marks, M.B. 262, 274
Marockie, Mary 26, 40
Martel, Leon 140
Marx, Gary 300, 315

Maslow, A. 213, 224, 249
Masoner, Paul H. 315
Mattingly, P.H. 261, 274
Mauro, L. 206, 265, 274
Maxey 285
Maxey, P.F. 285, 292
Mayer, R.170,182, 213,
    214, 215, 217, 224
Mayo, S.T. 254, 255, 274
McCaleb, Joseph L. 187,
    206, 265, 274
McCarthy, Bernice 191,
    206
McCarthy, Henry 324,
    333
McConaghy, T. 259, 262,
    264, 274
McCutchan 181
McDonald, Frederick J. 42
McKee, B.G. 256, 274
McLellan, J. 216, 222
McPhail 218
McPhail, P. 218, 224
Mehan, H. 287, 291
Memphis State University
    73,132
Mentkowski, M. 220, 224
Messier, Paul 191, 206
Metropolitan Life Survey
    of the American
    Teacher 78
Miller, J. 210, 212, 218,
    223, 228
Millies, Suzanne   25, 26,
    34, 81, 91
Malitza, 153
Mitzel, Harold E. 336, 349
Model Teacher Induction
    Program 38
Moeser, M. 220, 224
Molenda, M. 113
Moll, L. 287, 291
Moore, Richard W. 65

Moral Education Forum
    231
Mosher 221
Mosher, R. 224
Moy, R. 256, 273
Murphy, B. 286, 293
Murray, Frank B. 72, 77,
    92
Myers, Norman 316
Naisbitt, John 118, 120,
    121, 122, 127, 130,
    140, 144, 155
National Board for
    Professional Teaching
    Standards 14
National Center for
    Educational
    Information 78
National Commision on
    Excellence in Education
    5, 21, 49, 206
National Consortium for
    Humanizing Education
    238
National Council for the
    Accreditation of
    Teacher Education
    (NCATE) 12, 15, 72, 73,
    93,130, 262, 280, 281,
    301
National Council for the
    Social Studies (NCSS)
    280, 292
National Education
    Association 50
National Endowment for
    the Humanities 72,163
National Governors'
    Association 15, 21
National Teachers
    Examination (NTE) 77
Neill, A.S. 164, 216, 224
Newman, K. 25, 30

Newman, D.C. 255, 256, 258, 274
Noam 213, 225
Noll, V.H. 255, 275
North Carolina State University 220
Notar, Ellen Elms 26, 31
Nutter, Norma 125, 127, 134, 136

Oakes, J. 167,182
Oakeshott, M. 163,182
Odell, Sandra 43
Ohanian, Susan 337, 349
Ohio State University 262
Oja, S. 220, 224
Okorodudu, C.P. 262, 267
Oliva, Peter 194, 206
Orlich, Donald D. 336, 349
Oser, F. 227
O'Toole, Thomas 128, 138
Overton W.F. 213, 225
Owens, Robert 196, 206
Pacheco 283
Palaich, Robert 114
Palomares, Uvaldo 306, 316
Paolitto, D. 218, 225, 229
Paradise, M. 221, 224
Parekh, B. 280, 292
Parisi, Lynn 316
Parker, Jackson V. 151, 152,155, 206
Parker, Linda 81, 93
Parker, Walter C. 162,179,182,189, 307, 316
Patterson, Jerry L. 151, 152,155,189, 196, 206
Patterson, C. H. 250
Pendergrass, R.A. 349
Pestalozzi 69
Peters, R.S. 209, 225

Peterson 234
Peterson, Ken 43
Pfeifer, Jeri. 340, 349
Phillippy, S.W. 256, 272
Phillips, Gary 322, 332
Piaget, J. 216, 225
Pierce, R.M. 237, 248
Pines, Maya 123,140
Polin, L. 256, 273
Porter 264, 275
Postman, N. 304, 316
Professional Dynametric Program (PDP) 335, 340, 342, 343 349
Pulliam, John 153
Purkey, Stewart C. 151, 152, 155, 189, 206
Ramirez, M.A. 288, 292
Rauth, M. 264, 275
Ravitch, D. 163, 164, 167, 182
Redner, H. 261, 275
Reese, C.C. 213, 262, 276
Reese, H.W. 225
Reimer, J. 218, 225, 229
Render, G. F. 235, 237, 238, 239, 241, 242, 250
Research and Development Center for Teacher Education at the University of Texas at Austin 38
Rest, J. 229
Richards, A.C. 250
Richardson, John M. 316
Robards, Shirley 27, 35
Robinson, Rhonda S 114, 116
Rocks, Lawrence 140
Rodriguez, F. 288, 292
Roe, Rachael 317

Roebuck, F.N. 234, 235,
  237, 238, 239, 242,
  243, 244, 246, 248,
  250
Roeder, H.H. 255, 275
Rogers, C.R. 218, 225, 229,
  234, 235, 237, 239,
  241, 242, 250
Roper, Susan 36
Rosenholtz, Susan J 26,
  43, 56, 66
Rosenshine, Barak 169,
  182,192, 194, 206,
  336, 349
Rossetto, Celeste R. 44, 93
Rossiter, C.M. 250
Roth, Robert 22
Rousseau 164
Roy, P. 170,181
Rudduck, J. 261, 263, 275
Rudner L. M. 255, 277
Rudolf, Frederick 8, 22
Rumstein, R. 263, 276
Runyan, Richard P.140
Russell, J. 113
Ryan, Kevin 25, 30, 44,
  188, 206
Saettler, Paul 115
Salomon, G. 112
Salmolz and Katz 317
Sanborn, Michelle 317
Sandefur, J. T. 77, 93
Sapp, G. 230
Sarason, Seymour B.148,
  149, 151, 155, 188,
  206
Saunders, Robert L. 73,
  93
Schafer, W.D. 255, 276
Schlechty, Phillip C. 45,
  150,155
Schon, D.A. 169,182
Schooling in America 148

Schramm, Wilbur 115
Schroder, H. 219, 223
Schulman 192
Schutes, R.E. 209, 225
Schwab, John 188, 207
Scott, Anne Firor 335,
  349
Seelye, H. Ned 317
Segal, Ronald 314
Seifert, K. 234, 251
Selye, Hans 325, 333
Sergiovanni, Thomas J.
  58, 66
Shane, Harold 134, 140
Shanker, Albert 94
Shaver, J.P. 218, 221, 225,
  263, 276

Shulman, L.S. 167, 169,
  175, 207
Siefert 246
Sikula, John 72, 94
Simon, S. 225, 230
Simonson, Michael R. 115
Sit down and listen 247
Sivard, Ruth 305, 317
Skinner, B.F. 214, 215,
  225
Skinner, Ray 324, 333
Slavin, R.E. 170, 183
Smith, B.O. 173,183, 225
Smith, David C. 45,
  192,207, 209
Smith, Gary R. 317, 338
Smith, Roberta 123,141
Snarey, J. 213, 225
Snider, William 116
Snow, R.E. 190, 207
Snyder, David. 189, 207
Soltis, J. 211, 222
Soriano, Barbara 124, 137
Southern Regional
Education Board 66

Sprinthall, N. 220, 224
Stafford-Clark, D. 215, 226
Stager, S.F. 255, 256, 257, 258, 270, 276
Stallings W.M. 255, 256, 258, 274
Stanford 85
Stephenson, B. 220, 226
Sternberg, R.J. 165, 179, 190
Stetz, F.P. 256, 268, 276
Strait, M. 220, 224
Strong, W. 218, 221, 225
Strother, Deborah Burnett 11, 22
Suchman, J.R. 170, 183
Sununu, John H 116
Svengalis, Cordell M. 139
Sweitzer, T. 197
Taba, H. 170, 175, 183
Tafel, Linda S. 146, 155
Tamashiro, Roy T. 73, 94
Tausch, R. 243, 251
Taylor, Harold 296, 317
Tchudi, S. 166, 183
Teacher Corps 71
Teachers for the 21st century 13
Temple City Model 51
Tennessee Career Ladder Plan 51
Thayer, Lou 324, 333
Theobald 118, 141, 144, 156
Thies-Sprinthall, L. 220, 226
Thompson, L. 221, 226
Thorndike, E.L. 164, 183
Tice, T. 215, 226
Tobias, S. 194, 208
Todd, R.F. 262, 276

Toffler, Alvin 118, 119, 120, 130, 141,143,144,156, 165, 183, 199
Tom, A.R. 169, 183
Trout, Thomas B. 313
Turiel, E. 230
Tye, Barbara 198, 208
Tyler, Ralph 94
Ungoed-Thomas 218, 224
United Nations 317
United States Civil Service Commission 254
University of Bologna 254
University of Minnesota 220
University of Southern California 262, 296
Valdez, Gilbert 116
Van Horn, Royal 116
Vasconcellos, J. 286, 293
Veenman, S 26, 46
Veitch, S. 264, 275
Villeme, M.G. 256, 272

Volker, Robert P. 115
Walkabout 322
Wangberg, Elaine G. 325, 333
Ward, Beatrice 26, 46
Wasserman, E. 221, 226
Weingartners, C. 304, 316
Wendt, Janice 339, 350
West, B. Bradley 318
West, Peter 116
Westbury, I. 208
Wheatcroft, Andrew 318
Wheeler, C. W 16, 22
Whiteley 220, 224, 226
Whitson, T. 167, 183
Wilkof, N. 208
Willard 335

Williams, E. I. F. 69, 95
Williamson, M.S. 348
Wilson , Garfield W. 45
Windmiller, M. 230
Wisenbaker 197
Wisniewski, R. 258, 259,
    261, 277
Witkin, H.A. 288, 293
Wolfram, Tammara119,
    123, 141
Wood, G.H. 172, 184
Woyach, Robert B. 319
Wright, D. 213, 226
Wright, Jill D. 65
Yates, Brock 6, 22
Yeh, J.P.254, 255, 277
Yinger, Robert, J. 47, 166,
    184
Zaharias, Jane Ann 47
Zahorik, J.A. 263, 277
Zangwill 282
Zeichner, Kenneth M. 25,
    48, 76, 95, 147,
    150, 156, 176, 184
Zimpher, Nancy 26, 27,
    37
Zola, John 319
Zumwalt, Karen K. 57, 58,
    66